The Journey

the Journey

Captivity, Wilderness, Promised Land

Where Are You Now? Where Will You Go?

JASON ANDERSON

 All emphasis within Scripture quotations is the author's own. Please note that Destiny Image's publishing style capitalizes certain pronouns in Scripture that refer to the Father, Son, and Holy Spirit, and may differ from some publishers' styles. Take note that the name satan and related names are not capitalized. We choose not to acknowledge him, even to the point of violating grammatical rules.

DESTINY IMAGE® PUBLISHERS, INC.
P.O. Box 310, Shippensburg, PA 17257-0310

"Speaking to the Purposes of God for This Generation and for the Generations to Come."

This book and all other Destiny Image, Revival Press, MercyPlace, Fresh Bread, Destiny Image Fiction, and Treasure House books are available at Christian bookstores and distributors worldwide.

For a U.S. bookstore nearest you, call 1-800-722-6774.
For more information on foreign distributors, call 717-532-3040.
Reach us on the Internet: www.destinyimage.com.

ISBN 13 TP: 978-0-7684-3628-0
ISBN 13 HC: 978-0-7684-3629-7
ISBN 13 LP: 978-0-7684-3630-3
ISBN 13 Ebook: 978-0-7684-9044-2

For Worldwide Distribution, Printed in the U.S.A.

1 2 3 4 5 6 7 8 9 10 11 /14 13 12 11

Acknowledgments

ALL GLORY TO GOD, first and foremost. He has dibs on this one. The Word of God is the only completely true book on the planet. Without His awesome and true Word, I would have not written even one letter of this book.

Thanks to my wife, lover, best friend, texter, facebooker, Bible-reading, devil-defeating, praying, fasting, mother, influencer, nurturer, birther, encourager, and of course, some constructive criticism ("Don't do that thing with your hand when you teach. It's distracting"), other half, helpmate and "rib," Kelli Anderson. What can I say except, "I love you."

Thanks to my children who inspire me not to drop the ball. Christian, Katy, Matthew, Logan (and of course, Meghan, who is hanging out with the Lord before us).

My father and mother. My pastors. You live life for the Lord, and show us how.

For Christians all over the world who don't settle for average or mediocre, but are interested in the deeper things of God. You mess up sometimes, but you are trying to make a difference in yourself and in others. Go get 'em.

Endorsements

Jason Anderson's book *The Journey* will lift you and make you laugh, but most of all it will give you a clear view of the power of God as He works His plans into your life.

Dennis Burke

The word *journey,* by definition, means "travel or passage from one place to another." This definition also holds true of our lives. While the length and ease or difficulty of each journey is different, we can rest assured that God is with us each step of the way.

In Deuteronomy 10:11 the Lord told Moses, *"Arise, begin your journey before the people, that they may go in and possess the land which I swore to their fathers to give them."*

Jason Anderson's book, *The Journey*, shows us compelling similarities found between the Israelite's journey from Egypt and the Christian's journey today. If allowed, this book will make a positive impact on your journey.

Dr. Marilyn Hickey
President, Marilyn Hickey Ministries

Jason Anderson's book, *The Journey*, is a creative work that challenges readers to move out of the realm of average into the realm of the extraordinary to become spiritually mature men and women of God.

Creflo Dollar
Senior pastor, World Changers Church International

Who am I, why am I here, and where am I going? It's a Journey we're all on, and Jason Anderson will take you from being a "slave in Egypt" to beyond the Promised Land into a haven of Rest. Let him take you to the next level in your own spiritual journey and truly experience everything God has for you!"

James Covell,
Acclaimed composer and best-selling author of
The Day I Met God and
How to Talk About Jesus Without Freaking Out

Jason Anderson has spoken to a very important topic in the days we live in. I've seen too many believers who are stunted in their growth as Christians and frustrated that they aren't seeing fruit in their lives. In *The Journey*, you will discover the truths that will set you free, deepen your relationship with God, and position you to fulfill the calling He has on your life. This understanding will help you develop a maturity in Christ that few achieve.

John Bevere
Author/Speaker
Messenger International
Colorado Springs/Australia/United Kingdom

Contents

Part 3: The Promised Land

Part 4: The Rest

Introduction

THIS BOOK IS NOT just about embracing positive change; it is about direction and a destination. As the title indicates, it is about a journey. *Your journey.*

Often, when God shows up in the Word to talk to someone, it is about taking them to a different place. *"David the shepherd boy, you will be king"* (see 1 Sam. 16:13). God sent Samuel to deliver that very message to young David. Centuries earlier, God visited Abraham and asked him to leave his country and go to a new place (see Gen. 12:1).

There are journeys in life. What if you were to take a step back to look at your journey—not just where you have been, but where you are going? You know what you are doing for the next five minutes, maybe even the next week. To find out what is going on after work, you might call home and ask, "Hey, what are we doing tonight?" (Well, at least that's what I do.)

Even our long-term strategies take us out only a year or so, maybe five years at most. We live second to second, and day to day. It's life under the microscope of *now.* But, what if your life were not just examined under a microscope? What if you saw it from a distance instead?

People walked the earth for generations without realizing that it was round. They were so close to it that it seemed flat. If only they could have stood back to see what God sees. If they had been able to move far enough away, they would have seen what we know to be true: the earth is round.

Your life is too close to your face for you to see where it is headed. If you can back up, even for a moment, you can see what God sees. Life is full of anticipated changes, and God has a will for your life. That means there is a journey for you that God wants you to complete. *The Journey* is a book that looks at life, not as an accumulation of random moments, but as a lifetime using God's Word.

There is such a journey in God's Word. It is a well-documented journey that moves from a starting place to a particular destination. It is described in detail in four books of the Bible: Exodus, Leviticus, Numbers, and Deuteronomy (and with a great deal of review). It is the story of the Israelites traveling to the Promised Land.

I have found a parallel between our Christian walk and the Israelites' journey from Egypt. The Israelites were slaves there. We were slaves to, well, not Egypt, but sin. When we were born again we were set free and were no longer slaves to sin. Did it happen overnight? Do you still sin some? If not, would you mind writing a book? I would like to read it.

The Israelites saw the Red Sea part for them, and then watched the Egyptians drown in that sea (see Exod. 14:21-31). Isn't that a picture of God redeeming us from our sin with the blood of Jesus, washing away our sins in the sea of forgetfulness?

Next, the Israelites traveled through the Wilderness. Where were they going? To the Promised Land. God is bringing us through the Wilderness, as well. Yet, some will stay in Egypt. Others will stay in the Wilderness too long. In the Wilderness, just finding a drink of water is a struggle—like living from paycheck to paycheck.

The Israelites got stuck in the Wilderness. But why? Will you get stuck there, or is there something more ahead? If their journey relates to ours, then what does crossing the Jordan mean to us? Why does the Ark of the Covenant go first? (And where is Indiana Jones in all of this?)

Moses didn't make it to the Promised Land. Will you? And what exactly does the Promised Land have for you? There is milk and honey, but frankly, you can buy those at the store. Furthermore, isn't there some fighting to do? Joshua fought the battle at Jericho. What is your Jericho? If your journey looks a lot like theirs, then how does it all work?

Now let me freak you out a bit. Abraham took the same journey. He went to Egypt, through the Wilderness, and into the Promised Land. What about Jesus? Yes! Remember when He was born? Joseph and Mary had to smuggle the Son of God out of the city because Herod was going to have all the two-year-old and younger children bumped off!

So where did they go? Egypt. After Jesus was baptized, the Holy Spirit led Him out into...the Wilderness. He was baptized in *what* river? *Jor*-something, wasn't it? That's right, the Jordan River—the same river Joshua crossed to enter the Promised Land. It's pretty clear that in our journey, we are to follow Christ.

I can't wait to get you further into this book. The patterns found in Scripture from each portion of the journey are amazing and exactly for you, *for your journey.* In His Word, God announces to you as He did to the Israelites that He will give you *rest.* This is the Lord's rest, described in the Book of Hebrews.

From born again...to rest...and every road sign and landmark in between—welcome to the journey!

Before We "Travel"

When teaching, I always try to remember that my human lips and brain don't always articulate everything just right. With that in mind, let me say that the views in this book are mine. You will find plenty of my strong opinions in the pages ahead. Yet, opinions are just that—*opinions.*

I believe that Scripture is the only real truth left on the planet. So, allow me a simple prayer before we dive in:

> *Lord, partner with me as I write. Help me to say what You have called me to say. Let only truth be taught. I pray that my imperfect explanations would not reflect on Your infinite wisdom. Let all of this be washed in the precious blood of Jesus.*

Part I

Leaving Egypt

Chapter 1

Grow up or Fall Down

AFTER 17 YEARS of marriage, my wife is still trying to change me. I think she likes me. That is, we have an amazing marriage. I know I like her.

Of course we love each other. But she has never stopped trying to change me. When we first got married it was about how I dressed. When we were dating I picked out all my own clothes, but after the wedding, a struggle ensued. I found out that I was incapable of matching colors or patterns. I had apparently forgotten my kindergarten lessons about colors and shapes.

I thought my wife liked how I dressed? Apparently not. Little did I know that she had a list of things she wanted to tweak. The list was activated with the words *I do.* It was like I was a project.

The list was still working after more than a decade of marriage. "Hmm… let's see. Year 12—oh yes, here it is" she snickers as she taps her chin with her finger and pulls the wrinkled list from her make-up drawer. "Change the way he drives. It's annoying."

Unfortunately, my wife found out that I don't change so easily. We all are pretty resistant to change. A year goes by, but did we grow? Did we learn? Are we still pliable? Are we somewhere different? Or are the problems still the same? Can I even change myself?

Human history bears out that, for the most part, I cannot change myself easily, if at all. Addicts remain addicts, even if they abstain. My clothes still don't match, although I don't let my wife dress me anymore. And I will forever be making U-turns, to everyone's dismay. (If you want to have a conversation with me while I'm driving, then I will probably miss my turn and pull a "U-ey." Deal with it.)

Yet God has different ideas for all of this. He created His Word for us. Its purpose is to help us grow and change. This growth and change is for *His* purposes. (More on this later.)

As we study the Word together and implement the changes it reveals, we will also address many of the seeming contradictions and questions Scripture presents: Does God want you to be wealthy? Does He want you to be healthy? Does God desire you to suffer? Will you ever know God's will for your life? There are many conflicting arguments surrounding these questions, but one thing is for sure: God's Word is true and has the answers we need.

This journey is a launch—from where you are and all the trials you are going through—to a destination outlined in God's Word. It's quite a journey; but applying the Word of God makes change palatable, undeniable, and completely fruitful.

One more thing: this book is going to be unlike anything you have ever read. So, buckle up and keep reading!

Change Is Hard

Society has this idea (as do many Christians) that when you become a Christian you are all finished. Whaa-laa! Like magic, you are fully baked. The microwave beeps; you fully express Christ's likeness; and you have a WWJD bracelet to prove it.

This is why it hits us so hard when a Christian falls into sin. It comes as a big surprise to us. The truth is that, although God desires for us to grow into His righteousness, it takes some time. It's a journey. By definition, that indicates movement. Unfortunately, there are a lot of directions in which we can choose to move. Yet, at its core, life is defined by growth. That is to say, babies get bigger and all of us change.

Society often frowns on positive change. For thousands of years, societies have stuck people into neat little categories and asked them to stay put. Historians call this a *caste system*. It assigns people to certain classes. You are either seen as peasant or nobility; poor or rich; lower- or middle- or upper class or even some classes in between.

Movement from one class to another is often discouraged. In times past, it was taboo for a nobleman to marry a peasant girl. Even in today's high schools, a kind of caste system prevails. Geeks are not supposed to move into the jocks' realm. (Please stick to your math club, thank you very much.)

We have all seen movies where the geek makes his move to a new social category. Suddenly, the whole world is at odds with him. Old friends resent him and new comrades reject him. Everyone is resisting change. The same is true when a working-class person tries to move upward. Upper-class folks get uncomfortable over it, so they try and keep you down. Working-class friends don't like the idea either, and try to hold you back.

The caste system is merely an example of the world's resistance to growth. In a large family, one child is often deemed as the "less intelligent" one—a bit slower than the rest. "The toy is missing from the happy meal" kind of thing. If this child decides to pursue ambitious educational goals, the family rises up to put the "lesser" sibling back in his or her correct role.

Everyone is trying to keep everyone else from changing, because change makes self and everyone else uncomfortable. The overweight individual loses weight and, all of a sudden, loses his or her overweight friends, too.

People try to keep other people from changing (except for my wife; she is still trying to change me). We don't want to change, and the people around us don't want us to change. But without change how can we possibly get to the next place God has for us?

There are places that God has for you along your journey. Getting there will require movement, growth, and change.

Feeling Uncomfortable?

Most change is uncomfortable. When you decide to do something better or create a better version of yourself, it is because you are trying to advance. Maybe you have decided to go back to school or are working on some personality things. Maybe you are planning to go on a fast or a cleanse. Maybe you are changing the way you look or redefining your financial status. Maybe it's about your occupation or a dream you are chasing.

Whatever the change, some people will get in your business and say, "Whoa, big fella. Easy does it. Your movement makes me uncomfortable. You keep getting better and, well, I'm not. I'm comfortable with the way I am. So stop it."

As I mentioned earlier, God has a different system altogether. He wants it to be uncomfortable for us *not* to change. That is what the Word of God does for us. The Word of God is not always nice. He's a sword. That means *sharp edges.* That is the nature of a sword.

The other day, I was opening a plastic package—that really hard kind of plastic package. It was just a toy (see-through liquid nails or something), but it was wrapped in indestructible material. This thing could have fallen off a truck on the freeway and come up unscathed.

You seriously need a hacksaw to get into these things. So I pulled and pushed at it with a knife and…*slip.* Now my hand was bleeding. My blood was being shed for a toy. That's what sharp things can do. They cut; and the cut can hurt.

The Word of God is a sword. If you believe it, it will cut you sometimes. You might get hurt inside. It is uncomfortable as it pushes you to change. God is a God of making you uncomfortable in regards to growth. He is not a God who wants you to do nothing. He requires us to make choices. Until we choose, obey, or stop listening, we are divided.

This is why many leave the Church feeling hateful. Those who resist change and growth will eventually be separated by the sword, separated from the Body. Then destruction ensues as a mechanism to push them back to the need for the Lord. This destruction is not from God, it is the result of resisting God.

"But wouldn't a church that preaches the truth in a godly way be loved by all?" you ask. Remember that Jesus in the flesh was not well received. He had some detractors. Any good, God-fearing, uncompromising Word of God teachers and leaders will have some vocal haters.

The sword cuts.

Four Seasons

Back to the journey. At times, it cuts, too. Why? Because it is about change. Just ask the Israelites. Their trek from Egypt to the Promised Land challenged them. It should challenge us, too.

As I said earlier, the Exodus of the Israelites is a pattern for our journey from the new birth to the Place of Rest. This journey is divided into four sections, each one representing a different season in the Christian life. Although each season serves a purpose, it is meant to be left behind so that we can enter the next season.

In the coming chapters, we will plumb the depths of the four seasons. In fact, we'll map them out, and mark them with elements from the Word that will help identify the road and the destination.

FYI, there are four seasons, but seven stages altogether, because there were seven days in creation. The other three stages are transitions—one between each of the seasons. (See Figure 1 on page 45.) Transition is just as critical as the seasons themselves. Why? Because we are so resistant to change in our lives and because transition is the conduit for change.

Seven Stages of the Journey

For now, let's stick with the four seasons—Stages 1, 3, 5, and 7 (Stages 2, 4, and 6 are transitions).

First, let's consider the significance of the number *four*. The fourth letter of the Hebrew alphabet is *dalet, which is also the Hebrew number four. Traditional Hebrew sages contend that is represents four ways of interpreting Scripture, as well as* having to do with four levels of spirituality resembling those already listed (four levels of our Christian growth). For this work it is the latter that I wish to point as relevant. In your growth as a Christian, we will discuss four places God is bringing us. God has worked the number *four* throughout His creation and His story; There are four directions: north, east, south, and west. There were four initial commands to Adam and Eve, and four rivers flowing in the Garden of Eden. There are four physical dimensions in creation. We will even discover four statements that keep us from growing!

Most important to our study are the four seasons. In our physical lives, there are four seasons: spring, summer, fall, and winter. Spiritually speaking, we have the four seasons seen in the Exodus of the Israelites and in our lives:

- Stage 1—Leave Egypt: You are no longer a slave to sin.
- Stage 3—The Wilderness: You live day to day, crisis to crisis. Yes, you have to go through this (can you say "Eeeeck"?), but you don't have to stay there.
- Stage 5—Enter the Promised Land: There is a lot of fighting and taking of territory. Plenty of work and sweat. Here you will suffer, indeed. But suffering here is different from

what you might think. Welcome to the land of milk and honey.

- Stage 7—Enter His Rest: The battle is the Lord's. You become the influencer in your world; you subdue the earth. Here you actually experience the milk and the honey in peace.

Of the four seasons, you are currently residing in one. As a Christian, you may still be hanging out in Egypt. Or you may have advanced to the Wilderness where you have barely enough to get by. You may be further in the journey. The question is: exactly where are you?

The Israelites and Us

Let me give you a brief summary of the parallels between our Journey and that of the Israelites.

Israel started out in Egypt, working for The Man. They were called by God to move out from that place and go to a place God would show them, where the eventual goal was *rest* from their enemies.

You and I are on this journey as well. We start out working for The Man, building someone else's pyramids. At my early Burger King job, I wasn't striving to become the burger "king." Instead, I helped build someone else's kingdom. My effort helped someone else to profit. I was gathering seed. I was in Egypt.

Now that is obviously a physical interpretation in regard to labor. Most of us can identify with it. But the four seasons we are studying can be applied to every area of life, both physical and spiritual. In fact, the spiritual always precedes the physical. You need to get your heart out of Egypt before you can take your body out of the place. Your heart needs to receive the blessings before you *become* a blessing.

When I refer to this kind of thing I'm not talking solely about money. I'm not a big fan of that approach. I think it can get people off track. At the same time, I'm not afraid to talk about money. This journey covers the whole package. It is for you physically, emotionally, mentally, and spiritually, so that every faculty of your being can be offered to God and dedicated to His calling for your life.

When you get saved, you can leave Egypt. As good as that is, you want to eventually get to the place where you can sleep even when the storm comes. You experience storms, but you recognize the fact that God's Word is more powerful than any storm. You can *rest.*

My Mini-Exodus

I went on a journey last summer. I called my journey *vacation.* Because we live in Mesa, Arizona, vacation for us is best enjoyed in cooler climates where there is water. We desert people often vacation at the ocean. Our closest ocean is in California, so off we went to San Diego.

I have four children and a most wonderful and somewhat high-maintenance wife, Kelli. She is "smoking" beautiful—and lots of work. For us, leaving Mesa is a lot like leaving Egypt. In Egypt we work hard. Where we are headed is *rest.*

Now, getting there requires some preparation. We need to find the best route. We pack. With four kids I might as well rent a U-haul for the luggage. But I don't. Instead I jam the top of the car and between every seat with all the imaginable unneccessaries a family typically packs for a week in the sun. It is a lot of work leaving Egypt.

Some Christians leave Egypt and don't know where to go next. I have a map, though. We drive and drive and drive. This is not a sprint. Most men who live in Mesa, Arizona, will tell you it's a four-hour drive. That's what men do. They don't ask whether the destination is fun or relaxing. They will ask what all men really want to know, "How long does it take to get there?"

Now let the exaggerating begin. The reality is that, with four kids, 64 potty breaks, and three grande Caramel Macchiatos, you have yourself a six-and-one-half hour trip—that is, if none of your stuff falls off the top of the car on the interstate.

When we arrive in San Diego, we enter the Promised Land. Now I wish in real life the Promised Land were only six hours from receiving Christ. Spiritual journeys tend to take a little longer. It took the Israelites 40 years. Even Jesus was 40 days in the Wilderness. I'm not sure how long you will stay there.

For me, the Wilderness is like Yuma. You pass through Yuma about halfway to San Diego, yet it is still full-on desert. This is Stage 3. Spiritually speaking, many Christians stop in Yuma. I do not stop; I packed for the big trip and I want San Diego-type Christianity, which is *rest*.

Now when I arrive in San Diego, am I at rest immediately? No. I have to check in, unload luggage, and repack everything the kids have taken out of bags. Sometimes I even lug sleeping children out of the car.

The work continues. This is the Promised Land, but there's still fighting to do. It is Stage 5. When the Israelites arrived in Canaan there was plenty to do. But eventually, the moment comes when the planets align, the kids roam the shore, and the cool breeze blows through our hair. You'll find me sitting in a chair, taking a deep breath and saying, "Mmmm...."

You know the feeling. Not a care in the world. Finally at rest. This is Stage 7—the ultimate destination. Of course, Christianity doesn't mean doing nothing on some beach. But the rest part...well, we will get to that soon enough.

Four Growth-Stunting Statements

The path toward rest is pocked with pitfalls. There are obstacles to overcome and wars to wage. Often, the fiercest enemy we face is ourselves. We think and say all kinds of things that bog us down. Four common statements come to mind:

1. "It's not my fault."

OK address it this way: assume everything is your fault. When you land in a pit, hole, crisis, or storm, look in the mirror and ask what you can do to make sure it never happens again. Is there something in your actions, way of thinking, or faith in God that needs adjusting?

Consider this: if you remain a victim of your circumstances, you will never change. A victim by definition is subject to the crisis and actually made to serve the crisis. On the other hand, being a ruler means having the authority to make changes and solve problems.

"Well, I lost my job because my boss is a jerk." Maybe your boss is a jerk, but Joseph's boss was a jerk, too. What can you do to make sure that even if your boss is a jerk, you don't lose your job? Daniel's boss threw him in with the lions. Joseph and Daniel found a way to succeed despite ungodly bosses. The key is to understand your personal accountability in every crisis.

2. "I'm comfortable."

Being comfortable will de-motivate you. Your mission isn't founded on comfort. Jesus hit a storm because He was going to the other side. Was He going on vacation? Retiring? No. He was on a mission. His mission made everyone with Him uncomfortable.

3. "I don't care."

Apathy is today's anti-growth drug. Many people just don't care. Deception is involved because we all think we care. Not caring isn't some inherent, deep-rooted evil; it is more shallow than that. It's the feeling that we can't make a difference—the world is too big and the problems too grand, so we are overwhelmed. Apathy isn't about people who don't want to make a difference, but about people who don't think they can.

This book is going to change your mind. God did not call us to be overwhelmed; He called us to overcome. Time and again God finds that He can change the entire world with just one person, if that person will accept his or her role and rulership. Jesus was called the King of kings.

4. "I already know everything."

Pride. (No really, I do know everything.) The funny thing about pride is that it is nearly impossible to recognize that you have it. Knowing everything makes you un-teachable. If the pastor says something you don't agree with, you have several options. The best option is to argue in your own heart on behalf of the pastor, challenging what you believe and why. Maybe you misunderstood the pastor. Maybe the pastor is wrong. Or maybe you are wrong. You are responsible to get it right.

We must remain teachable. *If we only listen to what we agree with, then we are incapable of learning.*

I was on the wrestling team in junior high and high school. It was a bad sport for me, but my older brother was a champion-level wrestler, so I followed. Another boy in my weight class was not as good as me and rarely wrestled in tournaments. This was the case for two years.

The summer before tenth grade we began training. I was excited. At my lightweight class I would wrestle varsity and get a letter if I could beat my just one challenger—the kid I was already whooping on. Training began and I continued to dominate this other boy in practice. I didn't need to train hard, so I played instead.

Wrestling was a big deal at my high school in Gilbert, Arizona. It was 1986. My mullet and my wrestling uniform found themselves in front of the entire school at an assembly, as each weight class wrestled for the varsity position before the first meet of the season. As I went toe to toe with the "lesser" wrestler (who had never beaten me), I was startled to discover that he had become my nemesis. He entirely dominated and pinned me! I was owned. Dismantled. In front of my friends and peers, this boy utterly destroyed me.

What happened? I found out later that while I was playing, this boy had been training to beat me. I thought I knew everything. He remained teachable. In practice, he flopped around like a fish to give me false confidence. I was out-trained, outsmarted, and defeated.

It's called pride. We need to know when and where we have done this in our lives. Maybe you wanted that promotion; you prayed and believed, but you were beaten. Why? I can't say, but I know this: we sometimes rely on God yet fail to do everything in the natural that is necessary to win.

Now if you think you are ready to get moving on this journey, well, so do I. If you are ready to change, keep reading, because here we go!

Chapter 2

A Magical Land

My son Matthew was often distracted in the morning. As the family bustled about getting ready for the day, Matthew would cozy up on the couch with an episode of SpongeBob (which, by the way, is not the most developmentally safe children's show).

The story was the same every day—either Mom or Dad would hound Matthew to move from one task to the next, in hopes that he would be dressed and clean for the daily departure to school. During this time you might hear things like: "Did you brush your teeth, yet?" or "Your hair, Matt, your hair," or "Where are your shoes? Get your shoes on."

One day I realized that we were training him not to think, but to perform tasks like a robot. So I changed the ritual. "Matthew," I said as I sat him down for one of those chats, "every school morning we leave at 7:30 A.M. Whatever you look like at 7:30 A.M. is how I'm taking you to school. If you are still in your pajamas, then you'll spend the day at school in your pajamas."

Now Matthew knows I don't mince words. He knows I'm crazy like that. Once I say it, I always bind myself to my own word and follow through. My son knows this. Clearly, the fear of finding oneself at school in one's—should I say it?—*underwear,* is a dread we all share.

The strategy has been very successful. For Matthew and all of us, even going to school requires us to change. The journey and change are partners. Going anywhere new indicates change. The following passage from God's Word is one of many that call us to move from one place in our lives to another. In it, God is calling us to change:

> *For this very reason, make every effort to add to your faith goodness; and to goodness, knowledge; and to knowledge, self-control; and to self-control, perseverance; and to perseverance, godliness; and to godliness, brotherly kindness; and to brotherly kindness, love* (2 Peter 1:5-7).

Man, this seems like a lot of work.

"I got saved; isn't that enough? Why all the adding? I don't think I signed up for this. Jesus is Lord and I'm going to Heaven. I thought that was it! What's this now? This sounds like work!"

And it is work. God has given us things to grow into. Blessings are available for us so that we can bless others. Now let me share one of those seeming contradictions in the Bible, comparing two statements by Jesus:

> *...I have come that they may have life, and have it to the full* (John 10:10).

> *For whoever wants to save his life will lose it, but whoever loses his life for Me will find it* (Matthew 16:25).

So, which is it? In John 10:10, Jesus talks about giving us everything we need for life. In Matthew 16:25, He tells us to lose our lives. (And did I mention that the passage from Second Peter 5 also talks about adding to our lives?) Aren't those statements opposites?

No, and here's why (please keep this in mind as you read this book). Whenever it appears that the Bible is contradicting itself, then there is something we are misunderstanding. We have to press in to find truth.

"...I have come that they may have life, and have it to the full" (John 10:10). Jesus is the one speaking here. To the *full* gives the sense of having everything we need for life. It is complete life—the kind described in the passage from Second Peter. It is not just living. It means resurrecting any "dead" places in your life. This is not just life for eternity, but for *right now.* Life to relationships. Life to lack.

This life leads to godliness. Is anything missing from the grandness of His infinite love? Of course not. He is expressing the whole spectrum of life for you. So, when Jesus tells me to lose my life, it is not a contradiction.

Let's say I buy my son Christian a video game. To him, that is life and life more abundantly, because he loves video games. Now let's say that he returns a few minutes after receiving the game and asks for another one.

"Dad, can I have a video game?"

"Sure, son. Here ya go." Then five minutes later he returns and asks for another one.

"OK," I reply hesitantly. "But what happened to the game I just gave you?"

"Well, Dad, I lost it."

"Lost it?" I'm curious. "Why would you lose it? What happened?"

Christian looks at me in bewilderment. His eyes narrow, "You told me to lose it. You told me I couldn't have life unless I lost it."

Why would God give us life, and then tell us to lose it? The answer is simple: There are seasons of growth. Each one calls us to learn something new so we can move to the next level. At some point, we must be willing to lose the old ways of life and embrace the new things of God.

Sometimes this feels a bit like dying.

The Land of Canaan

I trust that you are ready to be whisked away to a magical land. Well, maybe not magical, but supernatural, for certain. Our journey is going to start by taking us back 3,970 years ago as Abraham is approached by God.

> *The whole land of Canaan, where you are now an alien, I will give as an everlasting possession to you and your descendants after you...* (Genesis 17:8).

The land of Canaan is known more famously as the Promised Land. Here God has promised the land to Abraham and his descendants, the Israelites. This promise is given centuries before Moses leads the Israelites to Canaan.

Yet, even this is not where the "Canaan" story began. Let's go back a bit further. Ten generations and 400 years earlier, we can trace the Promised Land back to Noah. Noah had three sons and one of them sinned and looked upon his father's nakedness (see Gen. 9:22). That son's name was Ham; he was father to a boy named Canaan. Yes, the same Canaan from the land mentioned to Abraham. When Noah awoke to find out what his son Ham had done, he prophesied that the other two sons, the sons who protected their father, would rule over Canaan:

> *He said, "Cursed be Canaan! The lowest of slaves will he be to his brothers." He also said, "Blessed be the Lord, the God of Shem! May Canaan be the slave of Shem. May God extend the territory of Japheth; may Japheth live in the tents of Shem, and may Canaan be his slave"* (Genesis 9:25-27).

Canaan, the son of Ham, would serve Shem and Japheth. Shem is the forefather of Abraham and the Israelites. Giving the land of Canaan, which represents the world, to Abraham would be quite correct.

There is another son mentioned here. Japheth represents the Gentiles, or those of us who would inherit salvation. *Japheth* means "widely extending" or, in other words, spread out.[1] The promise given to the Israelites through Shem was that they would rule Canaan. This confirms the Israelites' exodus to the Promised Land and their taking possession of that land. But reading further, we see that Japheth would live in the tents of Shem, that the territory would be expanded even further, and that he, too, would rule Canaan.

This is us. When Jesus came, He created a scenario in which anyone who would believe would have access to the promises of God. So the inheritance became expanded, a bigger covenant that included more. I will describe these things in detail later. For now let's agree that the Promised Land, Canaan, is for you and me to rule!

Looking back at Genesis 9:27, we would live in the tents of Shem in that, as we have accepted Christ, we enter into the family of God. The Israelites were the chosen of God, but we were grafted into the family (see Rom. 11:17). If that isn't enough, consider this:

> *Christ redeemed us from the curse of the law by becoming a curse for us, for it is written: "Cursed is everyone who is hung on a tree." He redeemed us in order that the blessing given to Abraham might come to the Gentiles through Christ Jesus...* (Galatians 3:13-14).

The land promised to Abraham is yours. As a born-again Christian, you are the seed of Abraham and this is your promise. Abraham has a son named Isaac. Isaac has a son named Jacob. Jacob has many sons, each pertaining to 1 of 12 tribes of Israel, which includes two grandsons, Manasseh and Ephraim. Without retelling the entire history of the Bible, let me summarize by saying that one of Jacob's sons, Joseph, was sold into slavery, and ended up in Egypt. God used this tragedy to perform a miracle; Joseph became second in command over all Egypt during a time of great prosperity that was followed by great famine.

In the famine, Jacob's family, Israel, ended up in Egypt. They left Canaan. (See Genesis 37;39-48.) For four generations, Israel was enslaved by Egypt, showing us the power of reaping and sowing. They sold Joseph into slavery, and then they themselves were enslaved.

The promise was not enslaved, however. The Promised Land of Canaan was still on God's agenda. This book is going to take you with Moses on the

Exodus. We are going to take the Israelite journey from slavery to Egypt to the Promised Land and beyond.

The same land is for you, but now it is a *picture* of what that land means. This is your journey. As the Israelites cross each bridge, traverse each new obstacle, and see the hand of God move, we will equate it to our modern journey. Moses led the Israelites; so did Joshua and Gideon. Today, Jesus is our leader through the journey.

The Journey's Starting Point

Let's begin by going to the moment when the Israelites are to be freed from Egypt. It has been 7 generations since Abraham was promised the land for his descendants, and 17 generations since Noah prophesied this would happen. Egypt is a picture of us, enslaved by sin. The Israelites have been slaves now for 430 years, and God speaks to Moses in a burning bush:

> *The Lord said, "I have indeed seen the misery of My people in Egypt. I have heard them crying out because of their slave drivers, and I am concerned about their suffering. So I have come down to rescue them from the hand of the Egyptians and to bring them up out of that land into a good and spacious land, a land flowing with milk and honey—the home of the Canaanites...* (Exodus 3:7-8).

Here now is confirmation of our destination. It is the Promised Land. There is lots of space; there is milk and honey; and someone is already living there. Moses reluctantly accepts his calling from the Lord, and after ten plagues (see Exod. 8-12) the Egyptians agree to free the Israelites. (When we receive Christ we are freed of the world's systems and "Pharaoh" has to let us go, too.)

The Israelites then traverse the Wilderness for much longer than they need to. While there, they learn many important lessons. God desires for us to grow and mature just as they did. He is not calling us *to* the Wilderness, but *through* the Wilderness.

As the story goes, Moses and the Israelites wandered for 40 years. They lacked the faith and obedience to enter the Promised Land as God had designed. Eventually, Joshua (Moses' right-hand man), led the Israelites in.

They entered the Promised Land. Whew, finally done, right? Wrong, they still had much territory-taking to do. We as Christians can learn great lessons from their experiences. We see that many of our good Christian friends will choose to stay in the Wilderness and not move on to the fight.

Yes, the Promised Land sounds like a lot of work, but Jesus has already paved the way. He has finished the work. But remember: even the Promised Land is not our final destination.

Do I have your attention now?

Chapter 3

The Best Is the Rest

Destination Defined

Go to Google Maps. Click the box and type in the sentence: "I don't know; take me anywhere." Do you know what you will get? Nothing. Our God-given and often brilliant common sense tells us you need to know where you are going in order to *go* somewhere.

That sounds simple, but if I were to ask a group of people whether they have a clear sense of direction for the future, many would admit that they do not. Without a clear sense of direction—that is, *a destination*—we wander. We talk about the idea of destiny, and we enjoy the discussion, yet we make little progress. Given clear direction, I think most of us would gladly jump on board. Without it, we meander through the years, strolling through whatever door opens and hoping it's the right one.

In reality, some doors open randomly. Sometimes, the doors we really need to enter must be broken down. Random doors lead to a random life—not a life of purpose in any sense of the term. It is important as we engage in our journey, to look to the Word of God for our destination.

While our individual destinies are unique, we share a common destination. That is to say, if we are all following Christ, we are all going in the same direction. Now I'm certain that your destiny will impact the world differently from the destiny of the gal sitting next to you, but to hit your destiny, you will need to grow using the same Word of God as she does.

His Word assures me that God is bringing me somewhere better than where I currently am. Of course, as slaves in Egypt, anywhere would have sounded better. But just getting to the Promised Land is not the destination. Watch this:

> *...you have not yet reached the **resting place** and the inheritance the Lord your God is giving you. But you will cross the Jordan and settle in the land the Lord your God is giving you as an inheritance, and He will give you **rest** from all your enemies...* (Deuteronomy 12:9-10).

Ah, *rest.* That sounds nice. The resting place here is the Promised Land revealed to Moses by God. Notice that God's promise couples the inheritance of the land itself with the promise of rest. Just arriving at the Promised Land was not the ultimate destination. The Israelites' journey would be considered complete when they received both the land *and* the rest He promised to give.

Who will give you rest? God. God reiterates this to us in the Book of Hebrews. I want to impart this seed into your heart so that you will recognize the destination that is the core subject and purpose of the Book of Hebrews:

> *Therefore, since the promise of entering His **rest** still stands, let us be careful that none of you be found to have fallen short of it. For we also have had the gospel preached to us, just as they did; but the message they heard was of no value to them, because those who heard did not combine it with faith* (Hebrews 4:1-2).

The people who saw the message as having "no value" were the Israelites. God gave them a Promised Land. It was available to them, but they wandered 40 years in the Wilderness, instead. Was that God's plan? No!

"But," you ask, "doesn't God's will always get done? He is after all, God. If He wants them to get in, then they should get in, right?"

The fact is that the ones originally given the promise did not enter in (except for Joshua and Caleb). It was a blessed land and they missed it. Why? Because they did not receive it by faith.

Likewise, there are blessings for you. There is a place God wishes you to go to in your journey, but you might not get there. You might not experience all of the blessings He has for you. Receiving the blessings is going to be up to you. The Israelites didn't believe they could get in, and so they didn't. Are there promises God has for you that He wants you to have that you will not get? Yes. Some will stop growing in the journey and get stuck somewhere in life just like the Israelites. So, take note: today you are hearing His voice about this journey God has for you.

> *It still remains that some will enter that* ***rest,*** *and those who formerly had the gospel preached to them did not go in, because of their disobedience. Therefore God again set a certain day, calling it Today, when a long time later He spoke through David, as was said before: "Today, if you hear His voice, do not harden your hearts." For if Joshua had given them* ***rest,*** *God would not have spoken later about another day. There remains, then, a Sabbath-rest for the people of God; for anyone who enters God's* ***rest*** *also* ***rests*** *from his own work, just as God did from His. Let us, therefore, make every effort to enter that* ***rest,*** *so that no one will fall by following their example of disobedience* (Hebrews 4:6-11).

Verse 8 says that *"if Joshua had given them rest, God would not have spoken later about another day."* Joshua led them into the Promised Land, yet they did not enter that rest. Joshua battled all his life for the land and eventually settled down in it; yet he did not overcome as God had planned.

OK, so what does this mean to you and me? It means God is beckoning us to let His Word do the work in our lives so that we enter His promises by faith and enjoy lives of peace.

Jesus at Rest

There is a familiar story from Mark 3 I'd like to re-tell: Jesus has had a crazy, busy day of healings, parables, and misunderstandings. He stops for lunch at a house and so many people show up that He cannot even eat His meal. He is accused of being Beelzebub (I've been called a lot of things, but never Beelzebub). Then His family pays Him a surprise visit—right in the middle of a teaching. Let's just say, Jesus has His hands full.

Later on, Jesus decides to cross the lake in a boat with His disciples. As they are crossing, a huge storm blows up. But Jesus had already spoken a word:

> *...When evening came, He said to His disciples,* ***"Let us go over to the other side."*** *Leaving the crowd behind, they took Him along, just as He was, in the boat. There were also other boats with Him. A furious squall came up, and the waves broke over the boat, so that it was nearly swamped. Jesus was in the stern, sleeping on a cushion...* (Mark 4:35-38).

Jesus' word was, *"Let us go over to the other side."* The sea begins to churn and Jesus is sound asleep. The disciples are afraid the storm is going to kill them. Meanwhile, their fearless leader, the one they look to for security, is out like a light.

> *...The disciples woke Him and said to Him, "Teacher, don't You care if we drown?"* (Mark 4:38).

The disciples were sure they were going to die. Do you think He knew they were panicking? And yet He continued to sleep? What I want you to see here is the stark contrast between two reactions. In the midst of the crisis, one reaction is rest; the other is panic. Everyone involved is in the same situation, yet responding differently.

Let's assume for a moment that Jesus has decided not to wake up just yet. The disciples try to rouse Him, but He moans, rolls over, and in a slow, guttural tone says, "Leave Me alone, I'm sleepy."

Are they really going to die? The answer is, *no.* Jesus already said, "Let's go to the other side." He is the Word of God. Once He says they are going to the other side, nothing can stop them. Jesus knows this. Jesus knows He is going to die on the cross, not crossing a lake. They are going to the other side regardless of the storm.

When storms well up in our lives, we are more like the disciples than like Jesus. We cry, "Help!" just as they did. When the plane hits a bit of turbulence over Philadelphia, we grip the armrests, tighten our seatbelts, and look around to see whether anyone else looks worried.

My question is this: when things get tight, are we able to rest in the kind of peace Jesus displayed in the storm? Do we believe that rest is capable of changing the circumstances we face? This, my friends, is the destination this book is all about—resting in and out of crisis because we trust in God's Word to do the work.

So, we have established the point of our journey: *the destination is to enter the Lord's rest.* Now give me the rest of the book to explain, please.

Our job is to follow in the footsteps of our Savior. Jesus displayed authority that caused even the winds and the waves to obey Him. We tend to handle crises differently; when storms hit, we panic. That is what *we* do.

Our minds spew fear: "There is no way out of this one, no light at the end of this tunnel. In fact, there is not even a tunnel. We are going to die. Period."

Jesus showed us a better answer: He rested. Even when awakened from sleep, He took authority and subdued the earth—immediately. Have you noticed that we look to God last? For some of us we say He always comes through at the last minute, but maybe that's because we don't fervently seek His involvement until we are at our wits' end.

Not so with Jesus. He involved God from the beginning. He spoke the Word and, as a result, was unafraid. Even before He rebuked the storm, He slept undisturbed and unmoved by it. Why? Because Jesus knows something that we disciples don't: Christianity is not a storm-free zone. Storms are part of the journey (see John 16:33). Our level of Christian maturity will determine how we react to those storms. Simply put, the attitude that Christ exhibited is the answer to where we are going.

Let me continue to identify our destination a bit further by saying that Jesus mapped out a path for us. This path follows Christ with principal and power so that we might truly fulfill His command:

> *I tell you the truth, anyone who has faith in Me will do what I have been doing. He will do even greater things than these, because I am going to the Father* (John 14:12).

What Christ demonstrated in His ministry days on the earth is something He not only expects us to attain, but to exceed. That may sound prideful, but you will find in this book that you cannot bring pride with you on this journey.

Jesus' expectation for us points back to God's original command to Adam and Eve to subdue the earth (see Gen. 1:28).

Subdue the Earth

To fine-tune our destination, let's look to God's original plan. Remember that He referred to creation as *good.* So earth before the Fall—before Adam and Eve sinned—is a picture of how God intended things to be. By defeating sin, Jesus has restored us to this original state, so let's take a look at how God originally set things up.

> *Then God said, "Let us make man in our image, in our likeness, and let them* ***rule*** *over the fish of the sea and the birds of the air, over the livestock, over all the earth, and over all the creatures that move along the ground."...God* ***blessed*** *them and said to them, "Be fruitful and increase in number; fill the earth and* ***subdue it****..."* (Genesis 1:26,28).

What is the first thing God did *to* mankind after creating them? He blessed them. This was His first priority. His blessing came with instructions in the form of four commands:

1. Be fruitful.
2. Increase in number.
3. Fill the earth.
4. Subdue it. Rule over it. In other words, *rest.*

The first three commands were not three requests to have more children. They were part of a path laid out with a specific destination. Nor is it a coincidence that there were four commands with each one correlating to one of the four seasons.

Of course, the blessing came first so that Adam and Eve could carry out the commands given them. Everything created with a purpose in this world has been assigned the resources necessary to fulfill that purpose. The blessing is the resource necessary to produce the fruit of God.

Looking at the fourth command, we see that the final destination is to subdue the earth. We need the blessing in its full power to accomplish this task. The word *subdue* indicates that it is going to be a process. The people of God have to take steps in order to bring the earth into full submission and rule over it successfully.

Jesus' ministry shows that He lived in this authority. He acted within the realm of this original command. While Adam's sin caused man to serve the earth and be subdued by it, Jesus sacrificed all to restore us to the original command.

Let's be sure not to fall short of it! We need to see rest for what it truly is—acting in our purpose, being confident of victory, having the wisdom to be just, subduing the earth, and influencing the earth to the point that His will is done here as it is in Heaven. In other words, being like Jesus!

Our destination is to subdue the earth and enter the Lord's rest.

What Are the Steps?

I love the navigational tools that are currently available. My car has one that announces when I need to make my next turn. All I have to do is program in my destination and it gently guides me there. I can change the sound of the voice, so I chose a calm female voice, which, by the way, does not sound like my wife.

My "navi" gently instructs me with a lovely British accent: "In 250 feet, turn right." Her voice is so nice…so sweet.

What if there were a navigational system for marriage? You walk in the house and it says, "Please pick up your dirty laundry."

YOU: "Oh, that's easy. OK. Let me grab this stuff."

Then the navi says, "You can fix your own dinner."

YOU: "Great, I'm on it."

NAVI: "Tell her she looks pretty."

YOU: "Hey, babe, you look pretty today…"

This would make marriage easier, but, guess what? There is a navigational system for life; it is the Word of God. The Holy Spirit is the voice that will speak the Word into your life. The more Word you get inside of you, the easier it is to hear the Holy Spirit say, "By Jesus' stripes you were healed."

"Oh yeah!" you reply with joy.

The Bible *is* this navigational system for our lives. In coming chapters, you will hear the Holy Spirit's turn-by-turn guidance. It will reveal in a whole new light just how the complete Word of God is working to grow you. Let's touch on some of the guidance elements you are about to explore.

The Map

To take a journey, you need a map. Here is yours. Mark this page as you will need to return to this detailed road map often. It corresponds to the seven stages described in Chapter 1.

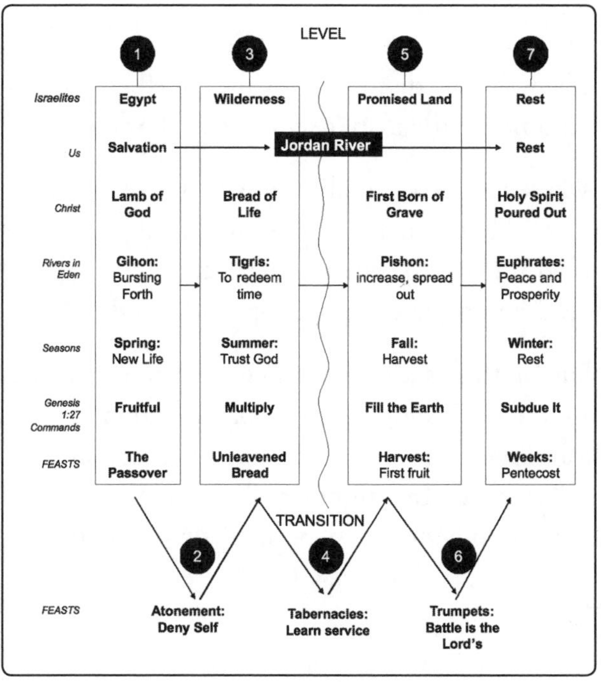

[Figure 1]

Remember the four seasons already mentioned and notice the placement of the three transitions:

- Stage 1—Leave Egypt: You are no longer a slave to sin.

- Stage 2—First Transition: Atonement
- Stage 3—The Wilderness: You live day to day and crisis to crisis.
- Stage 4—Second Transition: Tabernacles
- Stage 5—Enter the Promised Land: You still have some fighting to do.
- Stage 6—Third Transition: Trumpets
- Stage 7—Enter His Rest: The battle is the Lord's and you subdue the earth.

All seven stages will be discussed at length in the pages ahead. For now, let me briefly summarize the map, beginning at the end.

Stage 7 is where Jesus lived in His ministry. He recognized that the world was His; therefore, He commanded the earth to do certain things. For example, He turned water into something He could walk on. He also turned water into wine. He told the storm to stop, and it did.

Jesus is calling *us* to this level—not so we can run laps on the lake, but so we can influence the world and bring the manifestation of God's spiritual will into the physical dimension. This is possible, because all authority given to Him has been given to us. This authority, like all authority, is intended to put someone in charge of something—oops, there's more on this, but not yet.

Keep reading!

The Seasons

Looking at the map you see the four seasons of the Israelites' journey. Listed below each season are related items that apply God's wisdom in defining that season.

For instance, Stage 1 is named *Egypt.* Just below that is the corresponding starting point in the Christian journey, which is *salvation.* Below that, we see Jesus as the *Lamb of God* (the Passover Lamb) who frees us from Egypt (we are saved, born again). Below that you see the *Gihon,* the river in Eden whose name means "bursting forth," followed by the physical season *spring,* which is when rivers burst forth in nature (a picture of the new birth).

Keep tracking with me, now. Below the physical season is the corresponding command given to Adam. In this case, it is the first command, which is to be fruitful. Fruitfulness implies a time of tilling the soil and planting seed, which is typified in the Hebrew feast of the Passover.

There—you made it through a whole season! Now you can see how the diagram summarizes the others. We will revisit these items and see more about how they apply to us.

The Transitions

As I explained earlier, the transitions fall between the seasons. Each transition corresponds to one of the feasts of Israel: the Feast of Atonement (Stage 2), the Feast of Tabernacles (Stage 4), and the Feast of Trumpets (Stage 6).

Each feast provides a key element of our transitional phase. For instance, the Feast of Atonement is described in Leviticus 23 as a feast during which we must deny ourselves. In Matthew 16:24, Jesus also asked us to deny ourselves. This denial is critical to our getting out of Egypt!

Each feast is a stepping stone to the next stage. We need to understand them, in part because the most difficult phase of growth occurs in transition. It is a stage that is absolutely necessary to progress; it is leaving one way of life and moving into a new one.

Transition is not change. Change is the result of transition. Transition is the brief time between changes. If you sell your house and move to another house, transition is the packing, moving, and unpacking. The last time we moved we threw away items, sold some furniture, and donated some things.

Not everything we had in our old home was going to work in the new one. In fact, the greater the change, the less baggage you can take along. That's something we need to recognize, because, too often, we let the baggage hold us back.

What exactly is this baggage? It is anything you choose to hold onto because it is familiar or comfortable. In doing so, you reject (by default) whatever the Lord desires to bring you into. Pause and think of that, as the psalmist would say!

The appeal of familiarity causes many people to avoid transition altogether. It can be an awkward time when we feel as though we do not "fit." The trouble is that we try to shove too much baggage through the tunnel of transition.

Childbirth is an apt example. Imagine the transition a baby makes in passing from the womb, through the birth canal, and into life outside its mother's body. This is a strenuous time. The baby is forced through a tight place with barely enough room to breathe, let alone bring a binky! Whatever it takes, the transition must be completed or both mother and child will suffer harm.

In transition, we need to let go of some things in order to move forward. We can avoid transition, but it will hurt us.

The Sabbath

On our map of the journey, the four seasons are odd-numbered, while the transitions are even-numbered, with a total of seven stages. I mentioned earlier that the seven stages relate to the seven days of God's creation process.

What did God do on the seventh day? Exactly—He *rested* (see Gen. 2:2-3). God named this day of rest the *Sabbath.* Hebrews describes the Sabbath rest that God has for us:

> *There remains, then, a Sabbath-rest for the people of God; for anyone who enters God's rest also rests from his own work, just as God did from His* (Hebrews 4:9-10).

Now you have a broad overview of the map and its relationship to our journey and growth. As we move from chapter to chapter, we will examine the movement from one stage to another in greater detail and we will learn what each item means to our maturation.

It's a New System

We will also learn that there is a new system—God's system of growth—that does not come naturally to us. Many of us still operate under the old system. Instead of ruling, we are subject to creation, just as Adam and Eve were after the Fall. We work for the mighty dollar; the earth yields little, despite our labor; and calamity strikes without warning.

We have all been there: A big storm swells, real estate crashes, you cannot sell your house because values are out of whack. Because we are submitted to creation we live under the crisis and cry out to God to bail us out. We speak and think negatively, reacting to the crisis the same way as someone who does not believe in God. Instead of being positioned to influence our world; we have positioned ourselves to be rescued.

Church, God is calling us to mature so that instead of needing miracles we become the miracles other people need. That is how Christ lived—and we are following Him!

Are you ready for the first season? Great, because here we go!

Chapter 4

Finish Your Lamb, Then You Can Have *Desert*

KIDS CAN BE PICKY when it comes to food. Until I turned 18, I survived on five major food groups: pizza (cheese only)…macaroni and cheese…grilled cheese (notice the cheese trend)…peanut butter and jelly…and Waffle-o's. (If you don't know what Waffle-o's are, I am sincerely sorry. You missed something *amazing.*)

These were the five major building blocks for my life. My body managed to use them to build my bones, teeth, hair, organs—*me.* My metabolism must have been highly efficient to extract the nutrients I needed from such a limited menu. That said, I am pretty short.

My parents worked hard to get me to eat different foods, much as I do with my own children. Now that I am older, I realize that this sort of diet is not conducive to great health. I was stealing from myself the whole time! It was a sign of immaturity. Fortunately, I have since discovered new flavors to love. I'll never forget when my (future-at-the-time) wife introduced me to seafood. Wow! Turns out it's one of my favorite things to eat.

We can apply this principle to much of life. There are lessons we learn that, if followed, will improve our well-being *and* make life more fun. Life lessons are part of growth—they build one upon the other and they work together to keep us on track.

This is true of the journey. We need to learn the same lessons the Israelites did, and we need to take them in order, sort of like eating the main course before we get to dessert. In this case, though, to be perfectly honest, instead of getting dessert, you get desert.

Back to the Beginning

Let's set the stage again before we launch in earnest. Moses has been sent by God to lead the Israelites out of Egypt. For 430 years the people have been enslaved; now they are about to experience freedom.

The written record of the Exodus is traditionally attributed to Moses. Four books of the Pentateuch are devoted to the story: Exodus, Leviticus, Numbers, and Deuteronomy. In Exodus we read the play-by-play as Moses, Aaron, and God work to convince Pharaoh to let the Israelites go out into the desert to make sacrifices to God.

Pharaoh is opposed to the idea, fearing that, once the people leave, they will not return to enslavement. (Boy was he right about that one.) So God uses ten plagues to show that Egypt's gods are not trustworthy and the God of the Israelites is the Almighty God (see Exod. 7:14-12:30). After each plague, Pharaoh considers granting Moses' request, but each time he changes his mind. The final straw is the tenth plague, which brings death to Egypt, but new life to Israel.

These events symbolize that what was death to sin is life for all of mankind. This is the Passover, where we begin our journey. The event foreshadows our being saved by the sacrifice of Jesus Christ, the Passover Lamb!

Let's see how the Passover story applies to our Christian life and growth, as we join the Israelites in departing Egypt and walking toward the Red Sea.

Being Born Again

Many have heard this before: Jesus is the Passover Lamb. "Duh," you say. But don't skip over this chapter; we sometimes assume that we know certain things, but do we really know the depth of them?

The Passover is a representation of receiving Christ. Being born again is the starting line of new life. Jesus spoke to a man named Nicodemus about it:

> *...Jesus declared, "I tell you the truth, no one can see the kingdom of God unless he is born again"* (John 3:3).

Born again. The phrase screams *infancy*—and we know how slowly babies learn. It is usually a full year before they begin walking, and try as you might, the pee pee will not land in the potty until the child is around two to three years old. So listen carefully. This journey is not a sprint. It's not even a marathon. It is like 40 years of running, a trek of growing slowly and methodically, the way a baby does.

As babies, all of my children were dependent on me (or, actually, my wife) daily. We met their needs with diapers, bottles, and whatever else was called for—no questions asked. As my children mature, however, more is expected of them. The same is true of us, as Jesus explained:

> *...From everyone who has been given much, much will be demanded; and from the one who has been entrusted with much, much more will be asked* (Luke 12:48).

Once, my wife asked me to put on our son Logan's shoes. He was eight months old at the time. Typical dad, I was all thumbs trying to get the shoes on him. They seemed too small; I was afraid I would squish his little feet. I put Logan in my lap facing away from me and worked diligently for some time to get those tiny little shoes on his wiggly little feet, until my wife eased him out of my arms and said, "Here, let me."

Now imagine this scenario: I walk over to Logan, who is playing with his ball. His head is bobbling around the way infants' heads do. I throw his shoes over to him and say gruffly, "Here, put these on," and I walk away.

News flash to Dad: It's not going to happen. Logan is an infant and we need to put his shoes on for him.

What happens when our seven-year-old son Matthew asks me to tie his shoes? What do I say? Bearing in mind that I have taught him how to tie his shoes, I respond with a sufficiently annoyed tone, "Put your own shoes on, Matthew. You're old enough to tie your shoes."

When I'm ready to leave for work and Matthew is contending with his breakfast, I grab my keys and wallet from the counter, and glower with a look that says, "No, buddy, I'm not cutting up your French toast this morning, either. You are old enough to do these things."

As kids get older, parents require them to do more. To my 12-year-old I say, "You need to make your bed." I would never say that to my infant. Imagine striking this deal with a baby: "Oh, you want Cheerios, do you? Finish mowing the lawn and we'll talk."

That would be crazy! No sane parent would do that. As *the* ultimate parent, neither would God. His Word provides what we need at every stage of maturity, so that we can grow to the next level!

The First Passover

In Exodus 12 God visits with Moses and reveals the tenth and final plague, which will cause Pharaoh to release God's people. Each Israelite household is to slaughter a lamb that is without defect and paint its blood around the door frames of the house. That night, the destroyer will pass through and kill the firstborn of every household (including animals), but will "pass over" the dwellings marked with blood on the door frames.

Pharaoh awakens during the night to the cries of the nation and finds his oldest son dead. Pharaoh is broken; he allows the nation of Israel to go and make sacrifices to their God. The Israelite slaves are set free!

The Passover story pictures the Christ, the Lamb of God, whose blood washes away our sins. He is the firstborn and only-begotten Son of God who died on our behalf to set us free from slavery to sin, satan, and the earth. His blood protects us from the wages of sin (which is death) and gives us new life. Like the Israelites, we are free to leave our "Egypt."

There are some boring but important details here that show how awesome our God is. The Passover event happens on the fourteenth day of the first month of the Hebrew calendar, the month of Nisan. The Hebrew calendar is different from ours. Our calendar reconciles partial rotations of the earth by having a "leap" year every four years. The Hebrew calendar is reconciled seven times every 19 years.

For the sake of understanding, we can think of Nisan as being March to April-ish. The first Passover occurred around March 28, 1491 B.C., or the fourteenth day of Nisan in the Hebrew year 2270. The reason Easter Sunday falls on a different date each year is because Easter always falls on the Sunday following the fourteenth day of Nisan.

We know this was the weekend during which Jesus was crucified; it would have been April 14, possibly in the year A.D. 29. Again, many theologians dispute the year, placing it one year earlier or later. Quite honestly, the point remains the same. Scripture describes the timing:

> *It was just before the Passover Feast. Jesus knew that the time had come for Him to leave this world and go to the Father...* (John 13:1).

> *At the place where Jesus was crucified, there was a garden, and in the garden a new tomb, in which no one had ever been laid. Because it was the Jewish day of Preparation and since the tomb was nearby, they laid Jesus there* (John 19:41-42).

About 1,500 years after the Israelites' very first Passover in Egypt, they still celebrated the feast as the Lord instructed. The lamb they sacrificed was a picture of the Christ. Jesus Himself was crucified on the Day of Preparation—the fourteenth day of Nisan. This is no coincidence, as this was the day on which the Passover lamb was prepared. Not only was the Messiah prophesied to be the eternal Passover Lamb, but He was crucified on the day the earthly lambs were slaughtered (see Exodus 12:6). Wow!

It is important to understand that the story of Christ's crucifixion appears not only in the four Gospels but also in the Old Testament. In Psalm 22 David provides a first-person view of how Christ felt as He was crucified. Notice the phrasing in the following passages from the Gospel of Mark and the Book of Psalms:

> *At the sixth hour darkness came over the whole land until the ninth hour. And at the ninth hour Jesus cried out in a loud voice, "Eloi, Eloi, lama sabachthani?"—which means, "My God, My God, why have You forsaken Me?"* (Mark 15:33-34)

> *My God, My God, why have You forsaken Me?* (Psalms 22:1)

The psalm David wrote more than 1,000 years before the cross sends a clear picture of the Christ speaking the very same words Jesus did in Mark 15:34. Reading further into the psalm, you find phrases like *"they have pierced My hands and My feet"* (Ps. 22:16). This is undoubtedly the crucifixion prophesied!

Now take a look at Psalms 22:17: *"I can count all my bones...."* Interesting. Why is this important? Well, if we go back to the Passover lamb in Exodus 12, we see detailed instructions about the feast:

> [The lamb] *must be eaten inside one house; take none of the meat outside the house.* ***Do not break any of the bones*** (Exodus 12:46).

The apostle John makes clear the connection between the experience of the Passover lamb and that of the Lamb of God:

> *When they came to Jesus and found that he was already dead,* ***they did not break his legs****.... These things happened so that the scripture would be fulfilled: "Not one of His bones will be broken"* (John 19:33,36).

John refers here to the prophecy from Psalms 34:20, which says: *"He protects all His bones, not one of them will be broken."* The importance of these details lies in the fact that they leave a divine fingerprint revealing the awesome hand of God. His handiwork ensures that we recognize the connection between the Passover lamb and the Christ!

When Christ at the Last Supper broke bread, He said *"this is My body, which is broken for you"* (1 Cor. 11:24 NKJV). His body was broken, not His bones. What Christ said is that the will and desire of His flesh had been defeated and forced into submission. On the cross, Jesus defeated Adam's obedience to the temptations of his own body (which led to sin over a piece of desirable fruit). We must all follow Christ in this.

Jesus' bones were not broken. Instead, Christ broke down the strongholds!

Eating the Innards Changes the Outers

The details of the Passover Feast are relevant to your newly born-again life in a very basic sense: like a baby, your continued growth requires food. In this case, you need to feed on God's Word—that is, you need to hear it and read it.

Let's take another look at God's instructions to the Israelites:

> *The animals you choose must be year-old males without defect, and you may take them from the sheep or the goats. Take care of them until the fourteenth day of the month, when all the people of the community of Israel must slaughter them at twilight. Then they are to take some of the blood and put it on the sides and tops of the doorframes of the houses where they eat the lambs. That*

> *same night they are to eat the meat roasted over the fire, along with bitter herbs, and bread made without yeast. Do not eat the meat raw or cooked in water, but roast it over the fire—**head, legs and inner parts. Do not leave any of it till morning;** if some is left till morning, you must burn it. This is how you are to eat it: with your cloak tucked into your belt, your sandals on your feet and your staff in your hand. Eat it in haste; it is the Lord's Passover* (Exodus 12:5-11).

Remember that Jesus said, *"Man does not live on bread alone, but on every word that comes from the mouth of God"* (Matt. 4:4). We eat God's Word. Jesus is the Word. John states that *"The Word became flesh and made His dwelling among us…"* (John 1:14).

The first lesson of the Passover lamb is that we are to eat the meat roasted over fire. Jesus, the Passover Lamb—the Word of God—must be roasted over fire. The fire here represents the Holy Spirit. When you receive Christ, you receive the Spirit of God inside you.

> *You, however, are controlled not by the sinful nature but by the Spirit, if the Spirit of God lives in you. And if anyone does not have the Spirit of Christ, he does not belong to Christ. But if Christ is in you, your body is dead because of sin, yet your spirit is alive because of righteousness* (Romans 8:9-10).

The Spirit leads us to truth. The Spirit is a fire that refines us and the input we receive. The Spirit will give you understanding of God's Word. Chapters 14 through 17 of the Book of John describe this in great detail. John the Baptist also tells us in the Gospels that Jesus came to baptize in the Spirit and with fire (see Matt. 3:11; Luke 3:16). Malachi 3:2 says, *"For He will be like a refiner's fire…."*

Fire is used in purifying metals. When applied to meat it kills bacteria and burns fat (unused energy). Jesus, the Word of God, contains neither bacteria nor fat. However, when you read it, you can misunderstand it. A teacher of the Word might even get it wrong. This would most likely be unintentional, but human nature and denominational differences prove that truth is not always taught perfectly.

Let me give you an example. Let's say the Word of God is being taught and the teacher makes this statement: "God already knows your needs and has provided the answer. You just need to receive it. Therefore, you do not need to ask God for anything."

Now put the "fire" of the Holy Spirit to work on this "food." The Spirit only speaks what He hears (see John 16:13), which means you must *hear* the Word to compare any teaching to it. Let's assume you have heard the Scripture in which Jesus said, *"Ask and you will receive"* (John 16:24). Then you remember the Scripture in which James explained *"You have not because you ask not"* (see James 4:2). Do you see how the fire of the Holy Spirit begins to burn off the bacteria and fat from the teaching?

Bear in mind that either the teacher is wrong or you heard the teacher wrong. It would be dangerous and disrespectful to use even a genuine error from the pulpit as an opportunity to judge the teacher. Beware also of entering into pride or speaking against this individual. Humans will never get everything perfect, so be careful how you react.

Not only that, but even if a teaching error is made, there may be some real nutrition later in the teaching. Keep listening and relying on the Holy Spirit to feed you what you need and help you spit out the bones. We are to eat God's Word the way sheep eat their food. Sheep won't eat just anything. Goats, on the other hand, will eat *everything.*

In spiritual terms, eating like a goat means consuming all the worldly input available. While a sheep will find a nice church (a green pasture) to graze, a goat might go any old place for a meal. A sheep has four chambers for digestion, including three that process food before it gets to the stomach. This is a picture of our need to allow the Holy Spirit to refine whatever "input" we are eating. Eating everything is dangerous, but not eating anything is the wrong approach, too.

The Word of God—Jesus—is your food. Make sure the Holy Spirit "cooks" your food, or you might find yourself doing something like forbidding women to teach in the Church. While Paul said that women should remain silent (see 1 Cor. 14:34), the Holy Spirit reminds me that the prophetess Deborah was a judge in Israel and led the entire nation to victory. Good thing she wasn't silent.

When my food is properly "cooked," I look more closely at what Paul said and see where I misunderstood whom he was speaking to and what it was he really meant. After all, it was Paul who employed Priscilla to help in ministry (see Rom. 16:3). Priscilla *is* a girl's name, after all.

Then I remember Paul's admonition that, in Christ, there is neither male nor female (see Gal. 3:28). Little by little, as I allow the Holy Spirit to separate out for me the nutrition that I need, my understanding becomes complete. I'm feeding, not as a goat, but as a sheep. Therefore, I am able to mature in godly wisdom.

The second lesson from God's instructions to the Israelites is that we need to eat all of Christ, leaving none of Him till morning (see Exod. 12:10). If any is leftover it gets burned, which means we lose out on the value of that sustenance!

We cannot receive just a part of Christ; instead we must receive all of Him. It then becomes inappropriate to think that Christ will not heal us, since the Word says that *"by His stripes, we are healed"* (Isa. 53:5). Healing is a part of Him. So the question becomes, what are the attributes of Christ—and am I receiving all of Him?

This is part of our journey, learning to understand all that is available to us in Christ, so that we are *sure* to receive all of Him. We need to ask ourselves which Scriptures challenge us to the depths of our faith. We need to make sure we don't skip over them thinking, "I'm not interested in that right now," or "That one is inconvenient at the moment."

In my crusades in India, I have had a great many Hindus in the audience. Hindus are polytheistic, meaning they believe in many gods. It is easy for them to receive Jesus; they just throw Him into their mix of gods. At some point, the Gospel will reveal an age-old "Thou shalt not" and tell them that God is the only God. Here is where some Hindus reject Christ. Why? They are not willing to eat all of Him; they do not want the part that requires them to get rid of their other gods.

We can be picky eaters, too. Exodus 12:9 tells us to eat the "inner parts"—the *innards*. Eeeeek! Whatever these innards are, I doubt that any amount of garlic salt will make them tasty. Some Scriptures are like cake. They are pleasing to eat. Other Scriptures, however, are like asparagus: the pastor is preaching; you are really into it; then suddenly, he feeds you a long, nasty green thing. You can probably tell that I really don't like asparagus. Yet I know that it is the healthiest part of the meal. Pastor can season it a bunch and try to make it appealing, but it might still taste bitter.

The Passover Feast is so relevant to the Christian life. For one thing, it shows us the importance of hearing and reading God's Word. This is our first lesson after we get saved. Yet so many Christians are not going to church to hear the message. Their Bibles are collecting dust and so they stop growing.

If you have fallen into this trap, commit today to the growth God has for you. Clean off your plate, asparagus and all. Growing through life lessons is a hard way to live. If you want your pudding, you had better eat your veggies! God's wisdom is key.

So how does all of this taste so far? Well, keep eating!

Chapter 5

Turning up the Heat

When my son Matthew was four, I took him to Starbucks to have some Daddy-son time. I got my cup of fleshly, desirable sin (a Caramel Macchiato), and ordered him some juice and a muffin. We sat down and I began to share with Matthew, in the hopes of promoting his moral and spiritual growth.

We started with the basics. "Matthew," I asked, interrupting myself with a sip of joe, "do you know Jesus?"

He quickly answered in his best little-boy voice, "Yeah, Jesus is in my hut."

Perfect. He was ready for some real moral input now. I leaned forward with my cup in both hands, "Did you know that He protects you?"

"Uh huh," he replied, "He makes me do bad things."

Coffee came out of my nose with a really hard laugh that I tried to suck back. Needless to say, we addressed Matthew's misconceptions of what Jesus is here to do for us.

But how often do we adults misjudge what God does for us? Does God heal us or make us sick? Or is He indifferent about the issue altogether? What is His role in our lives? Do we settle for the destructive picture of God the Old Testament seems to paint? Are we focused on His harsh dealings with sin?

For some, the answer is *yes.* My point is that unless we really study the Bible, we do not understand the full picture of who God is. If our journey is to be successful, it is very important for us to keep track of who is in charge of what. Studying and reading God's Word, which was our first lesson for growth, will help us to rightly divide the roles and identities of God, satan, and ourselves.

Keep reading.

It's Time to Leave Egypt

The car is packed. The kids are loaded. Even so, the road ahead might look rough. It might even beckon you to go back inside to the comforts of home—the way things used to be...the place familiarly furnished with habits, patterns, and predictability.

Sin rules our lives before we receive Christ. It is a life of doing whatever feels good at the moment and whatever gets us through the week. We barely get to work; we drift along, barely working and barely living.

Before meeting Christ, sin is no big deal, because we don't know any better. Life's pleasures drive us to make the decisions we make. We are restrained only by what is socially acceptable or, in some cases, legal. Deep down, however, sin condemns us to death and destruction, in this life and the life to come. God's most powerful Word spoke that fact into existence; He said that if Adam ate of the tree, he would surely die.

Before Christ, we serve sin, the world, and satan; but when we receive Christ we are freed from that destructive hold. The spirit man is transformed instantly, but the soul grows out of the old ways slowly. When you awaken the morning after receiving Christ, you still have many of the sin habits you had the day before. Sin's desire to master you remains. However, the power of sin to separate you from God's safety and life is already defeated. Sin's power is gone!

Here is a picture of the power of sin to destroy and the power of the blood of Christ to redeem:

> *On that same night I will pass through Egypt and strike down every firstborn—both men and animals—and I will bring judgment on all the gods of Egypt. I am the Lord. The blood will be a sign for you on the houses where you are; and when I see the blood, I will pass over you…* (Exodus 12:12-13).

The blood is the redemptive power that removes the consequence of death from our lives. Destruction cannot enter our homes. So who is it that killed Egypt's firstborn?

God says in the passage above that *He* is going to do it. Now a teaching has permeated the Body of Christ for years, stating that God is a good God who isn't in the business of killing (especially children). He is in the business of saving. It is important that we assign the right attributes of God in our faith, so that we learn to understand His ways.

After all, Hebrews 3:10 explains that the Israelites did not enter the Promised Land because they did not know God's ways. The Amplified Bible says, *"they have not perceived or recognized My ways and become progressively better and more experimentally and intimately acquainted with them"* (Heb. 3:10 AMP). If we are to enter *rest,* then we need to gain an understanding of God's ways. We are using the Lord's name in vain when we are assigning to Him actions or words that are not His.

In Exodus 12:12-13, God clearly says that He will be the one striking down the firstborn. Later in the story, however, He describes the event like this:

> *When the Lord goes through the land to strike down the Egyptians, He will see the blood on the top and sides of the doorframe and will pass over that doorway, and He will not permit the* ***destroyer*** *to enter your houses and strike you down* (Exodus 12:23).

Enter a new character called *the destroyer.* Now I find in the Word that various terms are used interchangeably to mean the same thing. For instance, water typically represents the Word of God, as in Ephesians 5:26 where Jesus is seen washing us with water through the Word.

Other interchangeable terms are found when Jesus talks about satan. Jesus describes him as a thief (see John 10:10). Notice, by the way, that Jesus never connects an action to satan that would also be an attribute of God. God and satan share no similarities. For example, God's Word is truth, while satan is the father of lies (see John 17:17; 8:44).

Jesus also described satan as the one who comes to destroy (see John 10:10). So satan is the destroyer, not God. Now we can understand who killed the firstborn in Exodus 12. The Holy Spirit is "cooking" the Word for us and letting us in on a secret: satan and his forces are the ones who traveled through town killing kids.

We also know that God would not allow the destroyer into homes bearing the blood of the lamb on their door frames. So again, who was doing the killing? Did God shut Himself out of those homes? No! Satan and his forces were the murderers and God was the one who protected His people.

Destroyer on a Leash

As you can see, God remained in complete control of the event. So why did He say at first that He would be doing the killing? The answer is simple. God recognized His accountability in allowing satan to kill the firstborn. The Egyptians' firstborn would not have been killed if they had obeyed God and allowed the Israelites to leave.

Furthermore, the punishment was defined much earlier, when the Egyptians murdered Israelite babies during the time of Moses. Egypt sowed death and they reaped it. Satan has never had a free pass to randomly kill believers or unbelievers. If he did, we would all be dead. He needs permission—and the Egyptians unwittingly gave it to him.

Let's consider a modern-day, fictitious example of how this works. Our lead character is Todd Flanders. Todd is recently born again and just got fired from the lumberyard. When Todd asks why he is being fired, his boss explains that it is because he has been late for work 12 times in just the last three weeks. Although Todd is a good employee overall, he is still expected to obey company policies. That includes showing up for work on time.

Stunned by his dismissal, Todd asks, "Dear God, how could You let this happen to me?"

So, here is my question: Who fired Todd? Well the boss might say that he or she fired him. Based on the physical circumstances, that would be true. The company owner who wrote the lateness policy might say, "Well, I did it. They were my rules and he didn't obey them."

Yet, who really fired Todd?

Todd fired Todd. He fired himself when he chose disobedience. It's the way God's system works. God created it in such a way that sin curbs its own growth by eventually producing death. If it did not, sin would never stop growing.

At the time of Moses' birth, Pharaoh ordered the killing of Hebrew baby boys because he feared the growth of the Israelite population (see Exod. 1:8-17). Egypt sowed death, and because the Egyptians were not redeemed from sin, their disobedience led to more death (the ten plagues of disobedience).

This is a principle that God instituted. So of course He would say, "It's My rule. I did it." But who is the actual destroyer? Satan. So then the destruction came from satan. Once again, accountability leads us to the root by tracing the sequence back to whomever chose the path of destruction in the first place. Well then, that would be Pharaoh.

God is not afraid to be accountable as the ultimate authority for the systems He created. God readily stands up and says, "Yeah, I did it." But then we have to study the Scripture to find out why the system works the way it does. If we don't, the world will reject God on the basis of a misunderstanding.

I often hear people say they do not want to believe in a God who creates so much death and poverty. In reality, they don't understand how the system works. God does not create death and poverty; He helps us to overcome!

God Is Good

God is a good God. This idea continues to change the Body of Christ's thinking because the Scripture bears out this truth the more deeply you study it. Free will allows a drunk driver to enter a vehicle and smash into a car killing a child. Although God created free will, God did not kill the child.

Satan certainly had something to do with it, because he helped with the temptations and stupidity. There is a real battle with a real enemy and we must be prepared to fight. We must be vigilant and we must paint that blood over our doorposts. The Israelites were not perfectly obedient, but the blood over their doors brought protection, redemption, and forgiveness of sin.

Recognize in your life that you are protected by God, not because of how you live but because you have Jesus' blood covering your household. Jesus has provided this blood to keep the destroyer out of your home. Paint it on your doorframe. I pray the blood of Jesus over my children and family daily. I thank Him that they are fully redeemed from the curse of sin and death. It's a crazy world, but we need not fear, because Christ has overcome the world!

Now that we have clarified the role of satan as destroyer, we need to recognize our part. If you drink four diet sodas every day and develop a disease from the chemicals, this is probably not from satan (although he will gladly take credit for the diet-soda temptation). We do things that hurt ourselves sometimes, too.

How Good Is "Good"?

In Exodus 12:31, Pharaoh's oldest son has already been struck down by the destroyer. As the nation wails through the night, Pharaoh summons Moses and Aaron and tells them that the Israelites can leave. The agreement is that the Israelites will go worship the Lord in a three-day journey into the desert. Pharaoh is smart enough to know that if he lets them go that they will not be coming back.

So here it is—a free ticket to leave. The Israelites ask the Egyptians for clothing, silver, and gold before they go, and the Egyptians give it to them (see Exod. 12:35-36). After losing their firstborn children, the important things in life have become clear to the Egyptians. Wealth means nothing to them right now. *Just get these Israelites out of here!*

When Moses first arrived to convince the Israelites to follow him out of Egypt, they were hesitant. So God had Moses sell them on it. One of the great selling points was the promise of a new land flowing with milk and honey. God understands our nature; He knows that if He wishes to lead us somewhere, He has to find ways to motivate us. The land really is better, but it is important that we *understand* that it *is* a better place or we may not go.

In our journey God is taking us to a *"good and spacious land"* (Exod. 3:8), but just how good is it? And what is it like? Uh, it's really good. I think Moses would call it a *great land*. So then, let's define what *good* means to God.

Remember that when God created the world He called creation "good" (see Gen. 1). So, the word *good* here means more than what we might think. Consider this: If I wanted to convince my wife that we should move to Tucson, she would ask, "What's it like?"

If I say, "Well, it's good." She won't be very motivated to make the change. But if I used the Hebrew word *towb* that is translated "good" in Exodus 3:8, she would be more likely to pack up the house. *Towb* indicates something that is excellent and pleasant to the physical senses.[1] The definition also indicates sensual pleasure. Not just that, but the place will be spacious.

Suddenly, we are talking about a really nice place with a bunch of people living there who agree. Besides, it will be flowing with milk and honey. Sounds like an advertisement for Willie Wonka's Chocolate Factory—a land flowing with milk chocolate and nougat.

Scripturally speaking, the "milk and honey" description is better than that. The word for "milk" in Exodus 3:8 is *chalab.* It means to "suck the milk of nations."[2] One of the great things about the Promised Land is that when you arrive there, you will inherit cities you did not build, and wells you did not dig (see Deut. 6:10-11). This sounds more enticing than having a big river of milk, although that could be cool.

The word *honey* in the Scripture again represents delicacies provided by nature, and is symbolic of pleasure for our flesh. Wow. (Another wow.)

You see, the Gospel doesn't stop with "Jesus died for our sins"; that is where it starts. The Passover starts your journey away from sinful pleasures and toward godly pleasures.

Now in Christianity we are pretty cautious when talking about experiencing sensual pleasures. The world doesn't give us much credit for enjoying life's pleasures, either. According to the movie *Monty Python's Holy Grail,* if you want to follow Christ, you should starve yourself and bang your head on a stone tablet. The Bible, however, does not submit to religion or its theologies. The Bible promises us a land full of—watch yourself now—stuff you didn't earn and physical, sensual pleasure. That's a sales pitch that should get us moving!

I preached with an evangelist at a crusade once who in his altar call focused on all that a person must give up to follow Christ. By the time he was done I was thinking, "Geez, I'm not sure I want to be a Christian anymore."

But God in all of His wisdom sells the new place to the Israelites the way people should be sold on things, by offering hope of a better tomorrow. Jesus does the same with us. He doesn't introduce the Gospel by telling us of the sacrifice, but of the promises. The sacrifice will come. Imagine Moses telling the Israelites, "Hey guys, listen, God is bringing us out of Egypt into the Wilderness where we will learn through sacrifice and self-denial the power to love each other better. Oh, and there isn't much water."

Any religion residing inside of you wants to argue with me, but let's stay with the Word of God here. The promise that God used to motivate Israel was hope of a better place. Let me explain.

Money?

Uh—OK, so before we go anywhere, let's cut to the chase and deal with the question many of you have been waiting to ask. It's the money question.

"Is this going to be one of those money books?" you ask.

Well, no, this is a book about growth.

"Does God want me to be rich?"

That may be the wrong question. The real question is whether God wants you to be successful in fulfilling your destiny—the one He has ordained for your life.

The answer is, "Ah, yes. He does."

Your destiny fulfillment may require great resources. Or it might not. John the Baptist and Elijah did fine with very little, but then Abraham was really wealthy. We would consider them all to be godly men, right?

I will be sharing lots of Scriptures about all of God's promises for you, but not just yet. For now, let's just say that God is not the least bit offended by wealth. He created it.

Pleasures for the Flesh?

So what of these sensual pleasures we are promised? God invented great food. God invented sex. God invented sleep. God invented gold and had Eden flowing with it.

These are all good things. So let's look at sex for a second. (Here come the earmuffs.) Let's say a teenaged guy named Jimmy has been involved off and on in sexual relationships. He has even scored a few one-night stands. Sex to Jimmy has been a learning experience. He feels a lot of pressure to be seen as a good sexual partner. He really wants to be good at it.

However, there is much confusion in the bedroom. It's not like the movies or even the porn he has watched. In the end, the act is too short, not to mention uncomfortable in the morning. There's the fear of failed contraception and of getting AIDS. Nonetheless, a few moments of pleasure drive Jimmy relentlessly to score the next "chick."

Now imagine that Jimmy has gotten saved. Even though he doesn't know the rules of Christianity, he's pretty confident that one-night stands are not on the list of acceptable behaviors. Heck, they might even violate one of the Ten Commandments.

What Jimmy doesn't yet realize is that, if he matures in the Lord correctly, the Lord has a perfect spouse for him. He still has a lot of cleaning up to do, but if he stays on course and is patient, he will find himself in a monogamous relationship. Just keep it clean, Jimbo, and shoot for that wedding day. Love her enough to wait. When you are in the bedroom with the woman you love and are committed to in marriage, there is a level of intimacy that can never be achieved by sinning. It is a level of sensual pleasure, of learning and exploring each other's moods and desires, and passions and bodies, which porn can never duplicate. This is the intimacy where two literally become one.

Immaturity says, "Oh, marriage ruins relationships." This immaturity guards a person's heart so that they never fully give themselves to another. They don't realize that sexual pleasure is increased when you give yourself over to be fully engaged in commitment and trust and some good old-fashioned, healthy experimentation and communication.

Jimmy, if you stay the course there is *honey*, real physical, sensual pleasure that leads not to death, but to life. Here you become one with your mate—emotionally, physically, spiritually, and intellectually. She knows how you like it and you know how she likes it. There is no fear of disease and no insecurity. And let's face it, who you marry impacts greatly your ability to succeed and enjoy the ride of life.

The challenge is that, while God created these pleasures, satan offers shortcuts designed to destroy our lives. In our journey, godly pleasures require a bit more patience. But my friend, they are coming. And these pleasures don't lead to abortions or disease; they lead to life in the heart, fire in romance, breath from Heaven, and sometimes children, too.

I should know; I've got four.

Not Everyone Leaves Egypt

Some Christians never leave Egypt. They get saved by the blood of the Lamb, and that's it. Same life, same everything. Nothing changes. They ignore the call to maturity long enough that they don't even hear it anymore.

This may be your story. You waited for a change, but it never happened. Maybe you added a once-a-week visit to church, but your habits, desires, actions, emotions—*everything else*—stayed the same.

What happened? What went wrong? It's called *resistance*. Leaving Egypt is not easy. *Staying there* is easy, at least in the short run. I received Christ at age three. My mom told me to go in my room, ask Jesus into my heart, and then pick up my Lincoln Logs.

My journey was strange, in that I left Egypt behind as a toddler. I had to enter Egypt at age 14 or so, in order to leave it in earnest. By 15, I was full-on building pyramids, indulging the flesh in whatever ways I could get away with. Stole, lied, cheated, drank, cussed, and looked at my friend's dirty magazines. Son of the preacher, no less.

I tried to leave Egypt at age 15, after a great church camp. I even threw away my Def Leppard records. The effort ended in defeat, however. Three short days after my recommitment, I dug through the garbage to retrieve my copy of *Hysteria.*

At 18, I finally got out of Egypt for good. Why did it take three years? For a simple reason: it's hard to leave. As you read these words, many of you are thinking of people you know who are still in Egypt. You're all, "Yeah, Cheryl is still out partying on the weekends, playing it up. Then she goes all spiritual on Sunday. Some Christian she is."

Well, so much compassion, eh? Remember, it's tough to leave. Watch this:

> *When Pharaoh let the people go, God did not lead them on the road through the Philistine country, though that was shorter. For God said, "If they face war, they might change their minds and return to Egypt." So God led the people around by the desert road toward the Red Sea…* (Exodus 13:17-18).

God said that *if* they faced war they might change their minds and return to slavery. We can deduce two things from this statement: The first involves the concept of free will that I mentioned earlier. God is showing us the *power* of our free will.

It is a fact that man can be unpredictable. By this statement, I am not questioning God's omniscience. God has a good plan for your life that He wishes you to follow, but you might not follow it. He wrote the pages of His plan before one day of your life came to pass. But you can choose not to follow His script. That's free will. There is a lot of authority placed in your hands to change the story.

The second thing I would like to point out is that those who leave Egypt are fragile. God is aware that the state of those entering the Wilderness is unstable at best. Any resistance and they might just return to the old way of life.

When we get born again we, too, are fragile. The comforts of familiarity lie in wait to tempt us back to Egypt. Yet the pay-off from sin is always disappointing. In contrast to the life Jesus provides, Egypt is a place of physical destruction. For those who remain there, I can neither say that they are guaranteed a place in Heaven, nor that they have lost their salvation. Salvation is in the heart of the believer. Only the individual truly knows whether he or she is saved. But, what I can say for certain is that, in Egypt, destruction is a given.

It's no good to be a Christian and have no light to shine. Of course, let him who has no sin cast that first stone.

A U-turn

We fragile souls who leave Egypt behind are not left to our own devices. At this stage of the journey, God guides us with a cloud by day and a pillar of fire by night (see Exod. 13:21). A large ball of flaming gas and fire in the night sky beckon us in the right direction. The Holy Spirit is that fire and cloud to keep us moving away. Our common sense provides some guidance as well; as new Christians we know that there is a difference between the way we have been living and the new life we should be living.

God is serious about making sure we *know* which way to go. Interestingly, the Israelites do not head in the direction of the Promised Land at first. God leads them in what seems to be the wrong direction! They go south when they are supposed to go east.

God suddenly doubled backed on them. That's right; they made a U-turn. In Exodus 14:2, God said, *"Tell the Israelites to turn back."* Now when I make a U-turn, it gives the impression that I am lost or have missed my turn. If I'm an Israelite I'm thinking, "Ummm, who's driving here?"

Yet, God was sending a message to Pharaoh. He tricked Pharaoh into thinking the Israelites had been thrown into confusion. By doubling back, they pinned themselves to the Red Sea and were hemmed in by the mountains. If they had headed east earlier, they could easily have avoided the Red Sea problem.

Pharaoh saw an opportunity and he pulled out all the stops. He pursued Israel in hopes of taking them back to Egypt. You see, when you leave captivity, satan fears that sin has lost its hold on you. He has seen the movie before; he has watched folks like Billy Graham grow up and do terrible things to his work of darkness.

That is why sin chases those who have been freed from the captivity of sin. Temptation pulls out all the stops. Suddenly, a guy like our fictitious friend Jimmy has girls winking at him at the Jiffy Lube. His worldly buddy Charlie plans a big drinking party for Friday night. The alarm clock catches fire on Sunday morning and Jimmy misses church. Everything tries to get him back to Egypt.

Leaving Egypt is a struggle. When you first receive Christ, sin's master gets worried. Temptation works overtime. But don't worry; God is leading you. Not only that, but everything sin has stolen from you must be paid back.

The Fear of Leaving

Another reason people struggle to leave Egypt is because of fear. In Exodus 14:10 the Israelites see the Egyptians pursuing them. They are understandably terrified and cry out to the Lord.

What terrifies us? It's that feeling that everything and everyone we have believed and built our lives on has crumbled. Suddenly, you discover that you don't know everything. You wonder what you are doing. You might even argue with yourself, as the Israelites argued with Moses: *"Didn't we say to you in Egypt, 'Leave us alone...?'"* (Exod. 14:12).

The Israelites were sure they were going to die. Don't forget though, that they did cry out to God and received help from His representative, Moses. God has designed a system of authority: there are those to whom we submit, those whom we work alongside, and those who submit to us.

The Israelites had a God-given authority placed over them. That authority came from God. Moses, their leader, reassured them and said, *"Do not be afraid. Stand firm and you will see the deliverance the Lord will bring you today"* (Exod. 14:13).

God was *seriously* serious about leading His people to freedom and provided all the guidance Israel could ever need.

Authority on Earth

In the midst of this dramatic scene, God speaks to Moses, saying:

> *Why are you crying out to Me? Tell the Israelites to move on. Raise your staff and stretch out your hand over the sea to divide the water so that the Israelites can go through the sea on dry ground* (Exodus 14:15-16).

Apparently, the people aren't the only ones crying out to God. It seems Moses does too, because God asks him, *"Why are you crying to Me?"*

It's good to know that even our best leaders are human. We honor them because they are our leaders, not because they do everything perfectly. *Of course* Moses would cry out to God when the Israelites are trapped!

Now watch this important concept hidden in this exchange. God says, *"Tell the Israelites to move on. Raise your staff...."* It's almost as though God is asking Moses, "Isn't the solution obvious?" God's question reveals that the solution is within *Moses'* authority. "No need to bother Me with this one. Command it and the sea will part," God implies.

Moses has an action to perform. He is to raise the staff and stretch out his arm. But why must Moses do this? Can't God part the sea by Himself? The answer is a definite, "Yes!" Yet, because man has the authority to manifest God's will on earth, the action is not just an opportunity; it is a responsibility. In this instance, God is revealing that He will not move until man becomes a willing participant. Whoooah, there, big fella…let me continue before you get mad at me.

Can man stop God? Of course he can. Man stopped Jesus from performing miracles in His own hometown, simply by not believing. God wishes that none would perish, yet many do. Why? Because man *can* stop God— not because we are stronger than Him, but because God has created a system that involves both our authority on earth and our free will.

Here's an earthly example of how authority works: I directly oversee the financial division of our ministry. Yet, when a check needs to be written, no one has to call me and say, "Hey, we need a check down here right away."

They know how I would reply: "Why are you crying to me? Just cut the check."

The authority to write checks has already been delegated to our Finance team. If a check needs to be cut and no one takes care of it, I'll get involved. But instead of writing the check myself, I might show up in the finance office and say to the Accounts Payable director, "Stretch out your fingers over that keyboard and type in the data. Then print the check."

That is how God works with us. He has entrusted us with the world. He still signs the checks; it's His money, and we know we shouldn't be cutting checks He wouldn't approve of. We need to recognize the authority and power He has delegated to us so that we can take care of our "departments."

That is why God asked Moses, "Why bug *Me* about this?" Here's my paraphrase: "Just do what needs to be done with the authority I have given you! Part the sea. Walk on it, if you like. Just do *something*."

Getting across your Red Sea is not easy when sin is in hot pursuit, but you *can* leave Egypt. Want to know how? Just turn the page.

Chapter 6

"Are Your Peeps Eagles or Beagles?"

Moses stretched out his hand over the sea, and all that night the Lord drove the sea back with a strong east wind and turned it into dry land (Exodus 14:21).

HERE IT IS, your escape route, just when you thought you were trapped. Sin is about to overtake you, but if you cross over to the other side you will be set free.

Everyone at some point makes a second decision in their Christianity, the first being to receive Christ. The second decision is to leave sin behind. Does this mean you don't sin anymore? Of course not. Get ready to fall on your face a bunch more, because this is a decision to leave a *lifestyle* of sinning.

Once your decision is made and you cross over to the other side, the walls of water that were held back by the Lord come crashing down on your pursuers. The Egyptians are buried in a watery grave.

> *The water flowed back and covered the chariots and horsemen—the entire army of Pharaoh that had followed the Israelites into the sea. Not one of them survived* (Exodus 14:28).

What just happened? Well, you made it to the Wilderness. Doesn't look like much yet, but it is a time for great rejoicing for three reasons. The first is this: you have an opportunity to forgive and forget.

Forgive and Forget

Hebrews 8:12 quotes what the prophet Jeremiah wrote 550 years before Christ's birth: *"...For I will forgive their wickedness and will remember their sins no more"* (Jer. 31:34).

The Red Sea pummeling the Egyptians is the picture God wants you to envision as you consider His forgiveness. He has thrown your sins into the sea of forgetfulness. When you receive Christ and ask the Father for forgiveness, He is faithful to forgive you. You may still remember your sin, but He does not.

When Jenny was 15 years old she found out her boyfriend had gotten her pregnant. Her answer was to have an abortion. She was a kid. The government made it easy. Her friend had done the same. Without anyone's parents finding out, she had the procedure done. If only she had known then what she knows now.

Our society believes that a teenager is mature enough to make that decision. Whew. Jenny has kept this secret for some time. She is saved, and she feels terrible about the choice she made. She keeps rewinding her life to tell God one more time how sorry she is. "But God, I'm really sorry about what I've done."

Meanwhile, God is wondering what Jenny is talking about. He has forgotten it. "Seriously?" some would ask. "Could God really forgive Jenny her abortion?"

Religion asks that sort of question. Jesus says, "Jenny, what you did is buried in the Red Sea."

It is no coincidence that God used the *Red* Sea. Red symbolizes the forgiveness provided by Jesus' blood, the blood that washes us as white as snow.

Maybe not today, but one day you will learn to forgive yourself.

Salt and Yeast

The second and third reasons for celebrating your entrance into the Wilderness are connected. They are the metaphors God crafts with salt and yeast. Before we address these principles, allow me to set up a foundation for the concept of transition, beginning with the first transitional feast shown on our map from Figure 1, repeated here. This is the Feast of Atonement, which is described in detail in Leviticus 23:26-32.

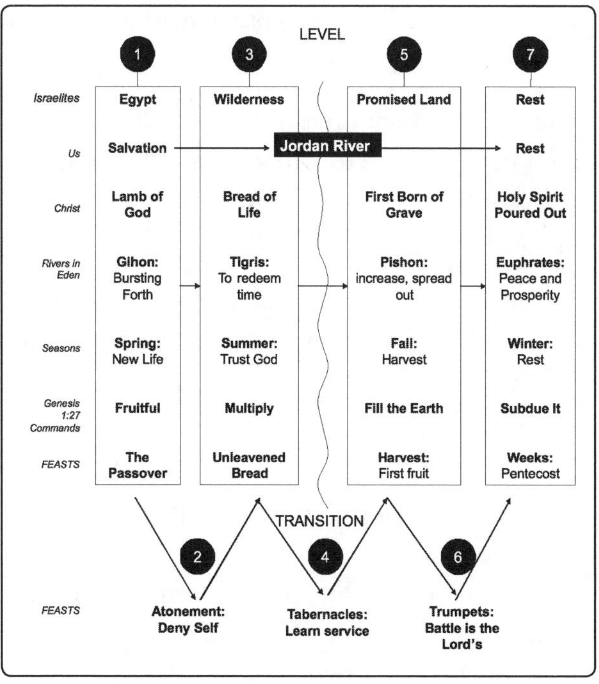

[Figure 1]

Notice that each feast includes one key detail that must be carefully followed or the people will be punished. This fact helps us to identify the key. In the case of the Feast of Atonement, the detail is found in Leviticus 23:29: *"Anyone who* ***does not deny himself*** *on that day* ***must be cut off from his people."***

The key in this Feast of Atonement is to deny yourself. It is necessary to hold fast this key in order to unlock the door, the transition to the Wilderness. What am I saying? Simply this: you must deny yourself in order to get out of Egypt.

In Matthew's Gospel, Jesus addresses the transition everyone must go through, as He did Himself:

> *Then Jesus said to His disciples, "If anyone would come after Me, he must deny himself and take up his cross and follow Me"* (Matthew 16:24).

Jesus here announces the idea of the cross before He has died upon it. This must have seemed more confusing to the disciples than it is for us now. Remember that the cross was Jesus' purpose. Christ asks us to deny ourselves and seek *our* purpose.

Taking up your cross does not mean dying for the sins of mankind. Jesus did that for us. Taking up your cross might, however, mean enduring some pain. Hard work is a form of pain. Your purpose will probably demand hard work, which implies denying yourself.

Although purpose is important in this transition, your purpose will unfold as more of a marathon, because it is part of your entire journey.

For now, we will focus on denying *self.*

You Are Not Yourself

As funny as that may sound, you are not yourself. You are a spirit, made in the image and likeness of God (see Gen. 1:26). You have a *self.* It is yours. Therefore you may call yourself *my*self.

Self is a pretty big deal. It embodies many of the tools you will need to accomplish your purpose and bring the Lord's will *"on earth as it is in heaven"* (Matt. 6:10). Your *self* is composed of body, mind, will, and emotions—tools God has provided to help you on your way.

Yet, these tools can malfunction or dysfunction, particularly when influenced by our desires. The body has four main desires: to eat, sleep, procreate, and experience God. All of these desires serve a purpose. For example, eating keeps the body nourished. However, desire can lead you to eat foods that are not nourishing. Therefore, the same desire that supports life can also make you bloated and sick.

The same is true for sleep. Sleep provides necessary rest and renewal for mind and body. However, this desire can malfunction, causing you to oversleep and become lazy and unproductive.

The yearning for God's presence is another powerful God-given part of *self*. Adam was created to live in God's presence. Every human being has the innate desire to experience God's presence. This is why a beer and a cigarette are so addicting. They are the body's counterfeits for the burden-removing experience of being with God.

Individuals who are built to lead worship have a passion and desire to be musical. It drives them to become skilled in music. The purpose of their talents and drive are to usher themselves and others into the presence of the Lord. When music does not accomplish its divine purpose, the soul is left empty and susceptible to counterfeits. This explains why musicians often struggle more deeply than others with cravings for drugs and alcohol, especially around concert time.

The human body also desires to procreate. This desire can malfunction in many ways (we don't need to go into detail here). These desires can bring life or death; therefore, our handling of desire will determine the outcome of our journey. If we fail to deny ourselves, desire will inevitably lead to destruction.

How does the denying of self relate to the Israelites journey or the ministry of Jesus? For starters, both were led by God. The Israelites followed the cloud and the fire through the Wilderness. Jesus was led there by the Spirit:

> *Then Jesus was led by the Spirit into the desert to be tempted by the devil. After fasting forty days and forty nights, He was hungry* (Matthew 4:1-2).

Jesus' ministry started when John baptized Him at the Jordan River and the Holy Spirit descended on Him like a dove. We will see in greater detail later that the Jordan is the same river the Israelites crossed (and we must cross) before entering the Promised Land.

Right after His baptism, Jesus entered the transition Feast of Atonement. In the Wilderness, He denied Himself the right to eat. Jesus lived the example that we must follow. All these centuries later, He is teaching us that we also must deny the flesh.

Jesus' Wilderness trip was 40 days long, symbolizing the 40 days of rain in the story of Noah. In our lives, this 40 days of rain (the Wilderness) washes us clean of evil influences, just as the Flood washed the earth of its sin. God uses our Wilderness experiences to clean us up.

The very idea of being in the Wilderness means denying the flesh; the place is hot and food and water are scarce. But, learning to say *no* to fleshly desires serves a longer-term purpose. It is like planting a seed, because denying the flesh produces the fruit of *self-control.*

When the Spirit leads you and me into the Wilderness, it is clearly not where we want to go, but where we need to go. God develops in us the ability to abandon ourselves to His will and to trust Him regardless of what we see before us. We must be willing to let go of everything that was familiar.

For the Israelites, everything changed.

YOUR INFLUENCE

How can we possibly be successful in learning to deny self? Well, let's get back to the topics of salt and yeast. The Red Sea is believed to be one of the saltiest bodies of water on the planet, with a salt content averaging 40 ppt (parts per thousand). This is a higher salt percentage than any ocean.[1]

It is not a factual coincidence that the Red Sea is this salty. Jesus said, *"You are the salt of the earth…"* (Matt. 5:13). His statement is profound, and here's why: Salt has many beneficial properties that we need to replicate.

For one, salt is a positive influence where flavor is concerned. We are to become a positive influence in our world. More importantly, salt is a preservative. Before the advent of refrigeration, meats were salted to keep them from spoiling. (We are the earth's preservative!) As such, salt was a valuable commodity. Roman historical records show that soldiers were sometimes paid with salt instead of coins!

Salt is necessary for life. Our bodies need it to maintain many functions, such as balancing heart rate and electrolytes. Likewise, God created us to bring balance to the earth.

You can see that the Red Sea is a picture of being *immersed* in the beneficial qualities of salt. The complete immersion that saved the Israelites destroyed the sin (Pharaoh's army) that was trying to re-enslave the God's people.

Immersion is a powerful theme in the Christian life. We just learned that the Wilderness experience parallels the cleansing action of the Flood upon the earth. We also know that water is symbolic of the Word of God.

> *Husbands, love your wives, just as Christ loved the church and gave Himself up for her to make her holy, cleansing her by the washing with water through the word…* (Ephesians 5:25-26).

Jesus is the Word; the Word cleans us up. So, while the salt of the Red Sea represents positive influence, the water represents the Scripture. When we get born again, we need both.

God is calling us to immerse ourselves for a time in the positive influence of God's Word. We are to be immersed—completely engulfed in—baptized in the water to where it is all we can hear or see. He is asking us to drown ourselves in His Word.

It will make us good and salty.

Get Rid of the Yeast

Now for the yeast, a big key in learning to properly deny yourself sinful habits. On our map, the Wilderness is in the same column as the Feast of Unleavened Bread. Unleavened bread is bread made without yeast. The Feast of Unleavened Bread was initiated on the day following the Passover. Notice what the Israelites were told to do as they began their journey:

> *For seven days you are to eat bread made without yeast. On the first day remove the yeast from your houses, for whoever eats anything with yeast in it from the first day through the seventh must be cut off from Israel* (Exodus 12:15).

The key to this feast is the total elimination of yeast from the diet and even from the house. The assigned disciplinary action makes this detail critical. If the "feds" found yeast in your house, you would be cut off from the nation.

Today, even non-Christians recognize the cardboard taste of a yeast-free communion wafer. But what is the big deal about yeast? Why does Exodus 12:15 make yeast sound like some sort of illicit drug or other vice? (Can you imagine people of that day sneaking off to do lines of yeast or rolling it in hyssop leaves to smoke it?)

Yeast is bacteria from the fungus family. It is a living organism. When yeast eats sugar it urinates and defecates alcohol. That is called *fermentation.* So, yes, alcohol is the fecal matter produced by yeast. The yeast itself slowly dies from the poison of its own waste. Downing a quick beer amounts to ingesting dead yeast.

Yeast serves another function: when it eats sugar, it produces gas. This gas is what causes bread dough to rise. Yeast creates activity, but yeast is not life-giving.

> *Your boasting is not good. Don't you know that a little yeast works through the whole batch of dough?* (1 Cor. 5:6).

In Scripture, yeast symbolizes sinful influence. It is infectious: just a little bit will work itself through a whole batch of dough.

The Israelites were to be yeast-free for seven days. Seven is the number of completion.[2] Being yeast-free does not mean we leave the world forever; remember that we are to be in the world, not of the world. God did not design Christians to completely unplug from the world. If we did, we would be unable to influence the world as salt should. What He is really asking us to do is to get away for a time and be set apart from the worldly influence for a season.

Having left Egypt, the Israelites are alone. There are no worldly peoples nearby to influence them. All they have left of the world are the thoughts and habits packed away in their hearts. Eventually, they will reenter a place full of perversion and sinfulness (Canaan). They will have to displace the worldly nations living there and possess the land.

For now, they are called away from all of that. This is a time for them to be strengthened in God. We need to submit to the same process. How long should you be separated from bad influences? That is up to you. Only you and God know how long it will take for you to become strong in your convictions. Be patient with yourself. It takes time to become the influencer rather than the influenced.

During this season, your sources of influence must change. Deny yourself by turning off the television—not forever, but for a time of denying yourself. If you think you should make a fast out of it, then deny yourself food for a time. Become immersed in the Word and deny yourself any negative or distracting influences.

For how long? The answer is, however long *40* is to you. It might be 40 years or 40 days. I can't say. I do know this: Rick Warren's *40 Days of Purpose* struck a nerve for this very reason: a time of separation is a critical part of our maturity. I have never met a powerful man or woman of the Lord who is changing nations who did not set aside such a time—a time to avoid bad influences and become dedicated to positive influences.

When the earth needed cleaning up, 40 days of rain kick-started the process. It's like rebooting the computer. Do you need a reboot?

Influencers Must Change

Now comes the hardest part of self-denial. Not only do we need to change our *influences*, but God also asks us to change our *influencers.* We may have to change some of the people with whom we associate. Some friends will allow you to go through your change; others will not be as flexible.

Some friends have a strong influence over your life. It could be time for some of them to go. It could be a boyfriend whom you love. You might need to borrow a phrase from NSYNC and say, "Baby, bye, bye, bye…Bye Bye."[3]

When I was 18 years old, I did just this. Friends, and even a high school sweetheart, got pushed out of my life because it was time for me to change. Not only were they not good for me; I was not good for them. Heck, I was a good example of why not to be a Christian.

Everyone was much better off as a result of my decision to change my influences and influencers. I went cold turkey, too. Even television was out. For me, it was the summer of change. It took me, not 40 days, but 15 months to gain some strength and resolve. (I will admit though, that I started watching *Star Trek* again after 90 days—the original *Star Trek,* that is.)

Now if you are married, you do not get to leave that key influencer known as your spouse. Salvation is definitely not a pass for divorce. God hates divorce. Your marriage supersedes the "do not be unequally yoked" Scripture (see 2 Cor. 6:14). God has promised you His strength. He has enabled you to be an excellent example of the change that is going on inside you.

You might be saying, "Rats! I thought I had an out." But, just trust God. Do this His way, and that spouse of yours just might get saved. Then the two of you *and* your relationship will all become brand new!

So far, the hardest part of leaving Egypt is this bit about breaking up with friends who are not good for you. They will not understand your decision; it will not seem to either of you a very "Christian" thing to do. My friends initially hated me for it.

Even today, people say to me, "Well Jesus hung out with the sinners." Well, that's not quite right. Those who he hung out with every day were his disciples, hand-chosen friends. Yet this line of thinking is exactly the trick the enemy uses to convince many to hang out with the wrong people. Remember also that Jesus went out to the Wilderness for a time away from everyone.

See, it matters which season you are in. We are currently in the season of separation. Right now, the best thing for everyone in the long run is to let go. They will see you transform over time and respect you for what you have done. One day, when they hit bottom, they will know who to turn to.

One day, soon enough, you will become the influencer, but first you have to get past the place of being influenced. Then you can start reconnecting with your friends if the Lord leads you to do that. When I was younger and hanging out with the world, I kept sinning. Now that I'm older, I hang out with the lost and they feel uncomfortable around me. "Oh, sorry about my language," they say. "I shouldn't really be doing this, huh?" they query. Funny, don't forget also that even mature Christians fall into sin from time to time.

The transition from being the influenced to the influencer will feel a lot like hanging on a cross. It will be hard to let go of lifelong friends or loves. *Very hard.* So immerse yourself in the Word. Get all the CDs, podcasts, and books you can find about the Lord. Read the Word, go to every church service there is. Make friends with people who are going somewhere, people who love the Lord.

Obviously, you still have to work. If your job is something like bartending, well, you still have to work. Ask God for help and direction concerning this. Quitting and sitting on the couch watching TBN 24/7 is not what I am suggesting. God is simply asking you to change all of your influences and influencers, for a time.

If you do not do this, you may develop a "yeast infection." That is no joke. A yeast infection (no matter how awkward to discuss) will greatly affect your ability to have intimacy with God and to produce the things of God in your life (godly fruit). Many Christians who work really hard to bear fruit do not realize why it is so difficult for them. They have yet to truly make this leap.

If we are to follow Christ, then we should be led by the Spirit into the Wilderness, just as He was.

Again, it is just for a time.

Salt Kills Yeast

In my extensive study of yeast (I'm kidding) I found a bread recipe via Google. The recipe specifically called for lightly salting the bread while being careful because salt kills yeast. What? That's right, yeast's arch-nemesis isn't bleach—it's salt. Good ol' NaCl.

Remembering my college chemistry class, salt is sodium chloride. The chloride part is chlorine. Living in Phoenix, Arizona, the land of the home swimming pool, I've learned that, if you don't want a pool full of algae, you need chlorine. Fill up the play pool without chlorine, let it sit in the sun for a couple of weeks, and watch what grows. It's pretty gross.

Lately, salt is being used in pools instead of chlorine, fostering a naturally occurring process that keep the pool fungi free. Somebody thought up this amazing technology by looking at the ocean. Salt is the reason the ocean doesn't look like your play pool out back.

God's use of salt is so applicable to our lives; His Word helps overcome any fungus in our lives. Let's look at a brief example. Todd, like Jimmy, is recently born again; only Todd is beginning to change his influences. He did not go to his buddy Charlie's Friday drink-o-rama. (First one he's missed in a long time.)

When Todd turned on his phone Saturday morning, there were no fewer than six messages. Five were from Charlie. Each one sounded less cohesive then the one before. One message was from Todd's old on-again, off-again girlfriend.

Todd is tempted to respond to the messages from familiar friends. He and his new Christian friend have, well, nothing in common. Conversation is uncomfortable; everything seems forced. Todd just doesn't feel like himself anymore. A very large part of him feels like it is dying.

It's no wonder that Todd has a strong urge to call Charlie, and make plans for the night. Todd's other alternative is to attend a meeting at his new church. Without a doubt, there is a tug of war going on inside Todd. Yet, he makes the right decision, even if it doesn't feel all that great.

Todd goes to the meeting and is renewed in his newfound faith. The pastor notes that faith comes by hearing. Boy, is he right! In that moment, Todd sees a clear line between his old life and his new life. Some of his favorite activities are on the wrong side of that line like those pay television channels he liked so much.

Little by little, Todd is maturing. The more he learns about the Lord, the better he feels about himself. Suddenly, instead of looking for pay-per-view, Todd wonders, "Where's that darn Christian channel with all the weird-looking people? Oops, can I say *darn* anymore?"

Todd chuckles to himself, but realizes the importance of the changes inside. "Heck, if a 30-minute message from the pastor helped me so much, I better get every bit of godly encouragement I can get my hands on right now."

Great going, Todd! Egypt is in your rearview mirror! Keep reading, reader—you are going places!

Part 2

The Wilderness

Chapter 7

On Time, on Your Dime

WHEW! YOU ARE OUT of Egypt, across the Red Sea, and you, my friend, are in the Wilderness.

Excited? Well, OK, I will admit the Wilderness is *nassogood* as they say. But God is bringing us to a *good* and spacious land. Thing is, there is only one way to get there from here, and that is through the Wilderness.

The Wilderness is a place with purpose. There are things we must learn along the way in order to get to the next level of maturity, which is the crossing into the Promised Land. Some will not even have made it this far, so *congratulations*.

Back to the purpose of the Wilderness. It is here to teach us six major lessons. But, it is also laden with traps. Over the course of this message, I will warn you of three specific traps satan has set for you. For now, let's start with a summary of the six lessons of the Wilderness:

1. The Word of God: In the Wilderness, you will have the opportunity to learn the importance of the water, which is the Word. You will also see how that message is flowing through the Body of Christ. Water is scarce in the Wilderness. Therefore, you must bring water with you—just like you would for any hike in the desert.

2. The Shepherd: The second Wilderness lesson is about the relevance to your life of the Shepherd and the people with whom you travel. We will redefine church; it will be far from the traditional model. Remember that the Israelites were a group of people journeying *together.* The Christian walk is not meant to be traveled alone. People who do not believe in the value of church are hard-pressed to balance this belief with God's Word. After all, the Church is the Bride of Christ. How important is a bride to the groom? Worth dying for, right?

3. Boundaries: One of the first things we need to figure out after we get saved is what the rules are. We desire boundaries for living. This is a natural part of our growth. Looking to Moses and the law will shed considerable light on the subject and on the enemy's third trap for Wilderness travelers.

4. Serving: The fourth lesson of our Wilderness journey involves servanthood. We are on the path to becoming rulers in the earth, but we came out of slavery. So how exactly do we become leaders? We will learn from Jesus that service is the first step.

5. and 6. Grace and Faith: Last, we will enter transition in our lives again as we cross the Jordan and are required to understand both God's (5) grace and (6) faith to make it into the Promised Land successfully. Oh, and don't forget the boundary of *time.* This is a very important boundary; it is the framework within which we carry out our destinies.

How Long Until the Promised Land?

Before we move on to these six lessons, let's take a broader look at the Wilderness and what kind of a place it is.

We have already discovered that being in Egypt is like being in infancy. The Wilderness is another phase of childhood: We have just been born again, but we are still children living at home with our parents. We don't work much and our food and travel expenses are covered. Clothing is provided and even laundered for us.

In the Wilderness, we are in the process of becoming more grown-up and self-reliant, yet we are learning to depend on God to meet our needs. It is the place where we always wonder, "How long?" It's like when our family drives to Disneyland and my daughter Katy asks, "Daddy, how long til we get there? Are we in California yet?"

We ask these questions because we know the Wilderness is not our destination. The fact that the Israelites were stuck there for 40 years makes them a bit like George Costanza from *Seinfeld*. (It's OK if you don't know who this is. It's not critical to your spiritual growth.)

Let me just say that the Israelites' story has a lot to do with their ability or inability to embrace God's perfect plan, which was for Moses to lead the Israelites from Egypt, through the desert, and into the Promised Land in far less than 40 years.

The Original Wilderness Timeline

We have already established that our disobedience can alter God's plan. The Israelites and Moses disobeyed God. As a result, they died in the Wilderness. In fact, it was not until Moses died that the "next" generation of Israelites (along with "old-timers" Joshua and Caleb) were permitted to cross the Jordan.

The idea of God's original timeline intrigues me. I've researched long and hard to find someone who has prepared such a timeline. I looked for accounts that clarify the time span between the Exodus from Egypt and the point at which Moses sent the 12 spies into the Promised Land. I even Googled it. I found no such research, so I did it myself. I muddled through all four books and constructed an accurate timeline from important dates mentioned in the Bible text.

Why do we need this information? I believe it helps us to understand two important points: (1) God doesn't intend to leave us stuck in the Wilderness for 40 years; (2) you can choose to stay stuck there if you like.

You may recall from our map on page 89 that the Wilderness is the stage in which we learn to redeem the time. (Go ahead and take a look at the map now.) This is where God teaches us the value and importance of time, the precious resource that is impossible to replace once it has been lost. (Until we invent a time machine, we are stuck with the cost in time of our mistakes and distractions.)

My point about the original timeline is this: The 12 spies were in the Promised Land for 40 days. Once they returned, the Israelites should have gone straight in and taken Canaan. But alas, the story takes a sour turn. The Israelites do not go in. Instead, they take the 40-year, not-so-scenic route.

Some Christians may be fine with sitting in the Wilderness for 40 years, but not me. I'm convinced we can learn from their mistakes. We can stick to God's original plan for us! That is why I pulled together the timeline in Figure 2. Keep a bookmark at this page. We will refer to this chart often during the next six chapters.

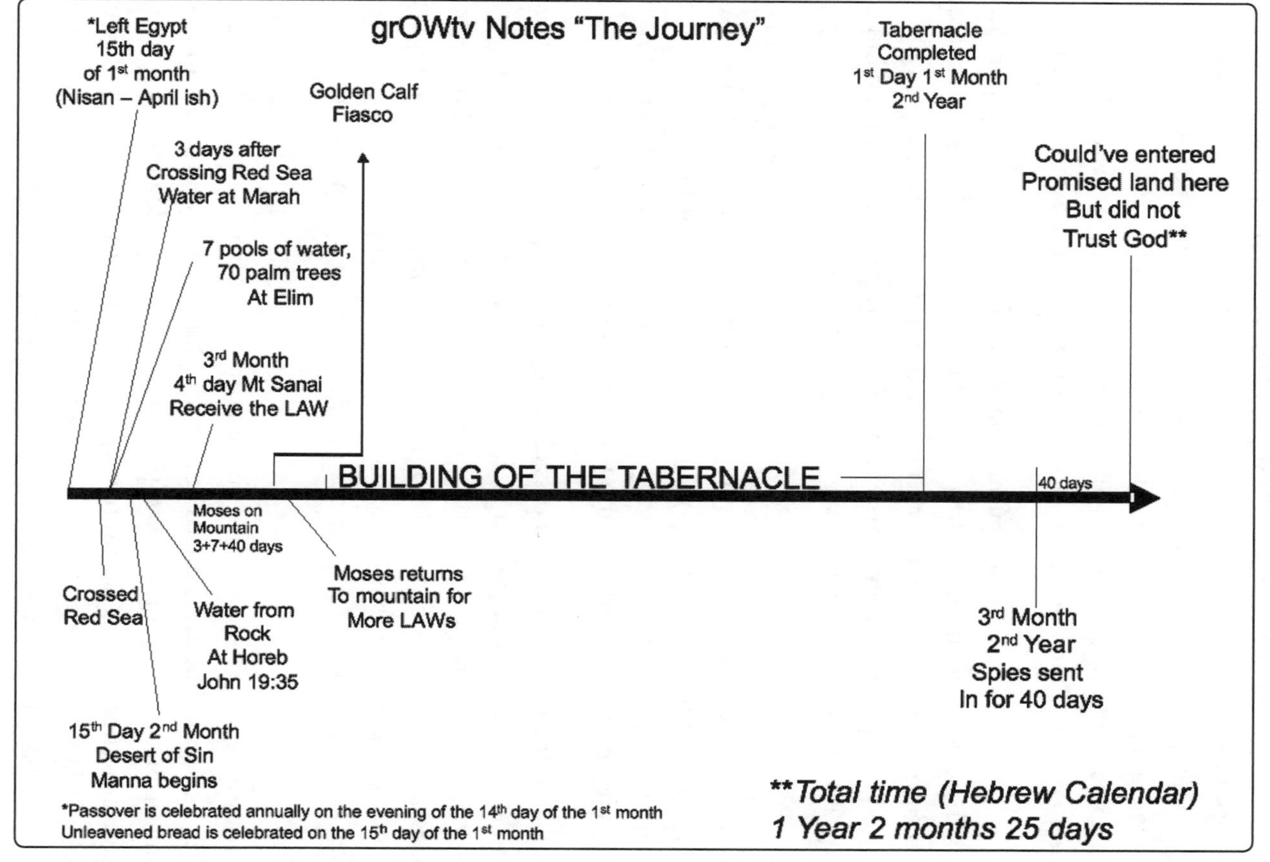
grOWtv Notes "The Journey"
*Left Egypt
15th day
of 1st month
(Nisan – April ish)
3 days after
Crossing Red Sea
Water at Marah
7 pools of water,
70 palm trees
At Elim
3rd Month
4th day Mt Sanai
Receive the LAW
Golden Calf
Fiasco
Tabernacle
Completed
1st Day 1st Month
2nd Year
Could've entered
Promised land here
But did not
Trust God**
BUILDING OF THE TABERNACLE
40 days
Moses on
Mountain
3+7+40 days
Crossed
Red Sea
Water from
Rock
At Horeb
John 19:35
Moses returns
To mountain for
More LAWs
3rd Month
2nd Year
Spies sent
In for 40 days
15th Day 2nd Month
Desert of Sin
Manna begins
*Passover is celebrated annually on the evening of the 14th day of the 1st month
Unleavened bread is celebrated on the 15th day of the 1st month
** Total time (Hebrew Calendar)
1 Year 2 months 25 days

[Figure 2]

Now I've heard it taught before (and I think I have even mentioned it based on hearsay) that the time span between the departure from Egypt and the commissioning of the 12 spies was three months. This is about a year off, though. I think people say this because Moses sent in the spies on the first day of the third month (judging by the time stamp given in Numbers 10:11 and adding the seven days that Miriam was sick in Numbers 12, plus three days of resting).

Still, the first day of the third month means that only two months have passed, not three. And it was actually more than a year before Moses sent in the spies. Let me show why I say this: The Israelites celebrated the Passover after the Tabernacle of the Lord was finished in the Wilderness (see Exod. 40:2; Num. 9:1). It was the fourteenth day of the first month in the year after leaving Egypt. So one year had already passed since the first Passover.

Now we add the two months (from Numbers 10:11) and 40 days (the length of the spies' stay in Canaan), and we see that the Israelites had been one year, two months, and 25 days in the Wilderness according to the Hebrew calendar; or one year, two months, and 20 days according to the Gregorian calendar.

Well that's enough to make a person's head hurt, wouldn't you say? But it is important to know that you don't have to wait 40 years. It is also important to clarify that this time span was longer than the three months that is frequently taught. Also, this chronology helps us to understand the major events and timing of this portion of *our* journey today.

Before we move on, and at the risk of surprising you, I must tell you that most Christians live comfortably right in the Wilderness. Remember that only two of the original millions of Israelites made it into the Promised Land. Likewise today, most Christians settle in the desert. Just as Egypt is the counterfeit of the Promised Land, so also the Wilderness is the counterfeit of our destination—the Place of Rest God is calling us to enter.

That's a sobering statement, but do not be discouraged my friend. Jesus has paved the way.

Attributes of a Wilderness Dweller

Now let's take a look at the characteristics of those who live in the Wilderness. Please take into consideration this important fact: Some areas of your life may be stuck in different parts of this journey. Your health might be in Egypt, while your relationships have the look of the Wilderness. Your financial matters may be in the Promised Land, or even the Place of Rest. What is in your heart governs where you live. Ultimately, if your heart is in the Wilderness, you will eventually find all of the areas of your life settling there as well.

So let's scan this abbreviated list of the six attributes of a Wilderness dweller. You need not display all six characteristics to qualify for Wilderness mentality; one of these features is enough to keep you wandering. We will cover these attributes in depth over the course of this and future chapters. *You will* learn how to be set free from each one of them, so stay with me!

The Wilderness dweller:

1. Blames God for problems and afflictions.

2. Lacks the resources to help others. These resources include money, love, and health.

3. Lives from crisis to crisis and paycheck to paycheck.

4. Switches focus from one thing to another; fails to finish projects; finds it hard to commit.

5. Is judgmental toward others.

6. Might understand purpose, but lacks the resources and focus to fulfill it.

You have made it this far; don't get mad at me now. We all need to be introspective about this, and I dare say that all of us can find one or more of these attributes at work in our lives to one degree or another. I'm also sure we can agree that all of them are detrimental, so let's go ahead and take the first one head-on.

Blaming God

In the Wilderness, the Israelites were often angry and bitter against the Lord and Moses. They were blaming God for their hunger and thirst. We sometimes do the same thing. Some people find it easy to identify their problems, but difficult to give credit where credit is due. Often, they blame God for problems they have instigated themselves or that satan has created.

There are lots of ways of accusing God: "I'm sick because God is teaching me something" is a common approach. Others say, "I'm not sure why the Lord took my son. I guess He just needed my boy more than I did."

What about telling a ten-year-old girl that God took her mom because He needed her in Heaven? That is a great way to teach a child to hate God for the rest of her life!

It is the thief, remember, who comes to steal, kill, and destroy (see John 10:10). We must get it out of our heads that God is the reason for *everything* that happens. God is the source of all that is good. Evil is merely the reaction to the existence of good, not something that God created.

Evil is the absence of good, just like darkness is the absence of light. God has given us charge over this earth. If we let companies put toxins in the water, how can we blame God when someone gets cancer from the pollutants? We need to take charge and administer justice.

That said, we can pray over the sick and see them recover (see Mark 16:18). Healing is from God. When we give God credit for the bad things, we undermine our prayers for deliverance. We are, in effect, praying against what we believe to be God's will. Subconsciously, our minds stop us from believing in the very answer that we want—the answer that God surely wants to give.

What if I choose to violate the speed limit? Well, I am likely to get pulled over. I can ask God to forgive me all I want, but I will still get a ticket. Whose fault is that? Mine!

Believing that God is to blame keeps me living in the Wilderness. Hebrews 3 says that the Israelites remained in the Wilderness because they did not know His ways. God is in the business of blessing us. He has gone to great lengths to get us into the blessing. He gave a great deal to reconnect us to the kind of life that can flow through us. That life is to be the light of men; it makes us the salt of the earth, the influencers of our environment.

Lacking Resources

The second attribute in our list is lack that leaves a person unable to help others. The Israelites only had enough manna to last them that day; they were not living in abundance. I have noticed in my life as well as in the Scripture that there are two types of Christians. The first is the Christian in need of help. When this person's car breaks down, there is no money to get it fixed. Now he or she is unable to get to work.

It's OK to live in this Wilderness lifestyle for a short time; but it is not OK to stay there. God is calling each of us to be the other kind of Christian, the one who can help someone else get their car fixed.

Jesus did not run around showing the crowds how He could heal Himself. "Hey, look everyone. I can make my hand shrivel and then heal it." No! For Christ, the miracles were always for others. He had more than He needed, so He was in a position to give.

There is another characteristic that tends to tag along with lack. It is a judgmental attitude toward Christians who are blessed. "See, I don't need a car like that to be happy." "Even if I had it, I wouldn't spend that kind of money on a dress."

We can all agree that buying "stuff" to be happy is not a good thing. But neither is it good to hold someone else to your self-imposed standards.

The Crisis-to-Crisis Lifestyle

Wilderness dwellers often live from crisis to crisis, generating endless cycles of problems and needs, just as the Israelites did. From extreme thirst to being attacked by a foreign nation, it was crisis after crisis.

As crazy as this may sound, we are most comfortable in panic mode. (Most of us grew up that way.) When one crisis is over, we invent a new one. Relationship crises are a common example. They often result from unbridled gossip as we chat on the phone about who said what and why.

Job-related crises often spring from a self-destruct mechanism that kicks in gear when success is near. Whatever the category of crisis, this kind of living stems from low self-esteem, which causes us to abuse and sabotage ourselves.

Why would we do such things? Often, it is because, deep down, we don't like ourselves. Whatever the nuances, causes, and results may be, this is nothing more than Wilderness mentality. It's a great way to stay stuck in the desert—maybe for a lifetime.

Inability to Commit

Another characteristic of the Wilderness dweller is the inability to truly commit and finish something. Like the Israelites, it is just a wandering through life. Commitment develops momentum in life. If you commit to anything with your whole heart, it will begin to improve.

On the other hand, if you only remain committed when things are going well, the situation will degenerate. It's a matter of taking ownership, come rain or shine. Ask any landlord about how renters treat property. Many renters will not take care of rental property. Why? Because they are not committed to it.

To succeed in any endeavor, whether a job or business venture, you must be committed. Wilderness dwellers often lack that commitment.

They don't hold down jobs very well. They dream of starting this or that business and begin with a lot of passion. They may even convince others of the merits of their idea. But as soon as the real work starts, they move on to the "next" thing.

Judgmentalism

The fifth and most prevalent attribute of the six, is being judgmental of others. It is in the wilderness the law was given, and harsh judgment passed for those who could not completely obey. A person wandering in the Wilderness will often sit in moral judgment of the world and will judge harshly Christians in every non-Wilderness stage of the journey.

When you converse with Wilderness dwellers, they will quickly inform you of what is wrong with every person you name. They will also let you know how they can be fixed. Wilderness dwellers are emphatically judgmental about Promised Land inhabitants, especially if they have any money at all.

A common refrain of judgment is: "Well you know, Jesus told the rich man to give everything to the poor."

No wonder I offended a Christian acquaintance when he found out how many televisions I owned (three at the time). Wilderness dweller. What's funny is that I was in the Wilderness at that time, too. In fact, I judged him for judging me!

What we have to remember is that most people are really trying to do the right thing. If I see a Christian coming out of an R-rated movie, or wearing a mini-skirt, or whatever, my moral judgment of them actually punishes me. It's a disease called *plankitis*—pointing out the speck in someone else's eye when you have a plank in your own (see Matt. 7:4). We do it because it makes us feel better about our own junk. Instead, we ought to love people! If someone gets a nice house, be happy for their success. Someday, it could be you!

There is an element of common sense missing from the religious sometimes; then a vague misunderstanding of the Scriptures is used to back it up. Proverbs 13:22 states that *"A good man leaves an inheritance for his children's children, but a sinner's wealth is stored up for the righteous."* On the other side of the coin, however, are those who use the blessings of the Lord as an excuse to live in greed. We will get to you soon enough. Yes, it is a very, very key part of the journey.

Unfunded Sense of Purpose

The sixth attribute in our list involves the person who understands his or her purpose, but has no resources to allow them to focus on it.

This person is in a good position to transition to the next level; with just one or two more revelations of God's ways he or she will be primed to cross over. This individual is *that* close to making the jump into the Promised Land.

The person may have a great idea for a business, outreach, or ministry; he may have made a pledge to the church missions campaign; she may have a plan to improve the culture of the workplace. Whatever the concept, it has been imagined and birthed, but there are no resources to implement it.

Because of this they will passionately seek outside resources to fund the mission, not realizing that the lack of resources is an indicator that the timing is not yet right. Be patient my friend, slow down. If you birth something prematurely you will have just that—a premature baby that requires a great deal of difficult care. Wait just a bit for the right season.

How are you going to get there? Give me six more chapters and I'll tell you how to have enough to get started.

Wilderness Trap No. 1

We will explore several traps the enemy sets in the Wilderness in order to hold us there or drive us back to Egypt. He generally uses a godly principle and then twists it just slightly to pervert it.

Remember, we all have within us the godly desire to enter the Lord's rest. Remember, too, that the Wilderness is a counterfeit of the Lord's rest. It is the place where God meets our needs the way a parent meets the needs of a young child.

Take a look at our map again, and notice the earthly season that is associated with the Wilderness.

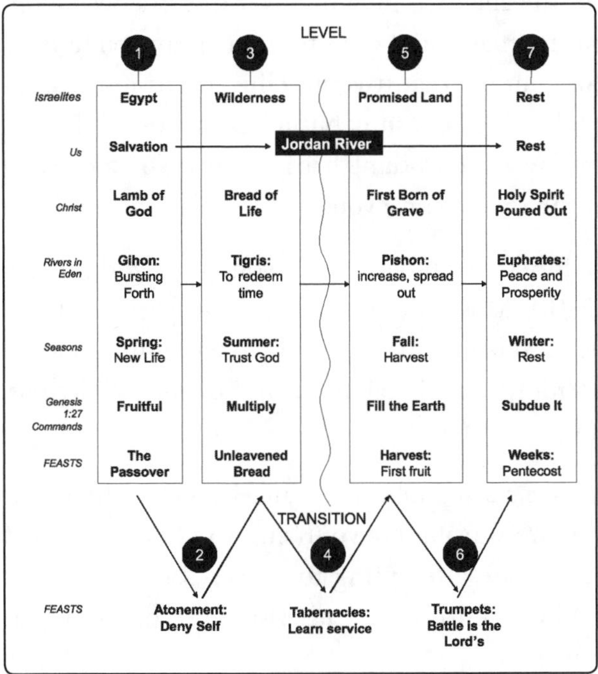

[Figure 1]

The Wilderness is our spiritual summer. In summertime, the farmer must trust God every day for the right atmosphere in which to grow his crops, relying on the perfect balance of rain and sunshine to produce a harvest. Summer is not the time for the farmer to eat the fruits of his labor. Nor is there any planting or harvesting to do. It is a waiting time—just sitting on the porch with nothing much going on.

During this time, God meets your needs every day. You have just enough. It is a season so many Christians misunderstand. Here comes the trap: they sit on the couch and wait for that miracle seed money to hit the mailbox.

You hear things like, "I quit my job and am trusting in the Lord to meet all my needs."

"Really? Are you sure about that?"

This trap of the enemy is high on his list. It is a deception loosely based on a few Scriptures that sound great to human ears, but are often misunderstood. God does not say that trusting Him means not working. You might think you are following Scripture, but in reality you are living off the Christians around you who are working hard. Because you are deceived, they have become the Lord's tools to save you.

Paul wrote it best when he said, "If you don't work, then you don't eat" (see 2 Thess. 3:10). Most of us will go through periods of hard times when we legitimately need help. This is nothing to feel guilty about. But we cannot stay in that position. God is calling us out of the Wilderness and into the Promised Land.

So, if you have started a business and it's not rolling yet; if there is no money and you are waiting for your ship to come in, then you might be out of season. You are attempting to harvest in the summer. The fruit is not ready yet. Go back to work, gather some seed, and replant. Work two jobs. Maybe three.

If you are resting and in need, you have a problem. If I'm talking about your husband, kick his butt off the couch and gnaw on him constantly until he gets some work. Do not permit him to continue like this. You are his helpmate, so help him not to be lazy.

Are you with me? We are on to Day One in the Wilderness. The good news is that we are going through the Wilderness with a sense of purpose: to get to the promises. So stay with me. The journey is worth it.

Chapter 8

I Like to Eat Eat Eat Apples and Ba-Mannas

As a pastor, I do weddings sometimes. Weddings are different to men and women. Men typically whine about having to attend weddings, while women find them romantically rejuvenating.

When I do a wedding, I try not to put anyone to sleep. That's a worthy goal. It's a small goal, but it's my goal. In reality, you can't really mess up a wedding. Regardless of how badly it goes, two people will end up married in the end. So my goal isn't just to marry people, it is to keep people awake—especially the men.

One Friday night I found myself attending a wedding, which is not nearly as much fun as doing a wedding. We were in an old-school style Methodist church, complete with pews, orange carpet, stained glass, and even hymnals in the seats. There were no 15-foot screens or smoke effects, moving lights, or big robotic arms lugging cameras for that sweeping crowd shot. It was church the way mom and dad would remember it. I found it very quaint.

That might sound funny to you, but I'm a big advocate of creating an atmosphere that excites people about the Lord. That is neither right nor wrong, it's just my flavor.

But if you've ever been to that little corner restaurant downtown in your city, the one that is so very small with tiny little tables draped with white table cloths and nestled in a wonderful little house from 1940 that is overgrown with vines and flowers—this church was like that. I loved it. This was church with the Ingalls.

I must confess that I couldn't keep my eyes open during the service. The air, the lighting, the entire experience was more conducive to an afternoon nap than watching football on Sunday. For me, this would not be my church. But it is someone's church. And I would bet good money (uh-oh, that's gambling) that every Sunday that you hear the message it uplifts you, reminds you of why we are here, reminds you to love, and feeds your soul. I sincerely liked this church. Of course, I love any church that preaches the truth, regardless of the color of the carpet.

We Need Water

The biblical account of the Exodus feeds the soul, too. The Israelites' troubles and experiences in the Wilderness are described so that we can learn from them. It is a complete story, and every element has meaning for us.

The first few trials in the Wilderness are powerful lessons involving the need for water. We find the Israelites running out of water not once, but twice. The first time is described here:

> *Then Moses led Israel from the Red Sea and they went into the Desert of Shur. For three days they traveled in the desert without finding water* (Exodus 15:22).

It is critical for the Israelites to find water. They are in the desert, pushed to the brink of dehydration. Survival is necessary if they are to reach the Promised Land. This is a picture for us. When we are newly born again, we need immediate sustenance. Just a few days without water can be deadly. We also recognize the need to change our influences and influencers. The nutrition we are accustomed to will no longer do the trick.

What we need is God's Word!

Marah and Horeb

Three key events occur in quick succession here. The first is the problem of the bitter water at Marah. Next is the manna falling from Heaven to feed the Israelites. The third event involves water again; this time it flows from the side of a rock.

All three events highlight the same foundational principle: *We need the Word of God.* Deeper still is the lesson about where our necessary provision—both water and food—comes from. That is the subject of this chapter, so let's dig in.

"When they came to Marah, they could not drink its water because it was bitter…" (Exod. 15:23). Imagine finding water to slake your thirst, only to realize that water was impossible to drink. That is what happened at Marah. The survival of the nation of Israel was on the line, and Moses knew it. Immediately, he turned to God:

> *Moses cried out to the Lord, and the Lord showed him a piece of wood. He threw it into the water, and the water became sweet* (Exodus 15:25).

We are also in need of water, not the bitter waters of the world, but the sweet water of truth. We need a place to drink individually and a place to come together and drink the water of the Word.

That is the picture God gives us here. The place we go to drink together is the Church. I will get into why the water was bitter later in this chapter, but first let's talk about the water from the rock at Horeb.

The Horeb story happens right after God sends the Israelites manna for their food:

> *But the people were thirsty for water there, and they grumbled against Moses. They said, "Why did you bring us up out of Egypt to make us and our children and livestock die of thirst?"* (Exodus 17:3)

Once again, the Israelites are thirsty. But where will they go? Often, we feel the same way. We might not be in danger of dying of thirst, but we are spiritually thirsty. God had a place for Israel to find physical water. In John 4, Jesus leads us to the source of *spiritual* water, saying, *"whoever drinks the water I give him will never thirst"* (John 4:14).

Psalms 1:3 tells me that God wants me to be *"like a tree planted by streams of water."* Wherever this water is, I need to plant myself there. Let's see where the water was found in the story at Horeb.

The people have grumbled against Moses and the Lord tells him, *"I will stand there before you by the rock at Horeb. Strike the rock, and water will come out of it for the people to drink"* (Exod. 17:6).

Moses is in his old stomping grounds; Horeb is the place where he saw the burning bush. It has now been a month since Moses led the people out of Egypt, and things continue to be challenging. The situation is serious and Moses needs a solution. God gives it to him: He tells Moses to strike the rock at Horeb with his staff. Moses does so and out comes water.

The rock is significant; Jesus is symbolized as the Rock. Metaphorically speaking, this water is coming out of the side of Christ. God is using a picture to show us where our source of water is so we can plant our tree by it.

This idea of life coming out of the side of the rock is important. In order to tie it all together, I need to share with you a whole mess of Scripture. Let's start at the beginning because, when you "get" this, it will set you free!

> *So the Lord God caused the man to fall into a deep sleep; and while he was sleeping, He took one of the man's ribs and closed*

up the place with flesh. Then the Lord God made a woman from the rib He had taken out of the man, and He brought her to the man (Genesis 2:21-22).

The word for "rib" here is the Hebrew word, *tsela`*, which also means "side."[1] In fact, the very next place this Hebrew word is used in the Bible it is to describe one side of the Ark of the Covenant (see Exod. 25:12).

So out of the *side* of man came woman, his bride. Because of the way God did this, the man and the woman are separate halves; they become one flesh again when they come together as man and wife. I bring this up now because it is a picture of the relationship between Christ and His Bride, the Church. Paul touched on the explanation by quoting Genesis 2:24:

> ***"For this reason a man will leave his father and mother and be united to his wife, and the two will become one flesh."*** *This is a profound mystery-but I am talking about Christ and the church* (Ephesians 5:31-32).

Notice this precedent regarding man and his bride. Now consider Jesus and His Bride, the Church. According to Paul, Jesus is the second Adam (see Rom. 5:14; 1 Cor. 15:45). The Bride for the second Adam is created the same way as the bride of the first Adam—from Jesus' own side.

Here is what happens as Jesus hangs on the cross:

> *The soldiers therefore came and broke the legs of the first man who had been crucified with Jesus, and then those of the other. But when they came to Jesus and found that He was already dead,* ***they did not break His legs.*** *Instead, one of the soldiers* ***pierced Jesus' side*** *with a spear, bringing a sudden flow of blood and water"* (John 19:32-34).

The soldier comes to break Jesus' legs, but instead randomly pierces His side, out of which His Bride is birthed. It is just as when Eve was taken out of Adam's side and just like all human births in this sense: both blood and water flow.

In human childbirth, the water flows before the blood, when a woman's water breaks and labor begins. In the case of the cross, the blood comes first. This shows the connection between our birth as a church, and His birth as a man. Because Mary was the only virgin ever to give birth, blood would have come before water in her case as well. This is also a testament to our purity as His Bride; our intimacy with Christ is unadulterated and is a blood covenant. Redemption comes through the blood first; then we are matured by the water of the Word.

Now we are getting a better picture of where the water flows from. It comes from the side of the rock, or the side of Christ. Christ Himself is the Word (the water) and the water flows from His body.

Church Is the Faucet

The Church plays a key role in God's redemptive plan for the earth.

> *And God placed all things under His feet and appointed Him to be head over everything for the church, which is His body, the fullness of Him who fills everything in every way* (Ephesians 1:22-23).

> *His intent was that now,* ***through the church,*** *the manifold wisdom of God should be made known to the rulers and authorities in the heavenly realms...* (Ephesians 3:10).

The Church, which is His Body, is going to reveal the manifold wisdom of God, even to the point that she will teach rulers and authorities in the heavenly realms just what God's plan is.

That is mind blowing! It also reveals the importance of staying connected. When you are disconnected from the Church, you are out of this flow of God's wisdom. So wisdom comes from the Scripture, but flows through the Church. Apart from the Church, your personal study time in the Bible becomes dry and unrevealing. You might read and read, yet squeeze out very little wisdom for your life.

Again we are finding that the water, which is the Word, is designed to flow out of the Body of Christ, which is His Church.

The Church, then, can be thought of as the dispensation system for wisdom. It is not the source. God's Word is the source. The Church is the faucet. Let's look at still another Scripture:

> *...you will know how people ought to conduct themselves in God's household, which is the church of the living God, the pillar and foundation of the truth* (1 Timothy 3:15).

The Church, God's household, is the pillar and foundation of the truth. Again, if you are not connected to the Church body, then you are missing out on the flow. The foundation is the starting point for building a life. The pillar is the strength to keep the house from crumbling around you. Being disconnected from the Church leaves you foundation-less and pillar-less when it comes to the truth.

The Word here also points out that the Church, the Body of Christ, is God's house. Where would you go if you wanted to eat my food? You would go to my house. Where then do we find spiritual food and water? Paul explained in Romans 10:17 that faith comes by hearing the Word of God. He asked the question, *"How can they hear without someone preaching* [the message] *to them?"* (Rom. 10:14).

So then faith flows through the message that is preached. Being connected to the Church will build your faith and make your personal study time more fruitful, thereby making your life more fruitful.

The answer to the question, "Where do we find this water and where should we plant ourselves?" is *in the Church.* In the Wilderness portion of our journey, the Body of Christ is the focus. If you are not plugged into a church, you will find yourself stuck in the Wilderness—or even in Egypt.

Do not be discouraged, though. Just make a decision for change. Realize that, in order to produce fruit, you need both bride and groom. When we are away from the Church, it is as though a husband and wife were living in separate states. They might call each other or share their love via email,

Facebook, or video chat. The romance could feel wonderful, yet because they are disconnected, they cannot produce fruit.

This is what our lives look like when we are disconnected from the Bride of Christ, His Church. It is one of the reasons Jesus told us to remain in Him, connected to the vine. Apart from Him we can bear no fruit (see John 15:4). God wants you connected. He wants you to drink the water from the side of the Rock or from the pool at Marah.

But wait—the water at Marah is bitter! It's a trap!

Wilderness Trap No. 2

The enemy has many traps set as we move along our journey. The first trap we discussed involved understanding when to rest and when to sow and reap.

Keep reading, as God points out another trap:

> *So the people* ***grumbled*** *against Moses, saying, "What are we to drink?"* (Exod. 15:24).

This is perhaps the most common trap the enemy sets for Christians in the Wilderness: grumbling and bitterness. The word *Marah* actually means "bitterness."[2] Satan wants you to be bitter about the Church and other Christians. He wants you to be angry about what someone at church said or offended because someone didn't say hi to you. If the enemy can accomplish this he can separate you from the Church and stunt your growth as a Christian, keeping you from God's wisdom.

My grandfather told a story about a man who had gotten some Limburger cheese caught in his moustache. He awoke from his post-lunch nap and said, "Man, it stinks in here."

He went to the living room and said, "Man, it stinks in here, too."

He ran outside and cried out, "Geez, the whole darn world stinks."

When everything stinks, we need to check ourselves. Maybe we are the ones who stink.

Grumbling and bitterness come easy to us. When things don't go my way, I can get to complaining as much as the next guy. If I'm going to see a Phoenix Suns game, it's a tough night, full of really uncomfortable seats; and parking—it's a literal nightmare. It's really, really loud. Not to mention the fact that they have no kids' programs, so we have to get a babysitter. I might grumble.

At church, however, that's another story. I never speak against it, only for it. This is the Bride of Christ, after all. We men don't like it much when someone criticizes our brides. I know I get upset when someone hurts my wife's feelings.

We shouldn't speak badly about Christ's Bride either. Instead of highlighting all her problems, we ought to become the solution.

The Water Is Clean

The water at Marah was bitter until Moses followed through on God's instructions:

> *Then Moses cried out to the Lord, and the Lord showed him a piece of wood. He threw it into the water, and the water became sweet* (Exodus 15:25).

The water becomes sweet. It is now drinkable. This pool of water represents the Church. The Church is made up of people. Sometimes, it is bitter. Moses throws wood into the water to make it sweet. That wood represents the cross. The cross made us holy. Without it, there is none righteous, not even one (see Ps. 53:3; Rom. 3:10). Yet, Christ died and made those who will believe on Him righteous. He gave Himself up for His Bride, the Church, to make her holy.

We the Church are holy. The water is sweet, so take a drink or jump on in. Oh, but be careful, there is to be no co-ed swimming (LOL).

> *Let us not give up meeting together, as some are in the habit of doing...* (Hebrews 10:25).

Alright. So much for the water; now on to the manna!

Relapse of the Old Life

Let's look at the third story, the story of manna. Remember, the Church has been made holy by Christ, but you and I are in the Church, and sometimes we do stuff that isn't all that holy.

In Exodus 16, The Israelites leave Elim and come to the *Desert of Sin*. No kidding, that is really were they went next. The Desert of Sin. "Sin" here is translated from the Hebrew word *ciyn,* which means "thorn."[3] That will be important throughout our journey.

Have you ever been to the Desert of Sin in your life? Often, it's the part where you have a relapse. It could be Jimmy one month into his Christian walk when he goes out with his old friends and gets raging drunk. He's not sure how much he wants to remember about that night. It is the place where you might question your own salvation, the place where you wonder, "Why did this happen?"

In the Desert of Sin, you hear echoes of your prior life. Ripples form in the smooth splash of your salvation. But there is a difference between a relapse and a lifestyle of sin. The difference is *guilt.* You didn't used to feel so badly about sinning. Now you do. What is happening?

Guilt is happening. Although you have been set free from guilt and condemnation, it is part of your journey. This guilt is what separates you from your old way of life; but it also makes you feel separate from God. Suddenly, you feel unworthy to stand before Him. You're in a maturation process; falling back into sin and feeling the guilt that follows are part of the Wilderness experience. It's one of the ways that we grow up. Eventually, the process will come to a head, but more on that later.

And, no, I haven't forgotten about the manna.

Manna Is the Word of God

Does God help us to deal with the Desert of Sin? Absolutely. The Israelites have been in the Wilderness for 30 days now. They are in the Desert of Sin and God brings them food to eat. Not just any food, mind you. This food fell from Heaven.

Moses explains that, *"The people of Israel called the bread manna"* (Exod. 16:31). It was something new to the Israelites, so God provided them with specific instructions for their manna.

We know that Jesus is the Bread of Life (see John 6:35). When satan asked Him to turn a rock into bread, Jesus quoted Deuteronomy 8:3, saying: *"Man shall not live by bread alone, but by every word that proceeds from the mouth of God"* (Matt. 4:4 NKJV).

God's Word is bread. It doesn't come from the earth; it comes from Him. The manna in the Wilderness represents God's Word. God provides the Word and He provided their manna—and He wanted them to handle it a certain way.

First of all, the Israelites were forbidden to gather more than one day's supply of manna. If they tried to hoard it, it would rot. This was true every day but one. No manna fell on the Sabbath, so on the day before, the people would gather two days worth of manna. Their Sabbath-day stash never rotted. It was God's provision for them and it remained fresh.

We, too, need fresh manna every day. Like the Israelites, we can't store up this nourishment for a rainy day. Jesus told us to pray *"Give us today, our **daily** bread"* (Matt. 6:11). It's not weekly bread or monthly bread; it's daily bread.

We need God's Word every single day of our lives. Most churches don't have service every day, so we need to get some manna on our own. In other words, there is going to have to be personal study time!

A Shepherd to Bring Understanding

When the Israelites first saw this strange new food on the ground, they called it *manna*. The word literally means "What is it?"[4] Moses answered this question in Exodus 16:15, saying, *"It is the bread the Lord has given you to eat."*

Moses knew what manna was. God had appointed and anointed him to lead the people. He gave Moses the revelation he needed to fulfill that calling. Moses is an Old Testament picture of the shepherd. Someone must lead us out of Egypt, and when our daily bread arrives, we need someone to help us get the revelation we need. That someone is a person—a physical shepherd who has been reading the Bible more than us. We need a teacher to help us mature.

This is so obvious where children are concerned. It would be ludicrous not to educate our children. Without a teacher to guide them, there would be no learning, or very slow learning at best. Those who decide to become doctors or engineers attend college. They learn from their professors, who prepare them in two ways: In the narrow sense, the professor prepares students to pass their tests. On a broader scale, the professor prepares students to fulfill their purpose and achieve their destinies.

The professor's responsibility is to present the necessary information. The student is responsible to retain the information and seek to understand it in order to pass this test. That is why students take notes. A good student will study the notes throughout the semester and pay close attention to the professor every day.

We must do the same things on the spiritual level. Remember, we learned from our study of the Passover Feast that the Holy Spirit is our teacher:

> *But when He, the Spirit of truth, comes, He will guide you into all truth. He will not speak on His own; He will speak only what He hears...* (John 16:13).

Keep in mind that He only speaks what He hears. This is a reminder that we must be hearing God's Word. Once we hear it and get it down inside us, the Holy Spirit will help us gain wisdom from that Word.

When a shepherd is positioned by God over a church, the Spirit of the Lord reveals to the shepherd (the pastor) the message that he or she is to share with the people. It is not a random process; there is a leading of the Holy Spirit. For example, when I prepare a teaching, a very clear path develops so that I know which message to bring.

Often, I will feel sick inside about going in a particular direction, but alive and passionate about sharing a different passage or theme. Even while I am teaching, I will sense the tweaks of the Lord. Sometimes a phrase will come out that I had not planned as part of my message.

This is the work of the Holy Spirit revealing the wisdom of God from Scripture through the message that is preached. As a shepherd who happens to be human, I'm not living a perfectly holy life. Nor are my words perfect. Yet, the message of God is perfected by the Holy Spirit in both the peoples' hearing and understanding.

This wisdom is delivered for the people. As you sit in the pew, you are being prepared for the tests that are ahead. You should take notes on the message. Then you should study your notes during the week. When you are absent for a message your pastor shares, it is like missing a class in college. You should get the notes from a friend so that there isn't a big empty place in your preparation.

The message not only prepares you for the tests that come up periodically; it also prepares you for your destiny and purpose as a Christian. It helps set the stage of your heart for the big picture of your life.

In all of this, it is important to remember the value of honoring your shepherd. Keeping your heart right positions you to receive from the wisdom the shepherd brings you. Grumbling against the shepherd—well, that is exactly what the enemy wants you to get into. Exodus 16:7-8 says, "*... Who are we, that you should grumble against us?... You are not grumbling against us, but against the Lord.*"

The Church is made up of imperfect people. What I mean is this: Don't try and paint in your own heart that a pastor is Jesus. Remember that "The Lord is my Shepherd." Jesus is your shepherd in terms of He who is leading you, and will chase you down when you fall. Jesus is the healer, and the answer. He is your High Priest. Shepherds cannot possibly fill the shoes of Jesus. They are there to feed you the Word of God through the preaching of truth. Also, there are people who are good members of the church who may not be helpful in your journey. Don't stand in their way, or sit in their seats (see Ps. 1:1). When they mock or grumble against a "Moses" or an "Aaron" they are grumbling against the Lord.

When they choose to be on the wrong team, make sure you don't follow in their footsteps!

Prepared for Our Test

In the 1984 movie *The Karate Kid,* Daniel LaRusso moves to California with his mom. He finds that the little karate he has learned is not working against the neighborhood bullies. He needs to learn to fight to survive. He needs a karate shepherd.

Life is full of bullies, and Mr. Miyagi is there to help. (We all need a Mr. Miyagi to prepare us for battle. "Show me sand da floor.")

You never know exactly when life's battles will come. The Israelites' first battle happened just after the three quick trials of water and food. Remember, Israel had never been at war with another nation. *Never.* They grew up as slaves. They escaped Egypt, but without fighting a battle. Now, after just a short time in the Wilderness, war was upon them.

> *The Amalekites came and attacked the Israelites at Rephidim. Moses said to Joshua, "Choose some of our men and go out to fight the Amalekites. Tomorrow I will stand on top of the hill with the staff of God in my hands"* (Exodus 17:8-9).

In battle you are either taking new territory or defending the territory you already have. We tend to prefer the territory-taking variety. Those are the ones we plan for ahead of time. The defensive battles are never the ones we choose. It's more like they choose us.

Either way, you can rest assured that you will have battles in every season of your life. Some of them happen when you step into something new. You are in unfamiliar territory and find problems that must be resolved before you can advance. Other battles happen when you are minding your own business. Suddenly, something or someone tries to destroy what you have. These battles may be from satan, or from something you sowed in your own life. They might even stem from fear or the random circumstances that occur in a random, messy world.

Battles experienced in the Wilderness tend to resemble the battle Israel faces with the Amalekites. The offenders attack Israel for no apparent reason, forcing them to defend land they don't even want. Talk about horrible timing! If I'm an Israelite, I am already up to my neck in paradigm adjustments. I'm eating bread (manna) from the ground (does the five-second rule apply here?); I'm thirsty all the time; and I am sleeping on the ground. I can remember the huge pots of meat we ate in Egypt. Some Promised Land this has turned out to be.

Oh, and now I'm being attacked. Great. And not by the nicest tribe in the neighborhood. *Amalek* means "nation of nippers," from the Hebrew words *'am,* meaning "nation,"[5] and *malaq,* meaning "to nip" or "nip off"[6] (see Lev. 1:15 which describes the priest wringing off the head of a pigeon).

The Book of Deuteronomy provides a few details about this war not found in the Exodus account:

> *Remember what the Amalekites did to you along the way when you came out of Egypt. When you were weary and worn out, they met you on your journey and cut off all who were lagging behind...* (Deuteronomy 25:17-18).

This was the Nippers' way. They went after the weak—the stragglers who did not stay connected to the group. When you disconnect from the Church, one of two things is true (or both): you are doing it because you have grown weary, or you are about to become weary because you did it. Stragglers are the Nippers favorite targets.

Have you ever watched the Discovery Channel's show, *Carnage at Midnight*? (It was the only show we found enjoyable when we were in India.) In one episode you might see a lion as he chases a group of animals. He works to separate one from the pack and then he eats him.

That's just the way the enemy works. He prowls about like a roaring lion, seeking out whom he may destroy (see 1 Pet. 5:8). Not only do staying connected to your church and honoring your shepherd prepare you for battle; they also keep you safely tucked in the pack where you are less vulnerable.

God has built his Church upon the rock, and the gates of hell will not prevail against it (see Matt. 16:18). Of course, if you walk outside the gates and play ring around the rosy on the freeway, well it's...ashes...ashes...we all fall down. That is why Christ (not your pastor—he is not Jesus) is so quick to leave the 99 to save one (see Matt. 18:12). He knows what happens to the one that wanders away from the group. The Nippers will attack.

During the battle with the Amalekites, the winner was determined by God through the shepherd, Moses, who went to the top of a hill to oversee the battle.

> *As long as Moses held up his hands, the Israelites were winning, but whenever he lowered his hands, the Amalekites were winning. When Moses' hands grew tired, they took a stone and put it under him and he sat on it. Aaron and Hur held his hands up—one on one side, one on the other—so that his hands remained steady till sunset. So Joshua overcame the Amalekites army with the sword* (Exodus 17:11-13).

Notice that Joshua defeated the Amalekites by the sword. The sword represents the Word of God, the sword of the Spirit that is sharper than any two-edged sword (see Heb. 4:12).

Jesus is the Word, but He is our Shepherd, too. We also need a physical shepherd like Moses. Both the spiritual Shepherd and the physical one are going to help us win. The former is the source of our victory; the latter is the one through whom the victory flows. We need them both. If we disconnect, well, we get nipped.

It is also important to see that the shepherd needs your help, too. He can't do it all, he is human, and his hands grow tired. Hold up his hands. Help your shepherd accomplish what God has called your church to accomplish. Remember that the Israelites are a picture of the family of God—a family that succeeds by staying connected in the journey.

The Amalekites are defeated and the Israelites are nearing Mount Sinai. They are about to embark on the important task of building the Lord a Tabernacle and an ark for His covenant. These are all tremendously important pictures for us to understand. The more we understand His ways, the more we will mature.

"So," you ask, "when do we get to the milk and honey?" It's coming. I promise. It's coming.

Chapter 9

Are You Distinguished or Extinguished?

WHAT IS THE DEAL with preachers' kids? Well, I can talk freely about PKs because I am one. PKs are a tough group. It seems that a high percentage of missionary and preacher children do not go on to serve the Lord. Somehow, the light of God within them is extinguished.

That is not God's plan. In fact, He wants to set each of us on a high place where His light burning inside us can be seen by all. His plan is to distinguish us from the world; He does it by teaching us how to live. Often, His lessons start at home.

An Old Testament promise is one we need to take a look at: *"Train a child in the way he should go, and when he is old he will not turn from it"* (Prov. 22:6).

Pastors have a difficult task that includes leading a congregation, ministering, counseling, praying, and caring for the family of God. Now juggle that with raising a family. I'm talking about pastors here, but you can apply these challenges to any Christian's life. Many families are so involved in ministry, they are lucky to have a free night. Christians who hit the mission field with children in tow—let's just say it can be a lot to manage.

The question is one of priority. To balance priorities in life, we must look to God's Word. We must be willing to make that which is important to God, important to us—and in the same order. The right priorities will help keep the light in our hearts burning brightly.

Wilderness Priorities

The Amalekite crisis is over. Israel is victorious. Still, Moses has his hands full just leading millions of ex-slaves through the desert. There is more to do than any one man can handle, and Moses must determine his priority chain.

What did Moses do? *"After Moses had sent away his wife Zipporah, his father-in-law Jethro received her and her two sons...."* (Exod. 18:2-3). He sent his wife and kids to stay with his father-in-law, Jethro, who was not with them on the journey. Jethro lived in Midian. Moses and his family are now separated.

Not for long. Just one verse later, Jethro brings the family back to Moses. "Oh no you don't, Moses. You married her and these are your kids. I'm not raising this family. This is *your* family."

It wasn't as though Moses had sent them off on a vacation. Instead, he cut them out of his schedule. He was too busy leading the nation to attend to the needs of his family.

Can you imagine the conversations between a modern-day Moses and Zipporah, his wife?

"Late home from work again I see. Oh, and guess what I made for dinner— a surprise. Manna *again.* So let's see if I remember this right. You and I were living comfortably in Midian, then we went to Egypt to get these whiny hoards and lead them to Canaan. Now I'm living in the desert. This is *not* what I signed up for.

"I need you Moses, but where are you?"

Moses has a lot on his mind. He is being pulled in every direction. People are blogging about him on the Internet. His Facebook page is filled with posts from grumbling and bitter Israelites. He's exhausted and has nothing more to give. His love cup is empty. He needs to rest for a moment. Maybe watch a little sand volleyball.

"That's it," he says. "I can't live like this. If being married to me is so bad, then go live with your father." (That isn't in the Bible, by the way. I just made it up.)

It has been about 50 days since the Israelites left Egypt, so what God presents here is a principle we need to heed early in our journey. The story of Moses and Zipporah is one of responsibilities and priorities. At first glance, it might seem that God's plan for Israel is more important than Moses' family needs. God comes before family, right?

Wilderness Trap No. 3

Of the three Wilderness traps, this is the most deceptive. The question is this: Who must make the sacrifice necessary for Moses to serve the Lord? Is this a cross the preacher's kids must bear?

The belief that God comes before family is the answer to a different question than the one Moses is facing. Let me explain. If my family disowns God and then asks me to do the same (under threat that they will forsake me if I refuse), then I will choose God over my family.

God is more important to me. However, that is not the question being posed by Moses' dilemma. What Moses needs to decide is whether ministering to others is more important than ministering to his own family.

God entrusts us with stewardship over many areas in life. So, how important is stewardship over a child? Well, a child is a life handmade by God Himself. Psalms 139:14 says that each of us is *"fearfully and wonderfully made."* That should give us some indication of the value God places on our children's lives.

What about responsibility toward a spouse? Let me answer the question with a question: if you can't love your spouse, how can you love others? How can Moses lead Israel if he can't serve his own wife and family? How can we instruct and relate to other people's children if we cannot raise our own?

Jesus says very little while on the cross, but He makes sure to take care of family. In John 19:26-27 Jesus arranges for one of His disciples to take care of His mother, Mary. Some might have said, "Well, God will take care of her." That is true, but Jesus also wanted someone on earth to take care of her.

How important is family to Christ? So important that He calls us into the family of God. Some leave their family thinking, well as I take care of God's business He should take care of my family. This kind of thinking is out of order. God wants you to be a steward over your marriage and children and finish what you have started. He doesn't want you to turn back once you have put your hand to the plow (see Luke 9:62).

In the Wilderness, Moses is about to learn a valuable lesson. After shooting the breeze with his father-in-law, they turn in for the night. The next morning Moses is off to work and Jethro follows along. Jethro has probably been briefed by Moses' wife as to why Moses sent her away. He watches Moses carry out a full day; Jethro's purpose becomes clear. Moses has been sitting as judge over 600,000 families and answering all of their disputes all day long, all by himself. You can imagine the issues that arise: who stole whose goat, who poisoned whose chickens, who broke a promise to whom. It is too great a burden for any one man to handle.

It is obvious that Moses must continue to shepherd the people. God made that crystal clear. So quitting his job is not the right solution. He doesn't need to be home in the tent with his family *all the time*. Yes, he needs to spend more time with them, but man must work. He just has to learn to work smart. Jethro helps Moses figure out how:

> *When his father-in-law saw all that Moses was doing for the people, he said, "What is this you are doing for the people? Why do you alone sit as judge, while all these people stand around you from morning till evening?" Moses answered him, "Because the people come to me to seek God's will. Whenever they have a dispute, it is brought to me, and I decide between the parties and inform them of God's decrees and laws." Moses' father-in-law replied, "What you are doing is not good. You and these people who come to you will only wear yourselves out. The work is too heavy for you; you cannot handle it alone* (Exodus 18:14-18).

Jethro then describes to Moses the art of delegation and organization. Moses needs to share the burden of leading with other capable people. Is this ringing a bell for you? Many of us simply need to organize and reprioritize our lives. In other words, keep that which is most important to God, most important to us.

Imagine that a certain man is having trouble with his marriage.

"How long has this been an issue?" the pastor asks.

"About two years."

What is wrong with this picture? Well, if your electricity went out, what would you do? Would you wait two years to ask for help? See, the problem isn't always the problem. Sometimes it's the priority level we assign to the problem that is the problem.

If my pay sports channel drops off, I'm on the phone faster than lickity-split (and that's fast). If my wife tromps through the house and starts slamming doors, what do I do? How do I show her that her emotions are important to me? Do I roll my eyes or turn off the game? (Maybe I can talk with her at halftime? Oh, wait, I have TiVo.)

Moses gets it. Jethro's idea makes sense. He delegates some of his workload and his family is saved. But how exactly does this relate to our Wilderness experience?

Simple. When we first get saved we are overwhelmed with zeal for the ministry. This is where your shepherd says, "Slow down, my friend, you are not spiritually mature enough to preach just yet. Let's produce some godly fruit first. Wait for the next season. Keep your priorities in order or you may do something you seriously regret later."

Learn to be great with your family first!

God Speaks Through Others

As Christians, we sometimes lose bits of our God-given common sense. Jethro did not come with a prophecy from the Lord. "Thus saith God, here are thy wife and childreneth back. Now leave your father-in-law aloneth."

Jethro was not even a child of God. He was the high priest of Midian. He was an important figure to his nation; nevertheless, he was a priest to idol worshipers. Jethro did not come to Moses as a godly man, yet God used him to speak some sense into Moses. Isn't it interesting to think that while God and Moses are on daily speaking terms, God chooses to speak to Moses through a third party? Why is that?

God uses many ways to communicate with us, so we need to be listening. Moses showed us his teachable spirit. He talked with God on an amazingly intimate level, yet he kept pride from entering his heart. He remained teachable. Because Moses was receptive, God was able to use Jethro to save his family.

Yet God did more than that. This relationship worked both ways. When Jethro first arrived, Moses told him everything that had happened. He told his father-in-law about the plagues and the Red Sea, and, well, everything. He told Jethro everything the Lord had done.

As new believers, we do the same thing. We aren't trying to teach in-depth Bible studies; we are just sharing our personal stories, the things God has done for us. Remember that Moses used to work for Jethro back in the day on the backside of the desert. Moses cared for Jethro's sheep (always the shepherd). Now listen to this:

> *Jethro was delighted to hear about all the good things the Lord had done for Israel in rescuing them from the hand of the Egyptians. He said, "Praise be to the Lord, who rescued you from the hand of the Egyptians and of Pharaoh, and who rescued the people from the hand of the Egyptians. Now I know that the Lord is greater than all other gods, for He did this to those who had treated Israel arrogantly." Then Jethro, Moses' father-in-law, brought a burnt offering and other sacrifices to God, and Aaron came with all the elders of Israel to eat bread with Moses' father-in-law in the presence of God* (Exodus 18:9-12).

What just happened? The high priest of Midian has just exalted God Almighty above all his gods. Then he offers a sacrifice and breaks bread with the elders and the high priest, Aaron, in the presence of God. In today's lingo, Jethro just got saved! Moses has just influenced an entire nation.

Later, in Judges 1:16, Jethro's sons join and live with the tribe of Judah in the Promised Land. They were grafted into the family of God. Pretty cool, eh? (BTW—Midian descended from Abraham through his wife Keturah, who he married after his wife Sarah died [see Gen. 25:1-2]. And if you really want to do some research, Hobab, Midian's son who joined up with the tribe of Judah, was called a *Kenite,* which means "Cain,"[1] as in the firstborn of Adam who murdered his brother, Abel.)

Make use of your Wilderness zeal. Redirect it into sharing your story with those you meet. Invite them to dinner. Invite them to church. Be especially zealous about your family. Moses shared his story of God's goodness with his father-in-law. You can, too! Just tell your relatives *your story.* No need to travel to the mission field in Yugoslavia just yet; let's get you anchored down a bit first.

Boundaries Separate Us From the World

It has now been 60 days since the Israelites left Egypt and they have arrived on Mount Sinai (see Exod. 19). God calls Moses to receive the commandments of the Lord and take them to the people!

Assuming we all know the story somewhat, I will stay with the concepts. Moses receives two things atop the mountain: the law to live by and instructions for the Tabernacle. He makes the trip up the mountain twice because, in the middle of his first trip he is interrupted when the Israelites get impatient, make a golden calf, and worship it (see Exod. 32).

So within the first 60 days, God issues boundaries. The very first thing God speaks is the Ten Commandments (see Exod. 20). The first two commandments speak directly to prohibitions against making idols and worshiping other gods (see Exod. 20:3-4). The Israelites hear these commandments from the mountain. After hearing the Ten Commandments, they are frightened; they tell Moses to leave them out of this encounter with God: *"...Speak to us yourself [Moses] and we will listen. But do not have God speak to us or we will die"* (Exod. 20:19).

The Israelites heard with their own ears the warnings against worshiping anyone but God. You would think that would have been the end of the golden calf, but they went ahead and made one.

> *Then the Lord said to Moses, "Tell the Israelites this: 'You have seen for yourselves that I have spoken to you from heaven: Do not make any gods to be alongside Me; do not make for yourselves gods of silver or gods of gold'"* (Exodus 20:22-23).

We know the rules as well. We know what we are supposed to do, but do we always do it? The boundaries are there because we need them. When we get born again, many of us begin a quest for the rules, asking, "What can't I do now?"

These boundaries serve many good purposes on our journey. At this particular stage, I want to consider just one of those purposes—the role of the rules in separating us from the world.

Whenever I take my children to visit Grandma and Grandpa's or anybody else's home, we run through the big speech in the car. Do you know the speech I'm talking about? It is the speech in which you mark out the boundaries. I want people's impressions of my children to be good. They should be able to distinguish my kids from the world's kids.

God gives the Israelites the car speech here. For 430 years they have lived under Egyptian gods and laws. Making golden calves and frolicking out of control had become natural to them. They were probably used to seeing the Egyptians do such things.

God's laws were put in to place to help the Hebrews live better lives. They were given sanitary laws, the first the world had ever seen, to keep them from living in their own filth. Other laws addressed covetousness, theft, dishonor, and murder. There were laws about which foods to avoid. (It was their version of the FDA...kind of.) There were social rules as well, including those about appearance and cleanliness. The law required circumcision for the men and forbade anyone from eating food sacrificed to idols.

God was differentiating His people from the Egyptians and the rest of the world. He wanted everyone to recognize that the Hebrews were different from other nations.

Of course, when Jesus died on the cross, everything changed. Jesus took the commandments up a level. Where the command said, "Do not to murder," Jesus says, "Don't even hate." He addressed the heart of the issue. The Ten Commandments remained intact, but the Mosaic law was superseded by the New Covenant: *"For sin shall not be your master, because you are not under law, but under grace"* (Rom. 6:14).

It is a good thing we are no longer *under the law*, for we are all in violation of the one that says not to cut your beard (even some of you ladies)—which, by the way, is the law just after the one forbidding tattoos.

The law focused on the externals; Christ changes us on the inside. Jesus didn't discard the law; He summed up the law and the prophets in His commands to love God and love others (see Matt. 22:37-40). Therefore, boundaries remain even for those who are in Christ; these boundaries are connected to the command to love. You see, God is still distinguishing us from the rest of the world. He wants the world to recognize us by our love (see John 13:35).

New Christians still need to know the boundaries: No more lusting! No hating. Pray for your enemies. Don't gossip. Don't be a drunkard. Don't get into pride. These are themes in the Old *and* New Testaments. The Ten Commandments are not passé; they are relevant. Now, however, our breaking the rules doesn't send us reeling to hell, or remove us from God's presence, or even remove our covenant with God and our authority. Instead, it makes us feel terrible inside. We don't want to continue on in our sin.

A new Christian wants and needs the rules. God uses them to distinguish the new believer from the rest of the world. Without that differentiation, the new believer's light can be extinguished, in part because the world won't listen to anything you say about Jesus if you look and smell like they do.

Your life *should* look different. The struggle to be sinless, however, is a losing battle. The rules teach us how to be separate from the world (they also teach another important lesson, one we will explore in the chapter on grace).

For now, when we sin, the feelings of guilt will prompt us to repent. We won't get it perfectly right, but trying to live perfectly is part of the journey.

Man-made Rules

For the Wilderness Christian, there is an inherent problem with boundaries: it is the temptation to invent rules that sound good.

This happened in the churches Paul wrote to. They would receive Christ by faith and then start adding all kinds of rules, until Paul would straighten them out. Observe the passion of a sound spiritual flogging administered by Paul:

> *You foolish Galatians! Who has bewitched you? Before your very eyes Jesus Christ was clearly portrayed as crucified. I would like to learn just one thing from you: Did you receive the Spirit by observing the law, or by believing what you heard? Are you so foolish? After beginning with the Spirit, are you now trying to attain your goal by human effort? Have you suffered so much for nothing—if it really was for nothing? Does God give you his Spirit and work miracles among you because you observe the law, or because you believe what you heard?* (Galatians 3:1-5)

An entire church had gotten a bit squirrely with the rules. We have seen the same tendency in our day; many American churches installed the no-makeup-or-you-are-a-harlot rule through the 1970s. Praise God, that's over. There was also the no-girls-wearing-pants-rule. Not sure why that would even exist. I remember as a kid the no-drums-in-church rule. "Those drums are the tools of the devil," we were told.

We still invent rules all the time—even though it is not our job. Let's keep it simple and remember why God gives us boundaries in the first place: His rules help us to live in ways that *distinguish* us from the world and ensure that His light in us is not *extinguished.*

Let's stick to His boundaries. There are plenty of those for us to mess up before we start concocting more of our own!

Chapter 10

Earn More When Paid Less

Buried in the pile of experiences a parent has when raising a two-year-old is a vein of genuine wisdom that applies to our journey.

Have you ever spent a year with a two-year-old? I have—four times now. When you are two (which I don't personally remember being, probably due to a couple of hard smacks to the head), the world is yours. Everything exists to benefit you. *Me…me…me…mine…*and *I want.* That about sums up the two-year-old's mindset—which, by the way, is eerily similar to the Wilderness mindset.

We are about to learn a new mentality. This one attacks the very core of the *me-obsession* mentality and addresses every speck of slave-thinking we may have dragged out of Egypt. Are you ready to take it on?

Do You Want to Give?

In just 60 days God has brought the Israelites out of Egypt, destroyed-Pharaoh's army, sweetened the waters at Marah, provided manna in the

Desert of Sin, brought water out of the rock at Horeb, and taken Moses up on Mount Sinai to give him the law and instruction for the Tabernacle.

The Israelites' minds must have been swimming—very much as ours do along this Christian journey! Moses treks up Mount Sinai for 40 days. Then he comes down, reads Israel the riot act, and goes back up for more. By the time Moses is done on Mount Sinai, God has issued command after command after command: "Thou shalt not do this," "Thou shalt not do that…."

"Uh—wait God. How do You spell *debauch*…errr whatever that word is?"

Suddenly, after a litany of shalts and shalt nots, God's tone changes from command to request:

> *The Lord said to Moses, "Tell the Israelites to bring Me an offering. You are to receive the offering for Me from each man whose heart prompts him to give"* (Exodus 25:1-2).

All these commands and then suddenly, "I want an offering, but only if someone *wants* to give." Say, what?

> *Then have them* [those whose hearts prompt them to give] *make a sanctuary for Me, and I will dwell among them* (Exodus 25:8).

> *Then the whole Israelite community withdrew from Moses' presence, and everyone who was willing and whose heart moved him came and brought an offering to the Lord for the work on the Tent of Meeting, for all its service, and for the sacred garments* (Exodus 35:20-21).

> *Then Moses summoned Bezalel and Oholiab and every skilled person to whom the Lord had given ability and who was willing to come and do the work* (Exodus 36:2).

God did not command everyone to help build the Tabernacle. He only wanted those who were willing to come and work on it.

But why not command them? They weren't busy doing anything. These people had no crops to raise. They had nothing to do except wake up in the morning and pick breakfast off the ground.

Yet, instead of commanding, God asks. It's like me telling my kids, "Look, no fighting in this house, we love each other. Respect your mother. Don't talk back to her. Oh, and who *wants* to do the dishes?"

Why not *make* the kids do the dishes? And why doesn't God keep on commanding things instead of asking, "Who wants to help?" He is Adonai, the sovereign God. He can tell people what to do and anything He wants them to do. (Of course, telling them what to do hasn't helped much so far. Remember the golden calf fiasco?)

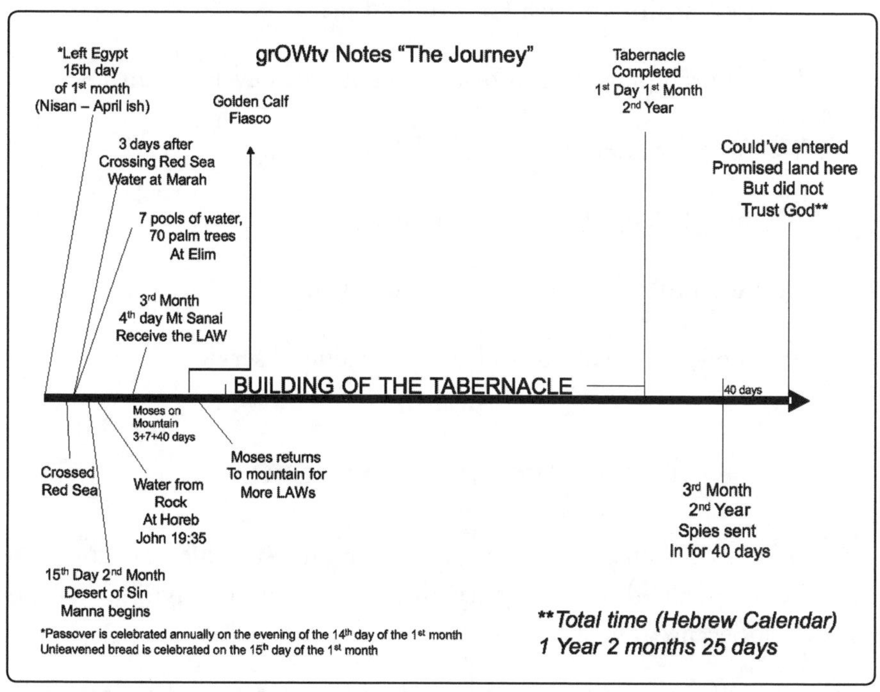

[Figure 2]

Looking again at our timeline covering the period from the departure of Egypt to the return to camp of the 12 spies, we see that the building of the Tabernacle comprises by far the longest portion of time. Just after finishing the Tabernacle (which takes two-thirds of the year), Moses sends in the spies. These things were done in a specific order: God needed the people to finish the Tabernacle first.

We must build God's house before he will build our house. In the Israelites' case, God's house must be completed before they get into the Promised Land. So what message is God sending by asking who wants to help?

Judging by the amount of time God dedicates to this particular Wilderness lesson, the point He wants to make is *major.* Before we tackle it, let's summarize seven concepts we have already considered:

1. Our influences and influencers must change.
2. We are learning to trust God to lead us.
3. The Church plays an important role in our development.
4. We need the Shepherd *and* the Word.
5. We must balance family and ministry.
6. God established boundaries for our lives.
7. And now, we are about to learn the value of service.

Attacking Slave Mentality

In order to directly attack our slave mentality, the idea of work must be addressed equally directly. Slavery amounts to day-in, day-out servitude. Slaves work because they have to.

The Israelites had been slaves for 430 years. Does God really need to teach them a work ethic now? They have spent their whole lives working. Josephus, the Jewish historian, notes that the Israelites built some of the pyramids.[1] So did they know hard labor? The answer is *yes. However,* Israel's productivity was tied to their slave mindset. Slaves will do the least amount of work possible in order to not be beaten. They are not motivated by pay raises, promotions, or bonuses. Just no beatings, thank you very much.

Joseph was the exception to the rule; he was self-motivated. He worked hard as a slave and did everything with excellence. Joseph tapped into something that the Israelites must learn before they can live the sweet life. Because of his exceptional mindset, Joseph found himself second in command of all of Egypt—and a brilliant leader at that.

Joseph was a slave with ruler mentality. The newly freed Israelites are called to be rulers, but have slave thinking. In a quick look at the map on page 116, the Feast of Tabernacles is our transition feast between the Wilderness and the Promised Land. The name of the feast gives away its key. God is telling us that in order to transition properly into the Promised Land without bouncing back into the Wilderness, we need to be willing to serve and give toward the building of the Tabernacle.

This is not a matter of compulsion, but of willingness—but *why?*

Successful Tabernacle Management Techniques

The tabernacle is tremendously important to build with excellence. The metaphors are a mile thick, each one explained in exquisite detail, God said "Make this tabernacle and all its furnishings exactly like the pattern I will show you." So no fudging room here. Now if you were reading the incredible writings of our leadership generals of today you will find the three important keys to successful leadership: talent (can I do it?), motivation (will I do it?), and attitude (how well will I do it?). This is the successful model. God has not been reading up on these books. I wonder if Moses should have advised God, letting him know that he can find talented people with good attitudes, but they will need some motivation. How about a promise for extra blessings for those who help? Maybe send them some cinnamon manna for a change, you know, if they help. Motivation is missing here. God just wants people who want to spend the better part of their year doing something for nothing. If Moses worked at the church today he might have said that this task would be impossible. I mean, who is going to WANT to do this?

In inviting His people to contribute voluntarily toward the building of the Tabernacle, God is not offering any motivation. He expects excellent work and perfect adherence to His design specifications—but there's no pay. The people are asked to donate money, gold, and other resources.

Why not compel them? Answer: God wants to change how they think. When you are a slave to this world, you scrimp, save, and hoard what little money you can get your hands on. This is slave thinking. The only way to cure this mentality is to give freely. When you give to the Lord out of the willingness of your heart, you attack the very root of the slave mindset. Willing service addresses slave mentality head-on.

When you are willing to serve for free, you demonstrate that you are becoming self-motivated, rather than driven by others.

If you are self-motivated, you perform with excellence *because you want to.* You may have spent your whole life doing things because you had to. You had to go to school. You had to get a job. You had to…had to…had to.

When everything is a *have to,* your *want tos* tend to be unproductive activities—you want to rest, you want to play video games, you want to "veg" out. Who wants to work when they feel they are forced into it? This is the weird part about Joseph; he was a great slave, a great prisoner, *and* he was self-motivated. This is ruler mentality.

Many people today want to start their own businesses so that they can "work for themselves." They think that being self-employed means you can schedule your own hours, sleep in if you like, take long vacations, etc. Being in business, then, is motivated by the desire to be less productive and have more time off. That is the wrong motivator!

If you haven't noticed, God designed a schedule where you work for six days and rest for one day. (Say *good-bye* to your five-day workweek!) In the Wilderness, He is about to dismantle the Israelites' slave mentality and install a genuine work ethic—a ruler mindset. *No more need for your two 15-minute breaks every day.*

In the process, the people who help Moses to build the Tabernacle are going to learn these three things:

Hard work...with excellence...because I want to!

If you are serving at church and are responsible to show up at 8 A.M., what happens if you sleep in and miss your assignment? Will someone call and yell at you? Will they write you up? Will your absence affect your Christmas bonus?

Of course not. So what is motivating you to be on time or even to show up at all? Nothing but the unbridled desire to serve the Lord! (Don't quit on me while I'm preachin' good.)

> *Whatever you do, work at it with all your heart as working for the Lord, not for men, since you know that you will receive an inheritance from the Lord as a reward...* (Colossians 3:23-24).

Now let's tweak the three lessons slightly:

Hard work...with excellence...because I do it for the Lord!

This is a rulership mentality. Your hard work is not motivated by thoughts of success, failure, money, or glory. You work hard because that is who you are. If you develop a habit of doing everything you do (even the stuff you don't like to do), diligently and with excellence, you will leave a trail of fruit and success.

How can you learn this concept? Simple. Serve at your church! Help build it with excellence.

"Well couldn't I learn that concept by serving anywhere?"

The answer is *no,* because you need to learn the concept by serving the Lord. He needs to start and finish as your motivator. Ladies and gentlemen, I won't lie to you. I am a pastor at a church and I speak from experience. Volunteer service at the church is a thankless job. You're lucky if you get the "Please stand up if you helped with this last week's conference," plug.

If someone quits serving because no one helped, or no one thanked them, then they did not learn the concept they needed to learn. It's going to be one more lap around the desert for them.

When you connect your labor to the Lord, you will challenge every slave thought that exists within you. It is the complete opposite of selfishness. It will be one of the first times in your life that you have worked hard for the sole reason that *you wanted to*. I promise you, it will change the way you view everything.

Now instead of doing just enough at work to keep your job, you find yourself dissatisfied with being average. You find that being an OK wife isn't good enough anymore. You want to be great and you are happy when working hard.

When self-motivation kicks in, life is never a grind. It's what keeps entrepreneurs going. Mind you, it's not easy. Any small business owner will tell you that 40 hours per week would be a fantasy schedule. They eat, sleep, and dream *business.* The first year involves the sweating of blood, and with little pay. Business owners never truly go home from work. It is a fight to the finish every day.

But there is a pay off. The business owner is taking territory—but only by willingly pouring heart, soul, and some tears, into the venture. You can see why starting a business in order to work less is a recipe for failure. If that is your motive, you aren't ready to rule. You were never built to be *less* productive; you were created to flourish in all you do.

That was a quick preview of the Promised Land mindset. Here's a summary of what we just learned:

We change what we "have" to do to what we "want" to do. It is a mental switch, because what we are doing does not change; but the way in which we address it changes completely.

Get happy—God is preparing you to lead!

I Will Dwell Among Them

In Exodus 25:8 God makes a profound statement you don't want to miss: *"Then have them make a sanctuary for Me, and I will dwell among them."*

Remember that, at Horeb, the Israelites asked, *"Is the Lord among us or not?"* (Exod. 17:7). Now, at Mount Sinai, God answers their question by telling them to build a dwelling for Him. God is aware of their need to walk in the light of His presence, just as He is aware of ours.

Under the New Covenant, God's dwelling is within His people: *"And in Him you too are being built together to become a dwelling in which God lives by His Spirit"* (Eph. 2:22).

Now there are two temples of God, spiritually speaking. Both must be functional. The first temple is you. Your body is the temple of the Holy Spirit. First Corinthians 3:16 asks: *"Don't you know that you yourselves are God's temple and that God's Spirit lives in you?"*

The Ark of the Covenant is inside you, just like it was in the holy Tabernacle. You have an inner court and an outer court. The Holy of Holies is within you.

The second dwelling place of the Lord is the Church, the Body of Christ. You must bring the Spirit in you and connect to the Spirit in the Body of Christ, which is the Church. Connecting to this temple where we, as a body, are being built together, serves to release the Spirit within you. In our corporate praise, the presence of the Lord is released. Jesus said it like this: *"I will declare Your name to My brothers; in the congregation I will praise You"* (Ps. 22:22).

If there is some praising to do, God wants others to join in. God told the Israelites that if they would build Him a sanctuary, then He would dwell among them. When you are at church, building the house of the Lord, God is dwelling among you. When an individual disconnects from church, they feel as if the Lord is not there anymore. It isn't because the presence of the Lord has left that Church. It would be ludicrous to think that God's presence would not be in the Body of Christ.

God didn't leave (assuming this is a Bible-teaching church and not some weird cult or something; and if it is, don't drink the water!) God is there. What happened is that the individual is not going to church to help build it. Connecting to a church is when you are attending it to build it. You might grab a flyer for the upcoming Christmas play or help raise money for the new youth hall. Maybe you serve by shaking people's hands or ushering. If you are a singer, then sing in the church…if you are a teacher, then teach…if you love to pray, then pray. Help build the Church—but only if you are willing. Don't do it because I said so.

Once we have learned service, the Promised Land is near. But there is something we need to do first.

Chapter 11

Forgiving the Unforgivable

I ONCE CALLED 411 to get a phone number. I'm not sure why they do this, but a computer-generated voice asked, "City and state?"

For some reason, I always panic at this part. "The Voice" is not very nice and not very patient. I made it under the wire this time.

"Yeah, for Mesa, Arizona," I answered.

The Voice asked, "For what listing?"

"Uhh...Target." All I really wanted to know was what time the store closed on Sunday. I don't know why I interact with the machine, because no matter how well I articulate what I'm looking for, a person shows up and asks the same question.

"City and state?" asks the woman promptly.

"Mesa, Arizona. I need the number for Target."

(Long pause.) "Can you spell it, sir?"

This is the part of the story where I'm not such a good pastor. I have a habit of designing and implementing a range of tactics I call "Annoying things to do when you're annoyed."

I was definitely annoyed. Can I spell Target? What planet are you from?

Don't you judge me, either. So I began to spell Target—well, sort of: "Double-u—" I paused again.

"Ugh," I said somewhat confused sounding, "I am not good at this."

"Double-u?" she asked. "Are you spelling *Target*?"

"Yeah," I answered, "I'm sorry, it's not a double-u, is it? OK, Let's go with Q— No, make that U—"

Suddenly the line made a clicking sound and I was connected back to the computer, which, in turn, transferred me to Target.

"Hah!" I thought. "She knew how to spell *Target* all along!"

Don't even think for a minute that this is a good example to set for a pastor or any Christian. We all react, do crazy things we don't mean to do, say horrible things to people we love. We are…human. We have addictions, quirks, even a cuss word squeaks out every now and then.

The question is: how is this reality reconciled with Christianity? We will find out soon enough.

Fully Obey?

For now, we begin our transition into the Promised Land. To do this, we need to jump back in time to when Moses climbed Mount Sinai to receive the commands of the Lord. Think back to Chapter 9, where we talked about boundaries. We want the rules. They are part of the natural learning process that, over time, will lead us to a revelation of grace.

At Mount Sinai, God gives an enormous number of commands, laws handed down to the Israelites that they were required to keep. There were promises of blessing attached to the law, but they were only attainable through perfect obedience. Here is what God, through Moses, told the Israelites:

> *If you fully obey the Lord your God and carefully follow all His commands I give you today, the Lord your God will set you high above all the nations on earth. All these blessings will come upon you and accompany you if you obey the Lord your God* (Deuteronomy 28:1-2).

To fully obey means you cannot make a mistake. If you obey, the fruit of your womb is blessed, your barns are blessed, and you are blessed coming and going.

Many of the blessings of obedience have to do with finances. Praise God—He wants to bless us! But here's the problem: who can fully obey *all* the commands? God goes on to say that if you don't fully obey, you are under a curse, and everything in your life will stink.

Great. All of us sin (miss the mark), because we are not perfect. This sounds like a lose-lose proposition. If I don't fully obey all the commands, I will come under a curse. No man or woman can fully obey all the commands, therefore, I am definitely under a curse.

Not anymore! In order to cross the Jordan into the Promised Land, we need to recognize that Jesus changed everything. The blessing represents the Promised Land, which is now open for business because Jesus broke the power of sin that would otherwise have separated you from the blessing.

That is a win-win proposition! Yet, when I sin, it is still true that destruction comes my way. If I shoot my neighbor's dog, trouble is headed my way.

"Didn't Jesus do away with the power of sin?" you ask.

Yes, He did, but sin still has natural consequences. For that, too, Jesus has made provision. It is called *grace.* Crossing the River Jordan will demand a revelation of grace. Paul had a full-blown *rhema* revelation of grace. His epistles lay it out. I can offer you the facts as he did, but grace has to come alive inside of *you*. I cannot make that happen.

You and God *can.*

Moses and the Law

Moses and the Israelites completed the Tabernacle. It was time to send in the spies.

> *The Lord said to Moses, "Send some men to explore the land of Canaan, which I am giving to the Israelites....* (Num. 13:1-2).

After almost 15 months of being in the Wilderness, the Israelites were ready to cross into the Promised Land. So are you. It is time to cross the Jordan River.

In the next chapter I will discuss the story in greater detail. I will ruin the ending for you now, though. Moses and the Israelites, who were adults when they left Egypt, do not get to go into the Promised Land. The Israelites lacked the faith that God would give it to them. Moses disobeyed God and was barred from entering, just short of Canaan.

This is where we see the two most important keys to entering the Promised Land: faith and grace. We must have both. If the people had believed God, they would have entered in. That was His stated plan—to lead them in! Because they lacked that simple faith in God, they died off in the Wilderness.

We need grace because, without it, sin disqualifies us from the blessing. Breaking one command banished Moses from his desired destination. In Numbers 20, he was instructed by God to bring water from a rock, this time by merely speaking to it.

At Horeb the striking of the rock was symbolic of Christ being pierced on the cross. But now, farther along in the journey, Christ has already resurrected and God's Word in us is sufficient to bring the desired results. The Lord is resting, because His Word continues to work. He called Moses into that rest, just as He is calling us. But Moses disobeyed God and struck the rock with his staff—twice. The water still came out, but Moses lost his chance to lead the people of Israel into the Promised Land (see Num. 20:11-12).

Moses is a picture of the law. I showed you just a moment ago that we cannot enter into the promises of God by obeying the law. None of us can obey it fully. Moses' death in the Wilderness is a picture of that reality. He did so many things right, yet one mistake cost him the Promised Land. We *cannot* enter the Promised Land through the law.

Joshua, Moses' aide and one of the 12 spies, is a picture of grace. After Moses dies, God speaks to Joshua:

> *After the death of Moses the servant of the Lord, the Lord said to Joshua son of Nun, Moses' aide: "Moses My servant is dead. Now then, you and all these people, get ready to cross the Jordan River into the land I am about to give to them—to the Israelites. I will give you every place where you set your foot, as I promised Moses* (Joshua 1:1-3).

Are you ready for this? It is a new day. Some old stuff has died, and we are ready to go in. It is going to be very important to pay attention to the details here, since we are in transition and transition is difficult to navigate. Read the following passage and make special note of the names of the locations that are affected as the people prepare to cross the Jordan:

> *So when the people broke camp to cross the Jordan, the priests carrying the ark of the covenant went ahead of them. Now the Jordan is at flood stage all during harvest. Yet as soon as the priests who carried the ark reached the Jordan and their feet touched the water's edge, the water from upstream stopped flowing. It piled up in a heap a great distance away, at a town called* ***Adam*** *in the vicinity of* ***Zarethan,*** *while the water flowing down to the Sea of the Arabah (the* ***Salt Sea****) was completely cut off. So the people crossed over opposite Jericho. The priests who carried the ark of the covenant of the Lord stood firm on dry ground in the middle of*

the Jordan, while all Israel passed by until the whole nation had completed the crossing on dry ground (Joshua 3:14-17).

This crossing was to happen at harvest time. If you look back to our map on page 116, the Promised Land is the fall, or harvest season, in our journey. Harvest is when we reap the blessings of the Lord in our lives.

Now for those details you just read in the passage from Joshua 3. As we follow the footsteps of the Israelites in crossing the Jordan, refer to Figure 3 often. You will see how the details pertain to sin and grace.

First, the word *Jordan* means "descender."[1] The Jordan flows down to the Dead Sea. The Jordan separates us from the Promised Land, the promises of God. This is a picture of sin's function. Sin wants to pull you down to death and destruction and separate you from God.

When the Ark of the Covenant was carried into the Jordan, the water piled up in a heap all the way to the place named *Adam*. This name is not a coincidence. Sin's power was defeated all the way to Adam for a reason.

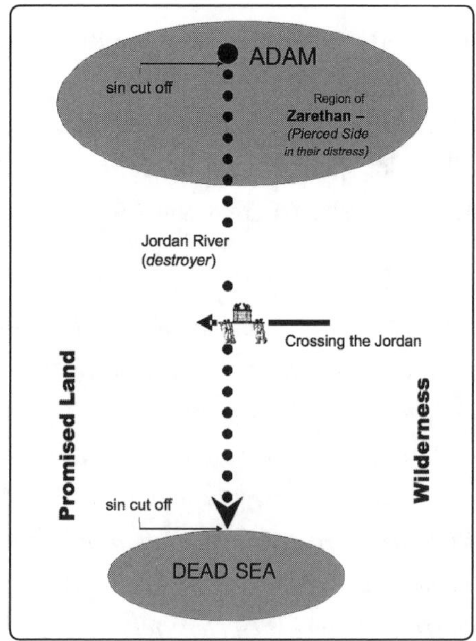

[Figure 3]

Sin entered the world through Adam and because of Adam's sin, all men sinned through him:

> *...sin entered the world through one man, and death through sin, and in this way death came to all men, because all sinned* (Romans 5:12).

Sin is passed down through the generations, because we were all in Adam when he sinned. You and I were there, like it or not. This is why we are all born sinners. It is also the reason that Jesus could not be born of a man. He descended not from man, but directly from God. Therefore, He was born sinless, as Adam had been.

Jesus never sinned, yet he died a sinner, so that sin would no longer have the power to separate you from God or from the Promised Land.

> *Consequently, just as the result of one trespass was condemnation for all men, so also the result of one act of righteousness was justification that brings life for all men* (Romans 5:18).

Justification is brought through Christ's life and death to us. We cannot earn it; it is a gift. Self-justification is impossible, because we were born sinners. Many people believe that if they live a good life they will go to Heaven, regardless of their faith. This is a one-way ticket to the Dead Sea. You and I were born sinners. We can try to be as "good" as humanly possible, but unless we receive Christ, we will die in our sins.

When we receive Christ, God forgives us and leaves our sin in the sea of forgetfulness. He doesn't even remember it. Jesus' death cut sin's power off all the way back to Adam and all the way down to the Dead Sea. Christ died for all sin and for all mankind—past, present, and future.

Sin can no longer separate us from God or His promises, but here is the catch: guilt can. Any guilt and condemnation that you carry with you will keep you from crossing the Jordan and enjoying all that God desires for you to have.

God has forgiven you, but you must forgive yourself, too; past, present, and future.

Further, the reason we stand in moral judgment of others is because we have not forgiven ourselves. We point out everyone else's faults and shortcomings because, deep down, we are disgusted with our own. When we forgive ourselves as God has forgiven us, we recognize that all have sinned. Then we no longer need to put others down.

This is how grace operates. Understanding grace will truly set you free of the burden of judgment and offense.

The Pierced Side

Looking again to Joshua 3:14, sin was cut off to the region of *Zarethan,* which means "pierced side in their distress."[2]

When the Roman soldier pierced Jesus' side, blood and water flowed. This flow takes the place of what use to flow in the Jordan, which is sin. Jesus canceled sin's power and took sin's property by flowing His blood into the water of the Jordan.

Let me explain. What once there was death, the waters now flow with life. This is a gift that is now called *repentance.* It is why John the Baptist baptized Jesus and others in the Jordan. Jesus came to John and was completely immersed there (see Matt. 3:13-17). This is a picture of leaving our sin behind as we repent and are reborn. Of course, Jesus had no sin and did not need to be reborn; He fulfilled the act and painted this awesome picture for us to follow.

Understanding grace requires us to realize that the price is paid in full. We are now baptized in the Jordan, symbolically speaking. When we are baptized, we go under the water and come back up again, symbolizing death, burial, and resurrection. Our death happens when we are crucified with Christ (at the point of salvation). We are dead, not physically, but to sin. The sin we carried into life has died—we no longer have sin in us.

All of these things are provided for us when we get saved, but like everything the Lord offers, we must believe and receive them. If we do not fully believe that we are forgiven, then we stay in the Wilderness.

"But Jason, you don't know what I've done. How can God forgive me?"

"Oh, geez, you did *what*? Yeah, maybe you're right. You might be out of luck there."

I'm kidding! Jesus died for all sin. The law will continue to increase sin in your life until you realize that you are dead to the law.

Moses and Mount Sinai

> *So my brothers, you also died to the law through the body of Christ, that you might belong to another, to Him who was raised from the dead, in order that we might bear fruit to God* (Romans 7:4).

You died to the law through the Body of Christ. Don't miss this most precious reference here to the Church. Now we see that wisdom, faith, victory, and grace all flow through the Church.

Through the Body of Christ you died to the law. Dead people are no longer bound by the rules in an agreement. Before you were crucified with Christ you had an agreement with God under the law. That agreement stated that if you would fully obey all the rules He would be with you, and you would be blessed. But when you died, your end of the agreement was made null and void.

That makes sense, right? If you are under contract with your employer to provide a service, but you die, you no are longer obligated to perform that service. (And if you continued to perform the service after you die, that would be really creepy. Dead people are not usually welcome in the workplace.)

God, however, is not dead. Therefore His end of the agreement still stands. His agreement states that He will be with you and He will bless you, your goats, and your grapes. By faith, you have been made holy before the Lord and are alive in Christ Jesus.

Under this New Covenant, your faith in Jesus is what holds up your end of the agreement—not your performance. You have to get out of your head the idea that you are a sinner. You are not your sin. Once you receive Christ, you are not seen by God as a sinner, even though you continue to sin. Instead, because you are in Christ, you are seen by God as being holy and righteous.

"But, Jason, if you sin after you are saved, then you lose the blessing until you turn from sin."

"Rats. Really?"

Now don't get mad at me, but that is just not true. If that were true, then no one will be blessed—*ever*—for all continue to sin. Paul comments on his quest to stop sinning in Romans:

> *For what I do is not the good I want to do; no, the evil I do not want to do—this I keep on doing. Now if I do what I do not want to do, it is no longer I who do it, but it is sin living in me that does it.... What a wretched man I am! Who will rescue me from this body of death?* (Romans 7:19-20,24)
>
> *Therefore, there is now no condemnation for those who are in Christ Jesus* (Romans 8:1).

What did Paul just say, except that he is saved but still sinning? It looks like he's sinning a lot, too. And his conclusion is that there is no condemnation for those who are in Christ Jesus. How much condemnation did he say there is? None.

Why bring this up? Because guilt and condemnation have the power to separate you from God and His blessing. You are holy, having been made holy through the sacrifice of Christ. You did not earn it and no amount of goodness or sin can change that. Only your faith can change it.

Grace then is the reason that God is with you and will bless you regardless of your sin. Now if you read this and use it as a free pass to continue sinning, then you are having serious heart issues. You must be *trying* not to sin. As I mentioned earlier, sin still has natural consequences. When you sin, you permit the destroyer to steal from you with natural consequences of sin. If you have an affair you will probably lose your family. But that does not mean God stopped blessing you. You just had the blessing stolen through some really bad decisions.

A word to the wise: If you sow drug dealing, you may reap a trip to prison.

God Is Not Disconnecting From You

God will never disconnect from you. You, however, might be disconnecting from God. Here is how: First, as I mentioned before, we must stay connected to the Body of Christ. That is done by being connected to the Church to help build it, to help her to influence the world.

The Church is Team Jesus, and we are supposed to be on the field, playing. Too many Christians are disconnected and cannot produce because they are in the stands of Christianity, watching the game, eating popcorn, and wondering why people feel the need to go to church.

But Team Jesus needs your unique talents and gifts to help influence the world. Let me ask you this: What if you were the greatest basketball player in the world, but you never joined a team? How much of an impact would you make on the NBA? The answer is *zero* impact.

The same goes for us Christians. You could be the best Christian in the world, yet be unproductive. Your impact on the world has no way to materialize, because you won't connect to the Body of Christ, His Church. Here's a clue: much of the New Testament was written to churches—at Corinth, Ephesus, Galatia, etc. There is a reason for that!

The second reason you are disconnecting from God is your faith. You honestly believe that He is far away, but you are the one who left town. Your guilt separates you from God. What Paul is saying in Romans 7 is that in his sin, *he* is not sinning. It is the sin that lives in him that is guilty of the sin.

Does this mean you go on sinning purposefully? Of course not. What we are doing right now is disarming the power of sin. As long as sin separates you from God, it has all the power. When your faith connects with the fact that sin is incapable of separating you from God or His promises, you will stop disconnecting.

> *"To Me this is like the days of Noah, when I swore that the waters of Noah would never again cover the earth. So* ***now I have sworn not to be angry with you,*** *never to rebuke you again. Though the mountains be shaken and the hills be removed, yet My unfailing love for you will not be shaken* ***nor My covenant of peace be removed,****" says the Lord, who has compassion on you* (Isaiah 54:9-10).

This prophesy from the Book of Isaiah foretold the change that Christ would bring when He died. God did not change; the circumstances changed. Earlier in the chapter the prophecy brings to light our Bridegroom, Christ, as our Holy One and Redeemer. Not all of the Old Testament is as encouraging as that. We find some places where God is pretty upset.

That was then. This is now. He doesn't get mad at us anymore. This is a promise from His lips. Really. He's not mad at you. Now, I've read stories where He was mad and, no, that's not where you want to be. Not only is He not mad, but He has also promised that His covenant of peace will not be removed. This is a promise. When you sin it does not disconnect you from God's covenant of peace, which is the blessing, the Promised Land, and rest from your enemies. God does not unplug His covenant. It will *never* be removed.

Whenever the Israelites would abandon God's laws, the covenant would be broken. But the covenant is no longer held together by obedience. Now it is bound by faith. You may be disconnecting from God every time you sin because you see yourself as unworthy. Still, the blessing is flowing toward you. But when you unplug and then plug back in, then unplug, then plug back in, the momentum of the blessing is disrupted and the blessing has a hard time manifesting.

It's like pouring honey on toast. It takes awhile for the honey to get enough momentum to exit the bottle. If you keep setting the bottle down, you have to wait for the honey to get moving again, so you can pour it onto your toast.

Quit putting down your bottle of honey.

JUSTIFIED BY FAITH

So can we enter the Promised Land as sinners? Yeah, we can!

Long before the law there was Abraham, whom the Lord credited as being righteous because of his faith. God makes a covenant of peace with Abraham. Abraham is a picture of our covenant with the Lord; it is a covenant that is based on faith. *"Abraham believed the Lord and He credited it to him as righteousness"* (Gen. 15:6).

Abraham was justified by faith, just as we are. We will take a good look at Abraham's life later, because he is one of the few people mentioned in the Bible who entered into the rest of the Lord.

God's promise to Abraham in the covenant was this:

> *I will make you into a great nation and I will bless you; I will make your name great, and you will be a blessing. I will bless those who bless you, and whoever curses you I will curse; and all peoples on earth will be blessed through you* (Genesis 13:2-3)

Two quick things to read here from Galatians:

> *The Scripture foresaw that God would justify the Gentiles by faith, and announced the gospel in advance to Abraham: "All nations will be blessed through you." So those who have faith are blessed along with Abraham, the man of faith* (Galatians 3:8-9).

> *He redeemed us in order that the blessing given to Abraham might come to the Gentiles through Christ Jesus, so that by faith we might receive the promise of the Spirit* (Galatians 3:14).

We are justified by faith, not works (obedience). Scripture invites us into His throne room so that we can make our requests boldly in faith (see Heb. 4:16). What entitles us to enter His presence, ask for His help, or receive the blessing? Faith.

In fact, Galatians 3:14 tells us that we were redeemed in order that the blessing of Abraham might come upon the Gentiles and we might receive the promise of the Spirit. If you want to assign an important value to the sacrifice of Christ, that is certainly valuable.

If you are not tapping into and seeing His blessing manifested in your life, you have probably discounted His gift and promise as being of no value.

It's like a kid refusing to open a birthday present from his parents, saying, "No thanks, I'm not worthy of this gift."

Oh yes you are. You have been *made* worthy.

Try as You Might

As a Christian you try and live right, even though many hang-ups seem to trip you up. You desire to overcome sin; that is why you are trying so hard.

The trying part is God's plan. Be aware that it is intended to lead you to grace; however, it can lead you to two possible destinations that are harmful: one is pride; the other is false humility. Pride appears when you feel that, through raw willpower, you have done a decent job of cleaning up your life. Your thoughts and emotions are still pretty messed up, but you have moved the majority of your sins to the back room. They become hidden sins, or sins that Christians find somewhat acceptable, like gluttony, gossip, and judgment.

As long as pride is operating, judgment will reign supreme in your life and you will find yourself forever wandering in the Wilderness. Your amazing self-control will have you looking down at all other Christians as being a bunch of weak sinners. Sadly, your only hope is that destruction will find you again so that you are humbled and begin searching for the truth again.

The path of false humility is the one that causes you to walk into church feeling guilty all the time. You start to sing a worship song and that voice rings loud and clear, "Who do you think you are, worshiping God? You are a mess. If anyone finds out what you are really like...."

And so you repent. Then you try harder. It's a vicious circle and shows a lack of understanding of grace. You show up for every service, lift your hands, and praise Him, but you still feel like you are on the hook for your sins. Like the pride path, the false humility path does not overcome sin. It can't, because sin still has the power.

As long as sin has the power to separate you from God then you will not defeat it. You cannot. You are fighting alone. Christ will defeat the sin when you finally realize that you cannot.

GRACE AND THE MOUNTAIN OF SIN

Trying to be perfect is intended to teach you how much you need grace. Understanding grace is necessary, because grace is the teacher of right living.

> *For the grace of God that brings salvation has appeared to all men. It teaches us to say "No" to ungodliness and worldly passions, and to live self-controlled, upright and godly lives in this present age...* (Titus 2:11-12).

You cannot defeat the sin in your life until you understand grace. Grace defeats sin, but only after you realize that you cannot justify yourself. The rules were given to bring you to the breaking point. They serve to prove that we must have a Savior. You and I *will* fail at being sinless. If we try to walk in self-justification, then we are stuck in Wilderness thinking. Eventually, we will fall to our knees and say to the Lord, "I can't do it. I can't. I can't. I can't." Broken, we finally realize that He already did it for us. He defeated sin and justified us before God!

I will be weaving grace through the next eight chapters because it is such a deep and important subject to understand.

First, let's go back in time just a bit, to where Moses is called up by God to receive the law:

> *The Lord said to Moses, "Come up to Me on the mountain and stay here, and I will give you the tablets of stone, with the law and commands I have written for their instruction"* (Exodus 24:12).

You may recall that these were the boundaries put in place to teach the Israelites to be different from the rest of the world. We as Christians want these boundaries when we get saved. But the boundaries are only there to teach us as well something far more important. They teach us that we cannot live sinless in our own strength and willpower.

God describes this wonderfully. The mountain from which the law was issued was Mount Sinai, which means "mountain of Sin." When I first discovered this I did not understand. In fact, I avoided mentioning it completely. Why would God not issue His most perfect commands on Mount Horeb, the mountain of God? They were at Mount Horeb only a few weeks prior. It would have been a much more insightful teaching.

Here on Sinai, the metaphor is that sin has been elevated above man, and will lord over him. Then I found this in Romans 5:20: *"The law was added so that the trespass might increase."*

Huh? This Scripture says that the law came to increase sin. The purpose of the law was to amplify sin. (I keep repeating it for a reason.) Now this fits perfectly with the law coming down from Mount Sinai. The Lord chose the mountain of sin to reveal that these commands were in fact amplifying sin.

God's point to all of mankind was to show them, through the law, that they could not save themselves. They could not keep all the rules. God knew that. He also knew that we would have to try to do it on our own before we would admit to our utter helplessness to self-justify.

Once we climb that mountain enough times, we find ourselves broken, looking to God and saying, "I've messed up *again*. Help!"

Remember that even if man could have obeyed all the commands, sin is passed down from generation to generation. Adam's original sin is in us, because we were in him when he ate the fruit. We were born sinners. Therefore, we are incapable of becoming sinless through our vain attempts at obedience.

Instead, as it says in Titus 2, grace is the teacher of godly living. We know that we must overcome sin and addictions in our lives as we mature. We cannot continue to live in sin or it will destroy us. But, as long as guilt causes us to separate from God, we are trying to defeat sin in your own ability.

It is impossible. We need God's help—His grace—to win. To enter the Promised Land we also need faith.

That is our next stop.

Chapter 12

Doing the Undoable

THIS CHAPTER AND THE LAST one overlap a bit because both grace and faith are necessary to enter the Promised Land. The two are married; it is difficult to discuss one without mentioning the other.

First, a story.

I had lunch with a friend at a nice Mexican restaurant. We were talking and eating. I was speaking emphatically, really into what I was saying. Then he glanced away and motioned to the waiter for something. At that moment, a sparkle of light caught my eye. A small strand of saliva left my lips mid-sentence and was now flying in the direction of his plate. The shiny strand seemed to float through the air in slow motion as I finished my statement.

I was captivated by the whole thing. If I had tried to accurately spit on my friend's ancho chile peach-glazed chicken, I could never have targeted it so perfectly. As it happened, my saliva alighted dead center on his plate, the splat of it echoing in my ears. The amazing thing was that my friend didn't know what had happened. He just glanced back at me, returning to our conversation at the very moment of impact.

"What now? Do I tell him? I have to, right? Oh geez, he's about to eat it. Nope, he just missed it."

Thoughts raced through my mind as I continued the conversation on autopilot, my mind focused on the gossamer thread of saliva screaming at me from across the table.

"No! Don't let him eat me!" it cried.

Now, I could see that my oral fluid was mixing in with his sauce. It was as though it were burning a hole in the chicken, through the table, and into my lying, cheating, blackened soul.

"So, what are you doing for Christmas this year?"

Was that all I could say? How about, "Oh, by the way, that delicious sauce you just sampled has been carefully seasoned with my spit!"

It was too late. He ate it.

I never did tell my friend what happened. I'm pretty sure that comes under the category of sin, somewhere between lying, failing to disclose, and violating spit-related etiquette. The thing is—my offense was not an act of my will. I was trying, however unsuccessfully, not to fall.

That is the thing about grace; it comes alongside my effort to do the right thing. As long as I continue to desire not to sin, then grace is active. The opportunity to not sin is always there, whether you're talking about a one-time sin or an addiction. The latter is a process of sin. It presents many opportunities to back away, but we often take the bait.

Once that desire has produced sin, the question is, do you still want to stop? Did you want to do what you did, or did you do something you really didn't want to do? Whether you engaged in an hour of gossip, or a full-on drinking binge, will you continue trying to stop?

This is what keeps grace active. It is only when we abandon the effort to stop sinning that we turn our backs on what Christ did for us. I haven't met a Christian yet who has chosen this path. Even the pastor who has a month-long homosexual affair is remorseful, wishing he could go back and undo his indiscretion.

Yes. That is an extreme example. An affair is designed to destroy all that that man has built. Yet, Jesus says His grace is sufficient (see 2 Cor. 12:9). When Paul said in Romans 7 that he keeps doing the things he doesn't want to do, he was trying not to sin. He was obviously sorry he had sinned. Therefore, grace was active.

I did not want to spit in my friend's food. I did not want to deceive him into eating my spit. I'm a good friend and I meant well.

Grace is the teacher that shows us how to say no to ungodliness.

Where Is the Blessing?

It was many years into my being a pastor that I noticed I was not being blessed. We were living paycheck to paycheck. My wife and I were making good decisions to avoid debt; I opened investment accounts in an effort to maximize a pastor's not-so-huge paycheck. I sought to be blessed so I could be a blessing.

My marriage was decent, still kind of crisis to crisis, though. As a singer, my throat was in and out of commission, depending on what my health was doing. I was attacked by storms pretty often in all kinds of relationships—friends with the ol' knife in the back kind of thing.

Every area in my life was livable, but just getting by. I was sure there was more. I believed that God wanted to bless me. I believed that He was capable of blessing me. I even partially understood what the blessing meant. I did not believe deep down, though, that I qualified. I was missing a revelation of grace. I was unworthy to stay connected to the blessing for any length of time. Sin relapse would disconnect me from the covenant, not because of my sin, but because of my guilt.

Then the Lord led me to Isaiah 54 in my study time. I stayed there for three months before I got a single thing out of it. I read it over and over again. Then suddenly, it sprung to life in me. *Grace.* That was my missing ingredient. Immediately, everything began to change. What was inside my heart began to manifest on the outside.

There were certain issues that had to be settled for my life to turn around. I had to know and believe certain things about the blessing. I can boil the heart of it down to just four simple questions we need to ask ourselves:

1. Does God want to bless me?

2. Is God capable of blessing me?

3. What is the blessing? (What's in it? What does it include?)

4. Do I qualify for the blessing?

In order to receive the blessing, we need to be able to answer these questions based on an understanding of grace.

Does God Want to Bless Me?

Why didn't the Israelites get to go into the Promised Land right away? God promised them the land, didn't He?

Yes, but they chose not to receive it.

"Oh no," you groan. "Has this book turned into a message about what we can get from God? Is this one of those use-God-to-get-rich-quick-books?"

The answer is a loud and clear "No." That is not where we are headed. But, if we are going to talk about the Promised Land and the Place of Rest, we have to talk about the ability to receive from God.

Stick with me. We are going to find some freedom—and the Israelites are going to help us find it. We are at the point in the story after the Tabernacle is completed. It is over a full year after the Israelites left Egypt. They set out for Desert of Paran. Then God had Moses send in the 12 spies to explore Canaan for 40 days.

Remember that Canaan is the Promised Land. It is where the descendants of Ham's son Canaan settled. The land of Canaan is inhabited by nations the Israelites will need to remove. It is also the land of milk and honey, according to God's promise.

The spies went in to check it out. Moses instructed them to find out whether the people in Canaan are strong or weak, few or many. In the natural, this seems a legitimate request. However, God promised them that He was *giving* them the land. How strong the people were should not have mattered.

Remember what God had already done to the Egyptians? He brought them to their knees, just as He promised. Now God is going to give the Promised Land to the Israelites. All they have to do is trust Him for it.

The spies return after 40 days with their report. They agree with God that the land is amazing, but ten of them are far more focused on the fact that the people there are powerful and the cities are well protected. Caleb, of the tribe of Judah, however, is adamant, saying, *"We should go up and take possession of the land, for we can certainly do it"* (Num. 13:30).

Immediately, the ten "doubters" beg to differ: *"We can't attack those people; they are stronger than we are"* (Num.13:31).

OK, here it is. *Fear.* Fear is faith in a bad outcome. Faith is the belief that we can do all things through Christ who strengthens us (see Phil. 4:13). What the ten spies have is not faith; they spread a bad report throughout the whole nation.

They say, *"We seemed like grasshoppers in our own eyes and we looked the same to them"* (Num. 13:33). The entire nation begins to grumble against

Moses and Aaron. They wish they were back in Egypt. They even talk about stoning their leaders (see Num. 14:10).

Many Christians hear the message of the Promised Land, but when they get to the point the Israelites are at here, they resist crossing over. They answer at least one of the four questions the wrong way:

1. Maybe God doesn't want to bless me.

2. He may not be capable of blessing me.

3. This may not be a blessing after all.

4. I just don't qualify for the blessing.

The result of this fear and doubt is anger. Anger toward whomever told them about the Promised Land. Anger toward anyone who is in the Promised Land.

Let the blogging in the desert begin. Those who speak about grace will be misquoted. Stones of hate will be hurled. The Promised Land will be declared a farce. Scriptures will be taken out of context to contradict the message of truth. Someone will say, "I tried that faith stuff. It doesn't work."

It's as though they have forgotten the Word of the Lord altogether. Let's listen for a moment to how this makes God feel.

> *The Lord said to Moses, "How long will these people treat Me with contempt? How long will they refuse to believe in Me, in spite of all the miraculous signs I have performed among them? I will strike them down with a plague and destroy them, but I will make you into a nation greater and stronger than they"* (Numbers 14:11-12).

Moses steps in and talks to God as a mediator between the Lord and His people. The insight provided into God's ways is so powerful. The Lord shows emotion and he allows Moses to show us a picture of our mediator, Christ, who stands before the Father continually defending against the accuser, satan, with four wonderful words: "I died for them."

What makes God angry enough that He would swear that this generation will not see the Promised Land?

> *Not one of you will enter the land I swore with uplifted hand to make your home, except Caleb son of Jephunneh and Joshua son of Nun* (Numbers 14:30).

In the previous chapter of this book I showed you that God has sworn not to be angry with us (see Isa. 54:9). He also says that if anyone attacks us it will not be His doing (see Isa. 54:15). What was it that used to make Him so mad? Was it that the people wanted more than He was willing to give? Or was it because they were receiving *less* than He was willing to give?

God was angry because they wanted something less than what He had given them.

If I say, "All this blessing stuff is not a part of my Christianity. I don't need that stuff to love God or be with Him. It's all so superficial," it would sound Christlike and humble to many people.

Well, that's great, but it really cheeses God off (or it used to). I do not want to do anything that makes Him angry.

The answer to Question No. 1 (Does God want to bless me?) is *"Yes!"*

Is God Capable of Blessing Me?

Once again, the obvious answer to this question is *"Yes!"* Yet this is the reason the Israelites did not get to go in. Of the four questions this appears on the surface to be the easiest one to answer.

Is God able? He is able to do exceedingly far and above more than you can ask, dream, or imagine (see Eph. 3:20). We would shout this out loud if you were in a service and I was preaching this message. You would echo with a loud, "Amen!"

Someone might even stand up and say, "Preach it, you wild short man."

Yet this is often where our faith falls short. It is interrupted by the natural circumstances that bring fear. Fear interrupts faith. Fear is not the opposite of faith, fear is faith. (Fear's opposite is love.) Fear is the belief in the opposite of what you hope for. It is faith in doubt. It is built on doubt; godly faith is built on God's Word.

When fear is operating, you entertain the idea that God's Word may not be true for you. The Israelites believed they would die if they went into the Promised Land. They doubted that God had given them the land. They doubted God's Word and they believed in the doubt, which manifested itself in the form of fear. They probably imagined the worst. They pictured it and thereby birthed fear in their hearts.

If they were to attack the inhabitants of Canaan while walking in fear, they would have lost. Don't believe me? Check it out for yourself. After the Lord passed His judgment for their unbelief, they got a group together and went into the land and tried to take it. They were still in fear, but were ignoring it. They didn't want to die in the Wilderness and were trying to pull a "do-over" on God.

Ignoring your belief in your own doubts (trying to deny your fear) is called *presumption.* Many people ignore sickness. They deny what is going on in their bodies and they die in presumption. Healing is not received by presumption; it is received by faith:

> *Nevertheless, in their presumption they went up toward the high hill country, though neither Moses nor the ark of the Lord's covenant moved from the camp. Then the Amalekites and Canaanites who lived in that hill country came down and attacked them and beat them down all the way to Hormah* (Numbers 14:44-45).

Presumption will get you beat up and shipped back to the Wilderness. The Israelites made a noble effort, but gained nothing. Their actions had changed, but instead of operating in faith, they were operating in denial of their fear. *The promises can only be received by faith.*

Now that I have your attention, what do we do to make sure our faith is rocking? (The good news is that unless you have ignored our previous chapters, you have already been doing it.) According to Romans 10:17, *"faith comes by hearing, and hearing by the Word of God."*

God asks Moses a question that reveals how faith is (or isn't) built in us: *"...How long will they refuse to believe in me, in spite of all the miraculous signs I have performed among them?"* (Num. 14:11).

Faith is not built by miracles. No one saw more miraculous signs than the Israelites did, yet their faith was lacking. In other words, *seeing* is not necessarily *believing.* At the same time, faith is not based on seeing. Faith is breathed into our hearts when we hear the Word of God.

People want to see a doctor's letter before they believe in a miracle. Why? Because they want to see it and then they will believe it. They don't realize that faith and sight are not connected. Faith is the result of sound, not sight. Faith comes by *hearing.*

Greater is he who believes and has not seen! We have a book of testimony at our church that is filled with documented doctors' reports of miraculous healings: a back that grows a new vertebra...a cancer that disappears...and more. The book is fun to read, but it doesn't build faith. The hearing of the Word builds faith. And here is what God says: I will protect you in the Promised Land. I will be with you. There is nothing to fear.

At some point as you enter the Promised Land you will discover areas in which you are operating in fear rather than faith. You might realize that you still haven't fully given yourself to your husband. You are afraid to. Your dad left when you were young. "Men don't stay," you carefully reason. But if you want a Kingdom marriage, you know you must face this fear. You must have faith in God.

Maybe you have started a business. It is kind of taking off, but you still work a full-time job. The hours you keep are crazy. It's time to fish or cut bait. Quitting your job to do your business might be scary, but have faith, my friend. (Just remember what we said about knowing which season you are in!)

Illness might be the issue that crops up for you. The doctor says your diabetes is not getting better, but you have been praying. You've had it most of your life, but you know that you must deal with it in the Promised Land—no more ignoring the fear that it desires to take your life early.

Remember, it is belief in doubt that contradicts God's Word. It's time to let go of the fear. God needs you healthy. He has a long life planned for you. No more fear. Just faith. You only need one rock to take down Goliath.

Back to Question No. 2: Is God capable of blessing me? The answer is an undeniable *"Yes!"*

How does that *yes* translate in our lives today? *Yes* means I'm not afraid of going into the Promised Land. The land may be well protected; there may be giants all over the place, but they are not my enemy—fear is!

An apprentice was asked to perform a very large task by his teacher. The apprentice tried but failed to accomplish the task. He said to his teacher, "You ask the impossible."

At this the teacher performed this great task in full view of the student. When the teacher was finished, the student exclaimed, "I don't believe it!"

The teacher replied, "That is why you fail."

Yeah, that story is from Star Wars. Good stuff.

Now on to Question No. 3.

What Is the Blessing?

The answer to this question cannot be covered in just a portion of a chapter. The entire Bible, taken from cover to cover, tells of the promises of the Lord, His blessings, His rewards, and more.

I do want to cross some controversial bridges here, however. It is probably not the greatest idea for an author, but very necessary in our journey. I actually do not want to spend this much time on this section, but I think in today's theological climate, I have to. Let me also say now that this section is not a mathematical proof of my view. The proof of what I am saying will unfold from this point forward, almost to the end of the book.

Many things that need to be said will not be said in this section because we are not mentally ready for them. We must create some foundations to build upon. If we are to go into the Promised Land, then we need to know what it is. We know that it flows with milk (the milk of other nations) and honey (physical sensual pleasure). We know it is a good and spacious land in which the Lord will give us rest from all our enemies.

What else is included in God's promises? We need to know and we need to set ourselves in agreement with them in order to receive them. Whether it is health or wealth, we must begin with the purpose of the promises. This is the only way we will be able to recognize what is and is not part of God's plan of blessing.

We have heard many things that reflect God's heart. Let me mention just a few. Jesus asked us to preach the Gospel to the ends of the earth and disciple all nations (see Mark 16:15; Matt. 28:19). God wishes that none would perish, but all would come to the saving knowledge of Jesus Christ (see 2 Pet. 3:9). God wants His will to be done here on earth, as it is in Heaven (see Matt. 6:10).

Now let's say for a moment that you are a teacher. If you are sick, are you capable of teaching? How about if you are dead? Probably not going to be productive right? The will of the Lord is going to require faith, action (obedience), and resources to accomplish. Jesus was born, and already wise men from the East were bringing Him gold. Why? Jesus would need resources for His ministry. If Jesus had been sick, would He have been able to impact the world for millennia to come in just three-and-one-half years of earthly ministry? Nope.

The promises of God are here to help us influence this world, conqueror nations, and administer justice. When I speak of conquering nations, I am talking about taking places of influence in this world (media, the arts, education, etc).

If you were in charge of approving scripts for a television sitcom, I'm guessing the writing would change substantially. Yes? Absolutely. So, if you took your place in that sphere of influence, we would eventually see that field reconciled with God's will on earth as it is in Heaven!

The blessing includes restoration!

There is more to the definition of blessing, so let's continue in identifying God's promises. Some clues of blessing are found by examining the world as it was before sin entered. The unspoiled world gives us insight into how God wants us to live. It reveals His original intentions.

In the beginning, God set up Adam and Eve in the Garden of Eden. God created this enormous earth to (initially) house just two people. It was a place of perfect beauty and splendor. There was no sickness, no pollution—maybe even no mosquitoes. (I hate those things.)

After making the earth, He called it "good." It was the ultimate good and spacious land. There were no crazy storms (until Noah's day). The earth was watered by underground springs. The entire world was covered with a firmament that regulated the harmful rays of the sun and kept the earth at a comfortable temperature. I imagine this was akin to an ozone layer on growth hormones. (The firmament collapsed in the Flood, by the way.)

Man would live nearly a thousand years in these conditions. Now if that weren't good enough, God hand-planted a Garden in Eden and put Adam in it. It was the best place on the planet. Adam was living large: God gave him something to do; He made a beautiful woman for him; He kept gold flowing in one of the four rivers nearby; and He sent animals stopping by so Adam could give them names (and they *did not* try to eat him).

Put yourself in Adam's shoes. He has more of everything than any one person could ever need. No lack. No sickness. No bad weather. And notice this: he was not in the desert eating manna. No. Adam was living in the world as God designed it. It is the picture of God's intent for us.

Because of sin, however, it takes some time for us to get back to the way it all started. But make no mistake—Eden is what God desires for us. It was His original plan, and He will restore it. If God were the way many believe Him to be, He would have taken man and put him in Yuma, Arizona. I happen to love Yuma, but I can tell you that Adam would have been picking thorns out of his feet all day long. Consider it pure joy, brother!

So The Garden was perfect and had everything man needed—in abundance! That brings us to an ever-controversial area of the promises of God. The question is: Did Jesus' finished work provide wealth for us? If so, He has some explaining to do because we see in Scripture that Jesus often addressed riches in a seemingly negative way. He once said that it is nearly impossible for a rich man to enter the Kingdom of Heaven (see Luke 18:25).

That is a strong statement that seems out of synch with the idea of wealth as a form of blessing. Yet, Jesus is not fighting Himself here; God's Word never contradicts itself. We just need to take a closer look:

> *For you know the grace of our Lord Jesus Christ, that though He was rich, yet for your sakes He became poor, so that you through His poverty might become rich* (2 Corinthians 8:9).

It sounds cut and dried. Jesus died so that you could be made rich. That is a big price to pay and I do not want to fall short of receiving the blessings God paid for so dearly. It used to make Him angry when His people did that.

Still, couldn't Paul be referring to some sort of spiritual wealth in the verse above? Maybe he was talking about being rich in love or health. Maybe this is not about money at all. Most Scriptures that seem to talk about being monetarily rich can also be interpreted as being rich in the things of God.

Sure sounds better, doesn't it, since the guy who is rich is going to have a tough time getting into Heaven? Well, not so fast. Let's look at First Corinthians 8 in its entirety. Go get your Bible, and let's make sure we get this right. Hold on, I'm reading it now. OK, this is definitely talking about money, because Paul is receiving an offering. (They sure spent a lot of time at that church in Corinth talking about money! LOL.)

Sorry, but that was funny. This was a financial offering. Paul was collecting resources. Why? Because resources are necessary to preach the Gospel. Ask any pastor or missionary what they need more of. I bet 95 percent will say they need more money to accomplish what God has put before them.

So God will meet the need, right? But who has ever seen God digging for gold? God needs His people to go get the gold. Then, when they give, God blesses them with an additional reward. Why? Because God knows that they will keep giving—and resources are needed to get the work done!

But what about the rich man who is going to have a tough time getting into the Kingdom of Heaven? Jesus is telling the truth here, but remember that He is addressing the rich man who is not saved. Once you become a child of the King, God begins your Promised Land journey. There the Lord will make you rich because Jesus became poor.

We need an outreach to the wealthy, because they will have a tougher time finding the Lord. The reason is mostly because money serves as a counterfeit for God. It can be relied upon and trusted to solve many problems. Solomon stated in Ecclesiastes 10:19 that money is the answer for everything. This is a bad thing and brings us to an ever-important passage in which Jesus spoke about money:

> *No one can serve two masters. Either he will hate the one and love the other, or he will be devoted to the one and despise the other. You cannot serve both God and Money* (Matthew 6:24).

Paul also had something to say about the issue:

> *For the love of money is a root of all kinds of evil. Some people, eager for money, have wandered from the faith and pierced themselves with many griefs* (1 Timothy 6:10).

There is no question: Second Corinthians 8:9 tells us that Jesus became poor so that we could be monetarily rich. Let us now reconcile that truth with the two passages above.

First, Matthew 6:24 contrasts the idea of serving money with the idea of serving God. Now let's change the word *serve* to something more in step with today's terminology. Let's go with the term *works for*. You cannot work for both God and money.

How many of us work for money? Ah, yes, now we are getting somewhere. Remember in Colossians 3:23 we discussed working with all our heart, as unto the Lord. This is a mental adjustment. You have to stop working for money. The promise then is this: as you gain wealth it will be important to make money *serve you.*

Money is meant to be put to work. This reconciles nicely with the parable of the talents (see Matt. 25). The men who were told "Well done, My good and faithful servant" (see Matt. 25:21,23)—the phrase we all hope to hear when we see the King—were the ones who doubled the money the Lord had given them. They made the money work for them.

This is called investing. We are commanded by God to invest in the Kingdom of God and to invest in the earth. The farmer can give as many offerings as he likes to the Lord, but he will have no crop unless he also puts some seed in the ground. Planting in the kingdom and in the earth is Promised-Land thinking.

We will soon spend an entire chapter on the love of money, which is sin. Wealth does corrupt some. However, we are not focusing on the trap of wealth here. My point now is to discover what the blessing includes. So does it include wealth? Yes, most definitely.

Was Abraham wealthy? Yes. When he came to a land the kings of the nations nearby sat up and took notice. Abraham had within his household 318 trained fighting men, his own army (see Gen. 14:14). That is quite a posse.

Was David, a man after God's own heart, wealthy? Yes. And he used that wealth to help fund the building of God's temple.

Was Solomon wealthy? Yes. Did wealth destroy him? No, his many wives led him astray.

Was Jesus wealthy? Not on the cross He wasn't. He did kick off his ministry around the age of two with treasures of gold and valuable perfumes.

Was Paul wealthy? He said in Philippians 4:12, *"I know what it is to be in need, and I know what it is to have plenty...."*

Wealth isn't given so you can be happy. And this is not a book about wealth. I must, however, attack the biggest fallacies concerning the promises of God. Controversial subjects must be addressed.

Remember that it was Judas Iscariot who in John 12:5 is saying *"Why wasn't this perfume sold and the money given to the poor? It was a year's wages."*

Even Judas, who would betray Jesus, sounded ever so humble and Christian. Jesus rebuked Judas for saying what he said about the perfume Mary used to anoint Him. Today, a man and his family might pull up to a humble church in a late-model Lexus. The members look upon the family in disdain. Even as they walk through the foyer, everyone checks out his expensive suit and his wife's Dooney and Bourke purse.

"Should've sold that stuff and given the money to the poor," their eyes say.

The wealthy man and his family are rejected. They might end up in hell, too. That might have been the only time they came to church.

We can choose to be poor, but when the time comes to raise money for a well to be dug in India, the best we'll be able to do is buy a bottle of water. Even if you want to dig the well yourself, the trip will cost you about $2,000.

If I'm talking to you and you have believed this way, you are in a perfect position to change your view of God's promise. You can learn to receive from God and then turn around and give of what He gives you.

God may need you to be wealthy. He has laid up the wealth of the wicked. Jesus died so that you might be rich! This way you can promote His will in the earth. Now here is an important thought. John the Baptist didn't need crazy wealth to accomplish his part in changing the world. But King David did need the wealth to help pay for the Temple construction. Both are godly examples.

Remember, there are two types of Christians: those who need help and those who can help. We are all on a journey to become the latter. We have the opportunity to get every area of our lives kicked into abundance—NOT JUST wealth, but also health, relationships, productivity, influence, and more. The blessings are so much more than just wealth.

So, regarding Question No. 3—What are the blessings of God? Are you ready for this? The answer is so simple it might just blow your mind: *The blessings of God are the resources you will need to change this world!*

And what about Question No. 4—Do I qualify for the blessing?

The answer is, *"Yes."* Jesus qualified you.

Now then, say good-bye to the Wilderness, baby. We are stepping into the Promised Land now.

Let's go!

Part 3

The Promised Land

Chapter 13

Milk It, Honey!

NOT EVERYONE ENTERS the Promised Land. Some stay in Egypt; others stay in the Wilderness. Before they entered the Promised Land, two of the tribes of Israel asked permission to settle east of the Jordan. They said to Moses, *"Let this land be given to your servants as our possession. Do not make us cross the Jordan"* (Num. 32:5).

So, when Joshua leads the people across the Jordan, the tribes of Reuben and Gad and half the tribe of Manasseh do not go. Their fighting men agreed to help with the battles that would need to be waged west of the Jordan, but any territory they helped take would not be theirs. At the end of the fighting they would return to their chosen lands east of the Jordan, in the Wilderness.

If there is one thing we have learned (and there are many), it is to be understanding of others and not judgmental. Judgment is the free pass back to the desert.

So what did we learn in the Wilderness? We have learned the importance of connecting with your church. We know enough to take notes when the shepherd gives a message. We understand the need to study our notes and have personal study time in the Word (because we are to meditate in it every day).

We discussed our need for boundaries that help us to live right. These boundaries (the law) will lead you to failure and, eventually, to grace.

We also know that we need to drop our slave mentality; we need to serve and give at our churches willingly. We understand the dangers of taking the path of least resistance and have determined that we will put our whole heart into everything we do.

We have discovered the value of honoring the shepherds God has assigned to us so that we may receive from them. We understand and have received a revelation of grace—we know that the promises of God are received by faith and not by works. Faith has been revealed to us as a key to entering the Promised Land.

Finally, we have learned to let go of fear and doubt and trust wholly in the Lord. We are aware that there are giants in the land, but we also know that God is bigger and more powerful than they are.

Let's pick up the journey from there.

Entering the Promised Land

So here we are in the Promised Land. Feel any different? Nah, me neither, and yet everything has changed. Here in the Promised Land the Israelites are to rule. They are commanded to displace the nations living there. They are to take the territory. This means much fighting. It's not an easy road, but learning to serve in the Tabernacle has taught us not to take the easy way out any longer. We will labor to enter the rest of the Lord (see Heb. 4:11). We cannot start skipping steps now.

Joshua is a picture of the battles we will be going through. Later, Gideon will teach us that the battle is the Lord's.

> *Remember the command that Moses the servant of the Lord gave you: "The Lord your God is giving you rest and has granted you this land"* (Joshua 1:13).

We have not arrived at the destination yet. Here in the Promised Land there are some things we must learn and accomplish before we can truly enter the rest of the Lord. God wanted Moses to make it to the rest. Now He is calling Joshua to make it into His rest. Eventually, Joshua entered that rest, but even he did not lead the people there.

> *For if Joshua had given them rest, God would not have spoken later about another day* (Heb. 4:8).

Sowing and Reaping

What has changed for the Israelites? Everything. Their parents are gone. They were children when they left Egypt; some were born in the Wilderness. They were too young to really understand all that happened. They have not had extensive battle experience and yet they are marching in for war.

In Joshua 5:12, the Israelites have just recently crossed over the Jordan. They celebrate the Passover, and, the very next day, the manna stops. No longer can they rely on food falling from Heaven as it had for decades.

Now, if the Israelites want to eat, they will have to plant. This is a picture of us learning the principle of sowing and reaping, planting and harvesting. The Israelites will have to learn, because they have little experience farming. God knows this and gives them the produce of Canaan for the first year.

Springtime has come and planting must begin. This is quite an adjustment from the Wilderness experience. The Israelites are like young people who have just moved out of Mom and Dad's house: it is time to buy a car; they will need insurance of their own; and the rent will have to be paid.

God is placing "adult" expectations on them. The umbilical cord has been cut (no more manna). They have already received the kick start of a year's worth of "free" crops—in other words they have "sucked the milk of other nations" by reaping this harvest that they did not plant. Still to come are the promised cities they did not build and wells they did not dig.

For the moment, however, they are learning to stand on their own two feet, as we must also do in our Promised Land.

On the Offense

There are many types of faith discussed in the Word: the faith through which we receive Christ; the faith to enter the Promised Land; the faith to enter the Lord's rest.

There is also the good fight of faith. For the Israelites, almost all the fighting till now has been defensive. Instead of reacting to someone else's actions and instead of defending their territory, the Israelites must switch to an offensive mode. They must take the Kingdom of God by force—and so must we. Jesus said in Matthew 11:12 that The Kingdom of God has been on a forceful advance since the time of John the Baptist.

Remember, John was baptizing in the Jordan. When we cross the Jordan, we join in this forceful advance. Now, instead of hanging out at the tent waiting for tomorrow's manna delivery and taking whatever life brings, we are going to go out there and take life by the horns. (I hope life doesn't have horns; that *would* be weird.)

The Promised Land is a place where you begin planning, setting goals, casting vision, and embracing the future with the hopeful expectation of glory. You will be exploring, spying, marching around cities, and attacking.

It is time to take territory.

Back in the World

For four decades, the Israelites have lived separately from the world in the Wilderness. Now they are back amongst the world, which is full of sin and bad influences. These nations are godless; they worship false gods, sacrifice their children on altars, and engage in perversion.

This was the kind of influence God pulled them out of 40 years ago. Are they strong enough to stand up to it? Are you?

The Israelites have a mission, though, and it isn't to hang out with all this mess. The mission is to go through and inflict change. They will possess the land. They need to be ready for it and so must we. The time has come for us to advance in our companies, influence the business world, change our government, be active in education, and do whatever else is necessary to return our world to godly ways.

Just as Christ changes us, we need to get in behind the walls and change the nations of influence from the inside out.

How It Works

Being called to take the territory indicates that God has extended trust to us. We must steward this trust. We *can* grow our own food. We can grow as much as we desire, in fact, because He will bless our fields.

Up until now, we, like Israel, did not have fields to bless. Before I could only collect as much manna as was allotted to me. Now, if I want to be greedy, grow lots of crops, and hoard them, I can. Luckily, God has already taught me not to do that...right?

Here again, God is trusting us. We have to accept the responsibility and excel in it. In the Wilderness, the law was given and life was all about what we *could not* do. In the Promised Land, it is all about what we *can* do. God desires productivity from us, but also restraint. When the manna flowed, God controlled our dietary intake. You cannot get fat on manna.

In the Promised Land, the Israelites can eat as much as they like (*if* they are working). The limits have been taken off and free will is even "freer" than before. If you want to supersize your McGrease order and drink your Diet Cokes every day, you can. It's your health, and God is allowing you to steward over it.

Of course, it is the equivalent of satan asking Jesus to jump off of the Temple so that the angels would save Him. To jump off is to test God. We are not to throw ourselves into the deliberate risk of clogged arteries and then ask God to heal us. Although, thankfully, He still will.

As we learned earlier, you have spent your life working for The Man at this point. You are a slave, working to build someone else's wealth. If you work at Home Depot, or Boeing, or wherever, you are building those kingdoms on your back, with hard labor. This, my friend, is still slavery. They will pay you as little as possible to post a profit and store up more wealth for the world.

For a transfer of wealth to take place and for us to make headway in removing this economy of greed off of us, we need to be starting the businesses. The world should be working for us and building the Kingdom of God in the process. We should be in the position to administer justice and not greed.

Let me just say that this kind of influence can also come from great promotions within the company. That is what happened to Joseph. The point is that God cannot transfer the wealth to us if we do not position ourselves to receive it. In the Promised Land the Israelites got cities they did not build. God wishes to do the same for us, the Body of Christ.

What is my point? God cannot bless your field if you don't own a field. We have to take some kind of action to change that. We have to take a look at our lives and decide what we are going to possess. Then we can expect God to give us whatever land we place our feet on.

What does that mean to you? It means you have to go for a walk. What are you good at? Politics? Go get it! Don't forget why you are doing it and don't follow the path of corruption. Your goal is to build the Kingdom of

God. Your connection to the Body of Christ puts Christ in a greater position of influence on earth.

This is how the Church becomes light and salt, wielding more influence each day. Are you an actor or a chef? Go get it! You're strong enough now. God will bless you. Are you afraid? Ditch your fear or you will be back in the Wilderness.

You have learned to work hard with excellence, so go show 'em what you can do!

Take the Territory

God is giving you the land. God gave them the land, but there were people in it. You would think they could just go up to Jericho and say, "Yeah, uh, I'm Joshua. Listen, this land is my land. God gave it to me. I need you to go over there to Gilgal. Oh, and please leave your llama with me. That's mine, too!"

When God gives you something you may still have to go after it. God has given you the perfect spouse. Now go get her. How? Chase her. If she doesn't respond, well now you're stalking her, and that's against the law.

You are in the Promised Land, which means you are ready. God will bring you the right one, but when you see her, go get her.

Attributes of a Promised-Land Dweller

Now let's go over the characteristics that describe a Promised Land dweller. There are seven here that I will discuss briefly.

The Promised Land dweller…

1. Has the Spirit of the Lord *on* his/her life

2. Prepares for battle and goes to battle

3. Actively sows and reaps

4. Often (unfortunately) falls into the blessings are for "me, me, me" mentality

5. Exercises self-control and perseverance, even if he/she does not always win

6. Becomes a land full of thorns and thistles, if he/she gives up

7. Loves the thrill of the fight

Are you getting a sense of what the Promised Land life looks like? Do you see yourself as one of its inhabitants? Great—but remember that the Promised Land is not our resting place. In fact, it may feel more like it is time to start your motor running.

We are just about ready to make our next transition through the Feast of Trumpets. First, we must look at *greed.* We need to be sure that the promises meant for good are not made good for nothing.

Make sure your sandals are buckled. We are moving forward!

Chapter 14

Half of Infinity Is Still Infinity

MY WIFE NEEDS ME. I'm thoroughly convinced that I am a necessity in her life, which affords me what I believe is a great marital longevity insurance policy.

Compare me, if you dare, to baby diapers. I serve a critical purpose; I must be restocked regularly; and frankly, life without me would be intolerable, as long as there is a baby in the house. (Of course, I'm probably the baby as well as the diapers.)

On any given day, my wife will call me at 4 P.M. to give me the after-work schedule. "Katy has dance and will need to be driven there. I need you to watch Logan during a grocery pit stop. Please pick up whatever it is you need so you can fix the garage door..." etc.

Without me, the door would stay broken, Katy would never learn to dance, and there would be no need to even own a refrigerator or buy groceries. Not to mention the fact that I'm the family Bible-study buff. Needless to say, I'm needed.

I need her as well. Not only is she oh-so-helpful in the income category, but she will change those poopy diapers without so much as a glance toward me. My socks are always clean and she can find a Scripture faster than biblegateway.com.

My wife is also the intercessor in our house. She regularly says, "We need to pray," or makes that most dreaded decree: "We need to *fast and pray*." Praying is commendable, but please don't take my food away. Please.

We need each other. When you reach the Promised Land, you have to win in some areas that you cannot win alone. You need a partner. A partner is strong where you are weak. In this case, your partner is God. You need God. Anyone can do what's possible. We are called to do the impossible.

Are you ready? Great, let's get started.

Why Now?

> *At that time the Lord said to Joshua, "Make flint knives and circumcise the Israelites again"* (Joshua 5:2).

If you don't know what circumcision is, I will describe it for you, from firsthand experience. I watched the circumcision of my youngest son, when he was just a few days old. Watching it was a bad idea. It scarred me for life (forgive the pun).

Circumcision is the removal of a bunch of skin from the end of the penis. They used a blade and a clamp to keep things from moving. In case you are wondering, there was bleeding involved. My poor son. He cried. I wept.

If you are a man, you probably work as hard as I do to keep sharp objects as far away from that particular area of the body as possible. It is instinctive. Maybe that is why circumcision is done when boys are babies. They can't say no.

Most children are circumcised out of a tradition that dates back to the Hebrews. The Israelites are commanded to reinstitute the practice immediately after they cross the Jordan. But, why now? For an adult, this is bad timing. All of the fighting men are included here. They have finally crossed into the Promised Land and they know they will soon go to war. Fierce battles lay ahead.

Yet, God wants the men to go under the knife. Imagine you are on an NBA team that is heading into a championship series. The day before Game 1, the coach says, "Let's all get circumcised." How does that timing sound to you?

For the Israelites, this primitive procedure (no doctors, no surgical steel instruments, no Advil) will ensure a greater level of difficulty in wielding a sword and winning a battle. The whole thing seems counterintuitive.

Yet God has a reason. The answer to "Why now?" is found in what circumcision represents:

> *On that day the Lord made a covenant with Abram and said, "To your descendants I give this land, from the river of Egypt to the great river, the Euphrates..."* (Genesis 15:18).

The land that God is describing here is the Promised Land that is for you and me. It is not a physical land of course, but an activation of the promises of God and blessings of God in our lives—milk, honey, and rest.

Back when God made His promise to Abram, he blessed him. Abram was blessed because he had faith in God. God actually describes His relationship with Abram as a *covenant.* The covenant at this point has God giving blessings and making promises to Abram. It's one-sided; Abram is not required to do anything in return. Later, God instructs Abraham that there is something that he must do in regards to the covenant:

> *Then God said to Abraham, "As for you, you must keep My covenant, you and your descendants after you for the generations to come. This is My covenant with you and your descendants after you, the covenant you are to keep: Every male among you shall be circumcised"* (Genesis 17:9-10).

Now Abram, whose name has been changed to *Abraham,* has his own end of the bargain to hold up. He must circumcise every male in his household—not just family, but anyone who is in partnership with him (serving him).

Circumcision is the sign of the covenant between God and us.

The reason for the Israelites being circumcised as they enter the Promised Land is to remind them of their covenant with God.

Since we have just arrived in the Promised Land, we, too, will spend some time reminding ourselves of the covenant we have with God.

A Big Picture

The first mention of a covenant between God and man was when God made a covenant with Noah. It was a simple covenant in which God promised never to destroy the earth by flood again (see Gen. 8:21-22).

A little history for context: There were nine generations from Adam to Noah. During those nine generations the people of the earth became so evil that every *"inclination of the thoughts of his heart was only evil all the time"* (Gen. 6:5). Only Noah was found to be righteous. Nine short generations from Adam and the entire human population is completely corrupt, save one family. Wow.

That's when God hits the reset button. The world gets a fresh start. Yet, simple math tells us that nine generations later, the entire world will be evil again—unless of course, something changes.

There are nine generations between Shem, Noah's son, and Abraham. At that time, God expands the covenant to include all sorts of new promises to Abraham and his descendants. God promises land, blessings, and generations to follow. He also adds circumcision to the covenant. This appears to be designed to keep the world from falling into evil again.

Yet, we know from the story of Sodom and Gomorrah that the world is steeped in sin again. Nevertheless, this covenant between God and Abraham is passed down until a nation arises from his offspring, the Israelites.

God updates His yet covenant again, seven generations later, with Moses. This time He adds the law given on Mount Sinai. In Deuteronomy 28, he lets the Israelites know that the blessing from the covenant is only available if they can fully obey all of His commands.

We learned in our own lives that this is in fact impossible to do. We cannot be self-righteous; we must take on Christ's righteousness. During Moses' lifetime, God brings the written Word of God. The first five books of the Bible are written and now the Israelites have Scripture.

This dilutes the evil in the world; instead of things getting worse as time progresses, things get better. Instead of just one believer in God (*i.e.,* Noah or Abraham), there is an entire nation of Israelites. This "big picture" is an outline of the Old Testament, the Old Covenant.

Christ came and gave us a New Testament. He brought a new covenant, not just for Israelites, but for anyone who will believe. It is not a covenant that reserves the blessings for those who fully obey or are circumcised; it is a covenant we enter by faith in Christ alone. This new covenant gives us access to all the blessings that were promised in the Old Testament, but through a new and living way, which is Christ.

This is a better covenant and, through it, we have access to better promises (see Heb. 8:6), especially the restoration of the authority that Adam lost. Christ has regained that authority and made it available to us. The authority brings us back into alignment with God's original command to subdue the earth (see Gen. 1:28).

God's covenant and His written Word are available to us through God's grace, so that now over half of the entire world's population confesses to be Christian. Not just one dude in an ark with his family, but half the earth. Do you see the power of the covenant now? The covenant of blessing fulfills its purpose as Peter described it:

> *Through these he has given us his very great and precious promises, so that through them you may participate in the divine nature and escape the corruption in the world caused by evil desires* (2 Peter 1:4).

Did you get that? God's promises help man to escape corruption. This is for us. I don't know about you, but I could use some corruption escaping every now and then. I want to stay out of that horrid Desert of Sin as much as the next guy.

What's Yours Is Mine

We now have a new covenant that is held together by faith. Still, the picture of circumcision remains an important one if we are to understand either covenant.

The use of blood in the covenant has been key since the beginning. God had Abraham sacrifice an animal to demonstrate the blood covenant. Then came circumcision, another sign that involves the shedding of blood. Under the law in Moses' day, the high priest would sacrifice an animal once a year and sprinkle its blood in the Tabernacle for the sins of the nation. This annual observance kept the covenant active.

Jesus died and bled for the New Covenant, making it a blood covenant. This bloodshed shows that God is making much more than an everyday agreement with His people. Giving and receiving of blood makes the strongest statement of commitment.

Blood has been used in this way throughout history. In ancient times and even in some parts of the world today, leaders cut their hands and shake hands, causing their blood to mix. This symbolizes covenant. It is a declaration that what's yours is mine, and what's mine is yours. It says that we are family now.

God's covenant with us does the same thing. It says He calls us His own and He is our Father. We are family sealed together in a blood covenant.

Let's look deeper into this. Remember from Chapter 8 that we are the Bride of Christ. Marriage is symbolic of our covenant and is itself a blood covenant. When a virgin woman has sex for the first time with her husband, she bleeds. This is a blood covenant in which the two become one in flesh.

Under this covenant, what's his is hers and what's hers is his (unless there is a prenuptial agreement to say otherwise). Whatever belonged to the husband now also belongs to the wife, and vice versa. This is true, for better or worse. For example, if you win the lottery, well then, your spouse won, too. But, if you don't have enough money to pay your mortgage, it is not just your problem anymore. It is your spouse's problem, too.

This is what God is trying to get across to us. Our Bridegroom, Christ, has some stuff. And guess what? It is our stuff, too! Too many Christians operate as though they have no one to help with their dilemmas. The truth is that your issues are just as much Christ's problem as they are yours, so let Him help you. Think about the importance of remembering this concept as you arrive in the Promised Land. There is territory to take; it is a tough job, but you are not alone. However, you have to *remember* that you are not alone. This is the reason God commanded the circumcision at Gilgal. He was reminding the Israelites and us that to get to the impossible, the unachievable, the incredible, we will need access to the supernatural.

Before you cross Jordan, you can walk out of your tent, pick some manna off the ground, and go back to bed. In the Promised Land, you become a member of the army of the Lord. Your assignment is to take back what the enemy possesses. It won't be easy, so it is imperative to remember that you have a partner who is going with you.

We are about to do some big things. Jericho has great big walls and we are going to bring them down. Many Christians think small: they run up to the walls and start scraping at them. The walls are too big for that. Unless we approach this differently, we will sigh in resignation and retreat to the Wilderness.

There is a better option: team up with God!

Location of the Blood

This brings me to the next point: the location of the blood in circumcision. First, we learned that circumcision is a sign of the blood covenant. It marks us as family. Now let's talk about the location of the blood.

To unpack this, we need to examine another covenant sign—a wedding ring, the outward sign of the marriage covenant. If a man forgets to wear his ring he is either forgetful or looking for trouble. Either way, he is in Dutch with his wife, because she wants the sign on his finger to say, "This dude belongs to someone else."

The woman wears her sign for the same reason. It is easy to see; people know immediately that you are in covenant with someone. Your ring does the talking for you. If you are Angelina Jolie, the paparazzi will notice immediately if your wedding ring is missing. The gossip columns will promptly announce that you are having marital trouble.

God does not use a ring as a sign of covenant with us. God uses circumcision as the sign of the covenant (we will talk about the New Covenant update to this sign in the next section).

"Hmmm…this seems like a strange place to put a sign," I say with a snicker.

People will not see this sign. Why didn't God choose to circumcise ear lobes—you know, so that people could see the sign? Why the male reproductive organ? What is God saying?

In marriage *we* use rings, but in God's eyes it is still a blood covenant. The blood that is shed by the virgin wife appears at her reproductive organ. The location of this covenant sign is meaningful because it involves the womb of a woman, which is sealed for only one man.

The woman is saying to the man and before God, "This womb is for your seed only. It is dedicated to production through your seed and no one else's."

Circumcision makes the same commitment to God. It says, "My ability to create is dedicated to You, to Your plans and purposes only. From this point forward, whatever we create, we create together. I do not create alone."

In the Wilderness we were far from worldly influences. In the Promised Land we become influencers, strong and victorious. Doing this means creating some serious God stuff. We are in this together with Him.

Circumcision of the Heart

Under the New Covenant, God has moved the site of circumcision. Knowing this is important, because we are now creating with God.

The following Scripture prophesied the New Covenant in Christ:

> *The Lord God will circumcise your hearts and the hearts of your descendants, so that you may love Him with all your heart and with all your soul, and live* (Deuteronomy 30:6).

Under the New Covenant, circumcision of the heart is emphasized.

> *No, a man is a Jew if he is one inwardly; and circumcision is circumcision of the heart, by the Spirit, not by the written code...* (Romans 2:29).

Why the heart? In the physical realm, our creative abilities are symbolized by our sex organs. The womb of creativity is the heart—the spiritual and soulish realms where true production takes place. No wonder Solomon wrote: *"Above all else, guard your heart, for it is the wellspring of life"* (Prov. 4:23).

God is changing us from the inside out. We now produce the seed of God in our hearts. That is where the battle takes place. We will see this more clearly, later. For now we need to know that Jericho lives in the heart.

Most every circumstance in your life, as well as all that you see (both blessing and trouble) results from what is growing in your heart. Addictions, unforgiveness, sinful desires, love, joy—all of these are birthed in the heart and produce the lives that we live.

No, not everything growing in your heart is something you planted. Yet, whatever the source of the seed, it will produce fruit for as long as it remains planted in the soil of your heart.

Yes, the source of the seed is important. God is showing us at Gilgal that our success in the Promised Land depends on what has been sown in the womb of mankind—the human heart.

Don't Leave God Out

Because God and you are going to create everything together now, you must develop a habit of including God in all of your endeavors. Just as my wife calls with my evening itinerary every day at 4 P.M., you must "phone in" to God.

You need to know which things are yours to do and which you cannot accomplish without Him. Do your bit and call God for the rest. *"The horse is made ready for the day of battle, but victory rests with the Lord"* (Prov. 21:31).

Great Christians often misunderstand their covenant role with God. This verse from Proverbs helps us identify who does what. In marriage, each partner should recognize who does what best and then use that knowledge to complement one another. This is a common sense success "formula."

On a basketball team, the guard does not play in the center position. The guard must know his role for the team to succeed. In football, the quarterback doesn't throw the ball to himself. If he did, the team would fail miserably.

So what is your role? You need to identify it in order to prepare for the battle. Know which horse is yours and make your horse ready. You can pray all day long for the horse to be saddled, but eventually you will have to saddle the horse yourself. God wants to grow and mature you. That's why He leaves you to do what you can do. He knows the task is in capable hands.

God will not do your part. Many battles await you in the Promised Land; you need to find the balance between God's role and yours. You can pray for a job, but you also need to look for one. If you have done your part, then wait on God to do His. Remember: your problem is His problem, and your victory is His victory.

Not long ago, I was overseeing some house construction in Cambodia, where we had also planned a Pastors' Leadership Conference. It was May 2009 and the Church in Cambodia was still very young and small. The day before the conference, my organizer informed me that, because the prime minister was going to be near the location of the conference, they were closing off that area of the city. The conference had to be canceled.

Now I had done everything I knew to do and was fully prepared for the conference. It is God who called me to help train these pastors. This circumstance was out of my hands; it was God's battle. I had done my part and I trusted Him to do His. I smiled at the organizer and said, "There will absolutely be a conference tomorrow. I am not concerned with this."

I really wasn't, either. This was not my problem. I called God. "Hey, You have hit a hiccup in the plan. Go get 'em, God!"

After a nice dinner at the hotel and before I went to bed, I learned that the conference was back on schedule. The prime minister's security detail had decided to open the area around the conference to normal activity.

Silly devil.

In 2005, during the real estate boom, I was buying and selling properties. We got into it because we felt like God had told us to buy a piece of land. When we were getting ready to build on it, God told us to sell it. The income from the sale was more than I had ever seen.

I was so excited about the transaction that I went and found another piece of land to purchase. It seemed like a no-brainer; the price was right and the location was great! I bought the property. Much to my dismay, I am still making payments on a property whose value is declining.

What happened? I left God out. I did something on my own. *Completely.* I really didn't even consult my wife. (A little prayer—her specialty—would have been helpful.)

A lot of Christians get themselves into scenarios like this and ask, "Where is God?"

Well, in my case, I left Him out. I call the deal an "Ishmael." Abram pulled an Ishmael, too; in fact, his Ishmael was the original. It happened while Abram was waiting for the son God had promised him. His wife Sarai got antsy waiting for a child. She had her husband sleep with her servant, Hagar. I can't imagine my wife ever having an idea like that, but Abram went for it.

Yeah, the great patriarch soon to be known as *Abraham* made a mistake. The result was a son, but not the son promised by God. The promised child had to come from Abram's wife's womb; it had to be from both of them.

Now Abram had a child, but it was not his wife's child. He named the boy *Ishmael.* What we get when we forget to ask God about what we are doing is an Ishmael. In terms of life—well, life is always a blessing, but the picture painted colored with an important lesson; be patient. Include God in everything you set out to do. That is the lesson of Gilgal!

A New Name

As part of the covenant, God gave Abram a new name—*Abraham*:

> *As for Me, this is My covenant with you: You will be the father of many nations. No longer will you be called Abram; your name will be Abraham, for I have made you a father of many nations* (Genesis 17:4-5).

God added *ah to* Abram's name. This comes from the last two letters of one of God's names, *Jehovah.* At this, Abraham fell on his face and laughed. Have you ever laughed so hard you fell down? That is a crazy amount of laughing, a real belly laugh. What a release this was, God was planting HIS joy in Abraham. We will revisit this fact later. The name change is important here, because you and I need one. We don't need a physical name change, but the concept of the change is important.

First, God has placed a part of Himself inside of Abraham's name. Today, we choose names for fun. Our parents probably got our names out of a trendy name book. In Abraham's day, however, a name was part of who you were. It truly meant something.

Through this covenant God is adding Himself into who Abraham is. God has done the same for us. We have a symbol of this in modern life. It is common for a married woman to take on her husband's surname. She has entered into a new family. As the Bride of Christ, we do the same; we take on His name. He has become part of us, literally living in us. We are asked to remain in Him.

This way, we can create together. Our remaining in Him means staying connected to His Body, the Church.

> *I am the vine; you are the branches. If a man remains in Me and I in him, he will bear much fruit; apart from Me you can do nothing* (John 15:5).

Of course we do things apart from Christ, but those things don't matter. What matters now is that each of us will be creating together with Christ, for God's purposes. The name change—God adding Himself to a man or woman as He did with Abraham—is a description of how this happens on the inside. God isn't just changing what we do; He is changing who we *are*. He is redefining us. He has placed Himself in us. How can we possibly fail now?

The final key in regard to this name change for now involves changing how you speak and think of yourself. The name *Abraham* means "father of a multitude."[1] At the moment of the name change, Abraham was not yet the father of many. But as he, his wife, and all those around him repeated his name in the course of the day, they described Abraham as the "father of a multitude," or, more simply, *the father of many.*

"Hey, Father of Many, dinner is ready."

"Hey, Father of Many, get in the right lane or you'll miss your turn."

You see, they were calling things that were not as though they were (see Rom. 4:17). It has an effect whether you say good things or bad. Christians often say, "I can't do it. I can't go on. I always lose." Those words produce results!

God is telling you right now that, in order to succeed in the Promised Land, you must change the way you think and speak about yourself. When the spies in Moses' time returned from the Promised Land, ten of them said, "We can't." And you know what? Even though it was God's desire for them to take possession of the land, their "We can't" turned into "We didn't."

Maybe every one of your ancestors got cancer, but if you are in the family of God, God says you will live a long and satisfied life (see Ps. 91:16).

Say and think only what God says about you.

Chapter 15

Hear the Light, See the Night

APPARENTLY OF ALL the genetic attributes that I could have inherited I seem mostly to reflect Italian when it comes to hair. I am Swedish, Norwegian, Italian, and then some other stuff. If you look at my hair though, it's Italian. Somewhere genetically, hair began to grow on ears. Although not readily accepted by today's society in terms of fashion, my ears have hair. Why? Not sure. Is it to keep ears warm?

Also, I have hair in my nose. More than you. (I say that with confidence.) I can clip, shave, and pluck the hair, but this doesn't find me getting into the source of where the hair comes from. It's coming from within. Deep down in my DNA I'm programmed to have hair growing from my ear lobes.

As a society, we are highly trained to address symptoms instead of the cause. In this chapter, we will literally get to the root of how the heart works. We'll take a look at the first enemy of the Promised Land and then see how the covenant operates within the heart.

When we address symptoms instead of cause, we are focused on *doing* instead of *being.* Being in the Promised Land isn't only about what you do and get; it is also about who you become. You and God are creating together now. As you seek His Kingdom first, then many good things will be added to you (see Matt. 6:33).

Again, the importance of the heart is primarily this; it is the production chamber of the things of God. From the heart, you empower the 100-percent spirit part of you to move 100-percent physical part of you, thereby bringing God's will to pass here on earth.

We Christians have not nearly tapped the potential of our God-ordained impact on this planet. In fact, all of creation eagerly awaits for the sons of God to be revealed (see Rom. 8:19). Yes, that is us. The whole of creation knows and expects us to impact the earth.

Remember that nearly everything surrounding your life can be traced to what is going on in your heart. If you attract the wrong men, then that is in your heart somewhere. Lost your job again? Believe it or not, your heart is the culprit.

God is so very concerned with the heart that it is where He chose to reside once Jesus made the way. The heart is where the Word of God and the fruit of the Spirit grow. If you are wondering just how powerful the heart is, well, it will be the primary topic for the remainder of this book.

Understanding the heart will open you up to understanding authority, rulership, justice, and (finally) rest.

Understanding the Heart

In the Promised Land and the Place of Rest, the wellspring of life (the heart) is the primary focus. Therefore, we must know how it functions.

We have already spoken about influences and influencers, the need to immerse ourselves in the Word of God, and our need to be in the Church.

All of this helps us to become salt—that is, to influence our world. And all of it happens in the heart.

From the time we received Jesus, the heart is where our journey has taken place. Now we are ready to explore the mechanics of God's production center. Let's first take a look at the heart's design, because that is where the unseen begins.

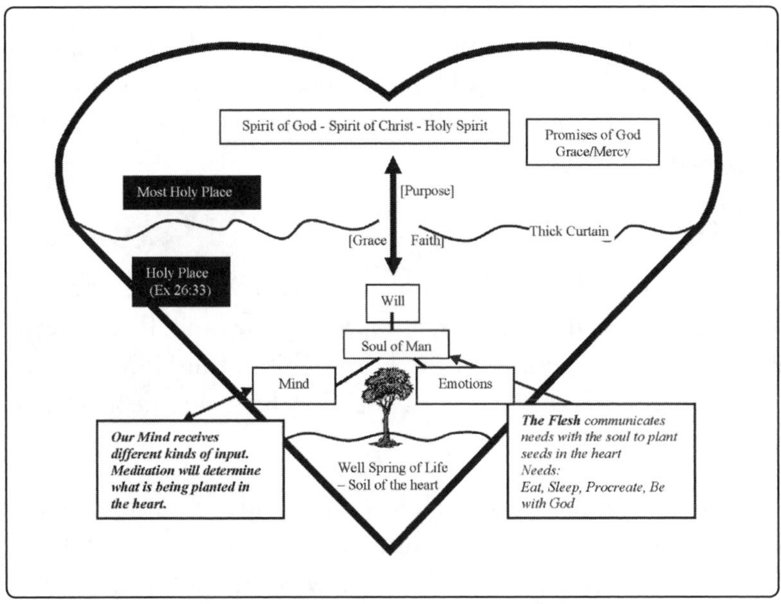

[Figure 4 depicts the heart as I understand it from the Word.]

> *The Lord your God will circumcise your hearts and the hearts of your descendants, so that you may love Him with all your heart and with all your soul, and live* (Deuteronomy 30:6).

The circumcision of the heart affects your soul because the heart contains the soul of man. A man's soul is made up of his mind, will, and emotions. The heart contains these elements, plus the soil needed to grow and produce fruit from the seeds that are planted in the heart. The Spirit of God dwells here, too. Therefore, the infinite things of God are contained in the heart.

Now let's visit the Scripture in Hebrews:

> *For the word of God is living and active. Sharper than any double-edged sword, it penetrates even to dividing soul and spirit, joints and marrow; it judges the thoughts and attitudes of the heart* (Hebrews 4:12).

The heart here is described as the container of thoughts, attitudes, soul, spirit, joints, and marrow. We also see that the soul and spirit are so closely knitted together that only an extremely sharp tool can divide the two.

You are described as the temple of the Holy Spirit (see 1 Cor. 6:19). The Tabernacle designed by God and built by man was a pattern of how the human heart works. The diagram above resembles the Hebrew Tabernacle as God patterned it for Moses.

Let's examine the parallels:

Your body is symbolic of the outer courts beyond the sanctuary. Your heart contains within it the soul, symbolized by the Holy Place. Deeper still, the Spirit of the Lord resides in the heart. This is the Holy of Holies (the Most Holy Place) where the Ark of the Covenant was kept. (There's that covenant again.)

The Ark contained the stone tablets, the budded rod of Aaron, and the manna. The stone tablets are a picture of Christ, described by Paul as the "chief cornerstone" (see Eph. 2:20). They were the principals of God that He is now writing upon our hearts. The budded rod of Aaron is a picture of Christ, who died and rose from the dead. Aaron's rod budded life as a picture of Christ's resurrection. The manna is also a picture of Christ, the Word of God, our daily bread.

All of these are now in you, in your heart. The priests carried the Ark wherever they traveled, including across the Jordan (see Josh. 3:17). You are a royal priesthood (see 1 Pet. 2:9), carrying the Ark of the Covenant within you.

The Holy Place and Holy of Holies were separated by two thick curtains. The Most Holy Place was where the Ark of the Covenant resided. Only the High Priest could enter the Most Holy Place, and only once per year, to atone for the sins of the nation. The curtain of separation was a symbol of man's separation from God resulting from the sin of one man, Adam.

Many Christians allow this curtain to stand as a separation between them and God. This is a matter of the heart that must be reconciled. In order to mature and advance on this journey, you must go through the curtain! Before we do this though, I want to introduce you to the first enemy of the Promised Land.

Promised Land Enemy No. 1

You already know about the three main Wilderness traps: misreading the seasons of sowing and reaping, bitterness and grumbling, and misplaced priorities.

Our first Promised Land enemy is the sort that must be dealt with directly. Anything short of a direct hit against this enemy will leave you stranded and stunted in life. Granted, this is your first crack at him. You were not allowed to defeat this enemy in earlier parts of the journey. Just the same, you cannot move on to the next place in your journey until you fight in this one.

Let me explain by returning to earlier in the Israelites' journey when God issued the following warning to Moses:

> *If you do not drive out the inhabitants of the land, those you allow to remain will become barbs in your eyes and thorns in your sides...* (Numbers 33:55).

Now God expects Joshua to drive out all the inhabitants of the land. All of them. Joshua is well aware of this order. God has already told him to meditate on His commands day and night (see Josh.1:8). Then in Joshua 8:32, Joshua copies the whole law on stones once again (a nice reminder).

I will now ruin the ending of the story for you by telling you that Joshua did not drive out all of the inhabitants of Canaan. I'm not knocking Joshua; I'm not sure I would have made it much past Gilgal, but the fact remains that the Israelites left many of the nations in the land and lived among them. These nations led Israel into sin, time and again throughout history.

This is an example we can learn from. We don't need barbs in our eyes and thorns in our sides. What we need to understand is that grace has already defeated these enemies for us. Sin no longer has the power to separate us from God or His Promised Land. What then? Shall we keep on sinning? Here comes the answer to the most prevalent argument against grace: "No. We are not to keep on sinning."

Many Christians cannot readily receive grace because they misunderstand it to be a free pass to sinning—and we know we are not called to sin. But Paul reiterated many times that grace is not an excuse for sin at all! (See Romans 6:15.) We are called to resist sin.

That is why the Israelites were instructed to drive out the inhabitants of the land. Now let's apply this idea to our journey. The Promised Land is within us. God has given us His promises already; their physical manifestation will depend on the functionality of our hearts, which is affected by the presence and absence of sin.

A word about sin. The word *sin* is taken from the Hebrew word *Ciyn,* referring to the Wilderness of Sin and also a town named *Sin* and described as the strength of Egypt in Ezekiel 30:15. *Ciyn,* as we saw earlier, means "thorn,"[1] as in the thorn in your side. You see, these other nations symbolize the sin in our lives. They are thorns.

The Promised Land you are taking is the soil of your heart. It is flowing with milk and honey! But there are peoples in the land that must be removed. The *Amorites,* whose name means "sayer" or "boaster,"[2] need to be removed. The *Jebusites,* whose name means "trodden underfoot"[3] (indicating a low value or esteem of self), need to be defeated. The Hittites, whose name involves the idea of terror, must be displaced, too.[4]

There are many more "Ites" to list, but I think you get the idea. They include gossip, pride, selfish ambition, low self-esteem, fear, and many other things that may inhabit places in your heart. They must be removed or you will forfeit the Promised Land God has already given you!

God has already blessed you and there is nothing you can do to earn that blessing. Still, any lingering Ites make it difficult for the things of God to manifest physically. An over-the-top example would be the case of someone with an addiction to abuse. Planted in this individual are the things of God from salvation, but if the addiction is allowed to continue, the blessing of a Kingdom marriage will be unable to grow. The Ites, or weeds, will choke out the Word from producing and defeat the good.

This is where the circumcision of the heart is so important. We know that God has delivered the Ites into our hands. Our job is to stand in the promise of that victory and allow the cutting away of anything that is not of God.

The "Ites" that must be defeated are within you.

So I guess you really are your own enemy, although it isn't you, it is sin living in you. Your Ites are remnants from your life before you met Jesus. They include anything that is not of God but has become part of you—opinions, thoughts, attitudes, habits, *anything* that does not perfectly align with the truth of God's Word.

These things will keep you distracted from your growth and purpose. They become thorns and barbs to you. When you have a thorn in your side, it is difficult to focus, no less accomplish anything. That is one of the attributes of sin; it has the power to distract you. It will eat up resources, including your time and money.

Take off Your Sandals

In the Promised Land, Joshua had wars to fight. I wonder if he was feeling a bit scared. Maybe that is why God instructed him to be "*very courageous*" (Josh. 1:7). We, too, have battles ahead. They can cause us to feel vulnerable, uncomfortable, and afraid.

Do not fear. God is with you and in you. The Ites are also within you, but the solution is found there, too. When Joshua's attack on Jericho symbolizes your attack against an Ite in your life. To attack these enemies means losing a part of you that you may be comfortable living with.

Let's see how it works so that we always find victory.

> *Now when Joshua was near Jericho, he looked up and saw a man standing in front of him with a drawn sword in His hand. Joshua went up to Him and asked, "Are You for us or for our enemies?"* (Joshua 5:13)

The key phrase I want to point out first is that Joshua "went up to Him." Overlooking the Ites in our hearts is the Spirit of the Lord, who holds a drawn sword just like the Man Joshua saw.

The sword of the Spirit is the Word of God (see Eph. 6:17). The man answered Joshua by saying "*Neither...*" (Josh. 5:14). God wishes that none would perish. He desires to remove all sin from our hearts, whether it dates back to our lives before Christ or even when we were born (this includes the original sin of Adam).

Nevertheless, His already spoken Word dictated the judgment of whom would survive and it was not going to be Jericho. The Word assigned to sin the outcome of destruction. This is the awful place in which Jericho found themselves. Their time was up. The righteous were due the land as a result of their inheritance.

Notice Joshua's behavior. He went up to the Man. The first step in our victory over Jericho is to "go up to Him," meaning the Spirit of the Lord. (See the heart diagram in Figure 4.)

> *The commander of the Lord's army replied, "Take off your sandals, for the place where you are standing is holy..."* (Joshua 5:15).

When you go up to the Lord, you enter the Most Holy Place where the Ark of the Covenant is. Why is it important for Joshua to remove his shoes? Is it like when you get new carpet and you tell your kids, "Hey, take off your shoes before you come in this house!"

It's not that at all. It's about the conduction of power. If you stick a fork in an electrical outlet, you will find out quickly that the human body is a conductor of power. (Of course, if you are prone to sticking forks in electrical outlets, you probably need to read some books about self-preservation.)

Throughout the law, God says that whatever is dedicated unto the Lord is holy. Anything that touches the holy things also becomes holy. If you touch electricity, you get electrocuted. By touching it, you become a conductor of its power. If you touch something holy you might get "holycuted." I obviously made that up, but you can see what I mean.

Joshua needed to remove his shoes so the holy ground would make direct contact with his feet. This is a picture of our being made holy, not by taking off our shoes, but by receiving Christ. He is holy, so now we are holy. We're holy because He lives in us, and we are conducting that holiness—not because we are perfect, but because we are connected to His perfection.

Our sandals also represent our past, and to be here you must have realized by now that your past is long gone, and you forgive yourself in the way that God has forgiven you. God is not concerned with where you have been, but instead, where you are going.

Entering the Most Holy Place

Let's now look at entering that Most Holy Place within our hearts, remembering that we need God to help us defeat our Jericho.

We have tried to defeat sin on our own many times, but to no avail. Even when we abstain, the desire creeps up on us from time to time, just like Paul said in Romans 7. Abstaining alcoholics will admit that they still deal with the desire every day, but have learned to control it. (What we really seek is freedom from even the desire.)

Whether your Jericho is alcohol, gossip, slander, or offense, you need God. You need to go up to Him as Joshua did. You need to enter in to see Him and so you need grace and faith. Let's begin with faith:

> *When God made His promise to Abraham, since there was no one greater for Him to swear by, He swore by Himself, saying, "I will surely bless you and give you many descendants"* (Hebrews 6:13-14).

God here uses the word "surely," to make absolutely certain we have no doubt that He will bless us. This same blessing that was given to Abraham is available to us. Now, more about entering in:

> *We have this hope as an anchor for the soul, firm and secure. It enters the inner sanctuary behind the curtain, where Jesus, who went before us, has entered on our behalf...* (Hebrews 6:19-20).

The inner sanctuary. Ah, this is where we are going. Hope goes before us. It is hope in the promise that God has blessed us. It anchors the soul and keeps us from being moved by currents or waves. The anchor of hope keeps us from being blown around by fear, worry, or unbelief. Hope is the precursor of faith; hope in God's Word becomes faith when we *believe* what we hear! *"Now faith is being sure of what we hope for and certain of what we do not see"* (Heb. 11:1).

Being sure is important. We must be confident that we can go in and see the King within our hearts! According to the law the High Priest would enter the Most Holy Place once per year to make atonement for the sins of the nation. He would enter through the thick curtain. At the very moment when Jesus died this curtain was torn from top to bottom. *"At that moment the curtain of the temple was torn in two from top to bottom"* (Matt. 27:51).

This indicates that God removed the separating barrier between Himself and His people. The barrier was no longer necessary once Jesus died for all sin for all time. So why am I mentioning the barrier that is now gone? So we go in and out to see God, right? Well, kind of.

You must realize and understand two things: You can go in and see God because of your faith in Him and His Word. You qualify to go in and see Him because of His grace! He has made you holy. Hebrews 9:11-12 tells us that this very ritual of the high priest entering the Most Holy Place was performed by Christ in the most perfect Temple in the heavens. The high priest atoned for the sins of the people for one year, but Christ redeemed sins for all man past, present, and future. This is all described in great detail and leads to this passage:

> *Therefore, brothers, since we have* ***confidence*** *to enter the Most Holy Place by the blood of Jesus, by a new and living way opened for us through the* ***curtain, that is, His body,*** *and since we have a great priest over the house of God, let us draw near to God with a sincere heart in* ***full assurance of faith,*** *having our hearts sprinkled to cleanse us from a* ***guilty conscience*** *and having our bodies washed with pure water* (Hebrews 10:19-22).

What is the confidence described in this passage? It is the place where the hope that anchors your soul becomes faith. You enter by the blood, which provides redemption. The curtain is His Body, which you may recall is the Church. The full assurance of faith is faith in what God has spoken.

We are told to draw near to God. God has sacrificed so much in order to remove sin's power to separate us from Him. How horrible it would be for Him to sacrifice His very Son only to have us miss out on drawing near to Him. Lest you think this is a cautionary tale for the lost, please realize that this passage from Hebrews is for believers.

You can be a believer and still remain outside this Most Holy Place. This passage tells us that many Christians dare not draw near to God with the full assurance of faith. Why not? After all, our hearts have been sprinkled to cleanse us from a guilty conscience. This is *grace*. Yet we must accept grace, or guilt and condemnation will keep us out of God's presence even after we have been invited in.

He knows that. Our hearts are not sprinkled to wash away sin (Jesus already did that), but to cleanse us from the thing sin leads to, which is a guilty conscience (the feeling that you aren't worthy). So, remove your sandals my friend and enter in. It has nothing to do with what you have or haven't done. It has everything to do with what He did for you!

> *How much more, then, will the blood of Christ, who through the eternal Spirit offered himself unblemished to God, cleanse our consciences from acts that lead to death...* (Hebrews 9:14).

To defeat your Ites (a guilty conscience is an Ite) you will need Him by your side. You will need to say, "I have a problem, and I need Your help." (Sounds like an episode of Dora the Explorer, doesn't it?)

If you are feeling lowly and unworthy, you will remain in the Wilderness. You will be doomed to your own efforts to abstain from weakness, therefore you will never be truly free. Instead, you need to approach God boldly, head held high, with confidence that says, "Hey, I'm loving what Jesus did for me. Thank You! Now let's go kick some booty together. I've got another "Ite" I need Your help defeating."

> *Let us therefore come boldly to the throne of grace, that we may obtain mercy and find grace to help in time of need* (Hebrews 4:16 NKJV).

We do not have a Father who withholds mercy and grace. We do not have a High Priest who is unable to sympathize with our weaknesses. Christ was tempted in every way (see Heb. 4:15). Our weaknesses glean sympathy from Christ, not judgment. He wants to help us with our Ites.

Let Him.

Grace for Others

Not only do you need faith and grace to enter in, but you must have grace for others. To enter into the Most Holy Place, you must operate in grace. This means recognizing the fact that God forgives you and expects you to forgive yourself and others. How can you expect God to forgive you if you do not forgive others? This is a deception many Christians overlook and it keeps them in the Wilderness.

> *Therefore I tell you, whatever you ask for in prayer, believe that you have received it, and it will be yours. And when you stand praying, if you hold anything against anyone, forgive him, so that you Father in heaven may forgive you your sins* (Mark 11:24-25).

Notice a few key points here. First, we are standing in prayer not as lowly, unworthy, nothing, nobody losers, but as children of God, a royal priesthood. Jesus' words are clear: if you have not forgiven your friend, it will not go well for you. In Matthew 5:23-24, Jesus says that if you are offering the Lord a gift at the altar and realize that your brother is offended with you, you need to be reconciled with that person first; then you can return and offer your gift.

Your brother may not want to reconcile with you, but you should give it a shot. The idea is to always approach the altar with active forgiveness in your heart. Remember that we enter the Most Holy Place by the blood of Jesus. Well, His blood is the *embodiment* of forgiveness. Far be it for us to attempt to enter in while withholding forgiveness from others.

This is one of the reasons the walls of Jericho refuse to come down in some people's lives. It is why so many people have difficulty getting their prayers answered. It is because they are not entering in—even though they have been personally invited by God!

He wants us to draw near to Him. We just need to believe and operate in grace! Then the curtain of separation will be penetrated!

The Unseen Becomes Seen

Now then, the sword of the Spirit, the Word of God, is available to defeat your enemies, as pictured by the angel holding the sword in the encounter with Joshua. Joshua continues to speak with this Commander of the army of the Lord, looking for help in defeating Jericho.

> *Then the Lord said to Joshua, "See, I have delivered Jericho into your hands, along with its king and its fighting men"* (Joshua 6:2).

God operates in the unseen realm. Here He asks Joshua to "see" that Jericho is already defeated. Of course, in the natural, it is not, but the unseen world is where Joshua needs to be living. Remember that faith is the evidence of things not seen (see Heb. 11:1). It doesn't mean that the victory doesn't exist. It just means you cannot see it with your natural eyes.

This "seeing" happens in the mind's eye. The Man is saying, "Picture it Joshua. It's yours."

We need to see the victory. We need to imagine it until we can actually feel the emotion of it. Did you know that your physiological and emotional responses are controlled by your thoughts? If you daydream about something horrible, you might break into a sweat and speed up your heart rate. If you think about your one true love, you can get that mushy, gushy feeling.

God is saying to you, "See, I have given this Ite into your hands."

Now imagine it. Imagine the victory and how everything in your life is going to change for the better when this Ite is defeated. Live it. Feel it. Breathe it. When you are standing in God's presence, you can do all three, because we take our souls into the Most Holy Place to see God. This means we take our mind, will, and emotions to Him.

Here is what happens when you take your soul to God. Your mind goes there to receive the plan of the Lord—in other words, to see the unseen. Your will goes there to be submitted to God in obedience regardless of your understanding or emotions. Your emotions go there to see God and be charged with the joy of the Lord (in the presence of the Lord there is fullness of joy, according to Psalms 16:11).

In the Most Holy Place, you experience the emotion of the victory before you physically have the victory. You are taking the spiritual territory so that the physical territory can come into alignment. Eventually, you will reach a place of maturity so that the curtain is always open and God and you are always occupying the same space.

The Most Holy Place is where spiritual things are made manifest before your very eyes, but of course, not to your surprise. Jesus lived with the Spirit of God in Him, and on Him. You have this same opportunity right in front of you.

When you hear the Word of God, as Joshua did here, you receive it through your mind and take it into the presence of the Most High. The Holy Spirit, who speaks only what He hears (see John 16:13), then brings wisdom and understanding to the seed of the Word. The seed cannot produce without this intimate interaction.

You may have lived your whole life struggling with diabetes, only to discover *today* that by the stripes of Jesus, you were healed (see 1 Pet. 2:24). Now then, you must take that Word into the Lord with faith, operating in grace, and allow Him to breathe life into it. Then you can draw from that the healing power to manifest wholeness in you.

The Word alive in you *will* produce what He promised. Your heart is, after all, the seed plot designed to produce the things of God. Many people are waiting for a word from God before they will take a step, but remember, the Word of God is at your fingertips. Read it. God says to you today "See, (insert your name here), I have given (name your Ite) into your hands!"

That is the Word. Now allow the Lord to make that Word alive in you.

Sleeper "Ites"

Ites left to roam the ground of your heart will eventually become barbs in your eyes, often when you least expect it.

Ites can make it impossible to see the unseen. They attack the very things that make you strong in the Lord. They get you to look at the circumstances. The enemy wants you to ponder just how impenetrable those walls of Jericho are.

How do you overcome these "giants" who work from within to keep you from taking the land? How do you keep from getting barbs in your eyes? I've never had a real barb in my eye, but I'm guessing it would hurt like crazy. I imagine you wouldn't be able to get out a cohesive sentence with a barb in your eye. You probably wouldn't be able to do *anything* until you got it out or downed a bottle of Advil Extra Strength.

God's mercy, however, has given us a great deal of time to conqueror each Ite before things get to this point. The Israelites lived among the Ites for some time before the mess set in. He helps us to deal with them one by one, in His timing. As the Holy Spirit reveals to you something that needs to change within you, then you must "go up to Him" to find the strength. There is no need for you to go searching for the Ites in your life. Instead, keep your eyes fixed on Jesus. When the time for battle comes, there is no room for delay. It is time to fight.

The Promised Land is a place of warfare, but your journey is leading you to rest, the place where the battle is the Lord's. You are not there just yet. You are still partnering with God in battle. God gave Jericho into Joshua's hands, yet when the walls fell, the Israelites still had to go in and fight. Joshua had to run in with sword drawn and slash away. He could not skip this step, and neither can we. We are going to learn some serious work ethic here. It is part of our maturing process. Blood and bravery are involved. There is going to be some suffering, some sweat, some carrying of a cross—even some dying to self.

One day, I asked my son to cut the grass. I then handed him a pair of scissors and went back into my office. When he approached my throne (which is a Staples-brand office chair worth $21.99), he didn't come in slowly on his knees saying, "Oh, Father, I'm not worthy to come into thy presence."

Instead, he walked in and said, "I think I can do a better job if you let me use the lawn mower." He was right. The lawn mower was available. It was one of the promises of, well, me. My wife lets me keep my promises in the garage. So I said, "You may, my son. Godspeed."

The promises pull down to you through your assignment; your assignment is a step toward your destiny and purpose. If we attack our Ites out of God's order or timing, we may find ourselves out there alone. Each of God's promises has a purpose and provision that is related to your assignment. "Mow the lawn. Here's a lawn mower."

God assigned to Joshua the battle of Jericho. Sing with me: "Joshua fought the battle at Jericho, Jericho, Jericho, and the walls came tumbling down."

The most important words we receive reveal the purpose associated with our assignments. I'm not teaching my son to mow lawns. I'm teaching him to finish projects with diligence and excellence. That is the purpose of the assignment.

Some of the most powerful Ites to overcome on the journey to rest are the ones you do not know are there (such as a lack of perseverance). This is why we must let God choose our battles. On your journey, you are being mentored and highly trained for a glory-filled destination. When Jesus went into the Temple with a braided whip, He cleaned out the place. That is how the Word of God works in you.

Chapter 16

Sow, Grow, It's How I Roll

In CHAPTERS 14 AND 15 we discussed our covenant with the Lord, the circumcision of the heart, God's desire to free us from the Ites in our hearts. The reason God has us addressing the heart as we enter the Promised Land entry is because the Promised Land is all about sowing and reaping.

In the Wilderness, there was no farmland and no crops. So God gave them manna. In the Promised Land, if you want to eat, you have to plant. This is true in the natural sense, but also, and more importantly, in the spiritual sense.

The Promised Land is within us. We will experience it in the physical realm as we take possession of it in our heart. Therefore, we need to get our hearts functioning at optimal level. A farmer knows he must prepare the soil before planting—if he does not, the soil will not produce to its potential. God paints the picture of Joshua defeating the Ites because He wants us to see the importance of creating a healthy heart environment in which to grow our "crops."

The cornerstone of our Christianity is salvation, which is in the heart of the believer. We typically define salvation as the eternal life that is available to us through Christ. That is correct; but salvation is more than the gift of eternal life. It is being saved from sin and death. The life we acquire through salvation is a good life; it starts when we receive Christ, not when we die.

You entered into that good and eternal life when you were born again. You can apply salvation to whatever is ailing you—in other words, whatever needs to be saved from death. Your salvation (the rescue that comes with life) is in your heart. Spiritually speaking, your heart is the reproductive organ in your life. This chapter is dedicated to getting your heart primed to produce the right crops in abundance.

Consider an apple seed. It is hidden deep inside the apple with several of its "sibling" seeds. Apple seeds are small, but each one contains enormous potential. What can one seed planted in the right environment produce? One tiny brown seed can produce an apple tree. In a single season that apple tree will produce multiple fruits, each with seed inside. How many seeds? Some 30-, some 60-, and some 100-fold.

In the realm of finance, if I invest $1,000 and receive a return of $1,000 (now I have $2,000), I have made a great investment. That is a 100 percent return. I have doubled my money. As multiplication goes, it's good, but it doesn't compare with God's multiplication—the kind we saw in the apple. If my money multiplied like the apple seed did, my $1,000 would have yielded a minimum of $30,000 in just one year.

That is how His creation produces. A single apple seed has the potential to produce tens of thousands of apple trees in it's lifetime, each having the ability to produce seed. God has put inside that little seed the power of the infinite—not just a two-fold return (a 100 percent gain), but no less than a 30-fold return (the equivalent of a 3,000 percent gain)!

Do you see the difference?

When we talk about money, the multiplication is easy to visualize, but the real seed power God has given us is His Word. He created in the seed the power of the infinite. He gives us the same kind of power to produce in our hearts. Money cannot produce what God's Word can. God's Word produces wisdom and, guess what? Prosperity follows close behind it.

Just ask Solomon.

You Are Not Easy to Change

Ask anyone, especially your spouse, whether you are easily changed. Ask yourself.

Yes, we already discussed this, but let's recap for a second. If we lack the discipline to stop drinking three Diet Cokes each day, how are we ever going to find the discipline to maintain a solid Christian attitude? How will we manage to be joyous in every occasion and trial? Or be salt and light to the world?

Not that Diet Coke is a sin. Diet Fresca is far more sinful (I'm kidding). My point is that we are creatures of habit, dug in deeply with our pleasures and weaknesses. As a pastor, I know that adjusting our service time by 15 minutes in either direction will cause four families to leave the church. I'm not trying to be condescending here, I'm pointing out our innate resistance to change.

Resistance to change is a godly attribute that is meant to keep us from being thrown around by every wind and wave. However, when this attribute prevents us from making good changes, it is malfunctioning.

One way that we resist change is to address adverse symptoms instead of their root causes. If I'm having headaches every day, I will take more Advil. The idea of cutting out all that caffeine I'm drinking (the cause of the headaches) is not an option.

Our society has trained us to medicate our problems. Depressed? No problem, here is a medication that will cause your armpits to bleed and your hair to smell like rotting walnuts, but you will feel oh so much happier. Depression is a real issue, and real people deal with it. Pills can mask the issue, but only God has the real solution, which is freedom.

God's power to change you is to address the root, the heart. His tools are the seed (His Word) and the power of the infinite. He will change you from the inside out! Many Christians continue to medicate because they haven't partnered with God to take the Promised Land. They hear the things of God, but they haven't taken hold yet.

The Sower and the Seed

Jesus tells His disciples a parable about a farmer sowing seed. He sprinkled the seed everywhere: along the path, on rocky places, among thorns, and on good ground. Of the four places he planted, only one place produced a crop.

When Jesus' disciples ask Him what the parable means, He replies:

> *Don't you understand this parable? How then will you understand any parable?* (Mark 4:13)

Ah, then this is a very important parable to grasp. It sounds like it is the beginning of understanding the things of God—the core, the very foundation of wisdom. You may recall from Hebrews 3:10 that the reason the Israelites did not enter the rest of the Lord was because they did not know God's ways.

The word, *know,* is often used in the Bible to indicate intimacy that produces fruit. Remember, Adam *knew* Eve, and they birthed their first son (see Gen. 4:1). To know God's ways is to produce His wisdom inside us and grow it into fruit.

Ground Type No. 1: Satan Steals the Word

In Jesus' explanation of the parable, we learn that the seed the farmer planted is the Word of God. The different types of ground represent different types of people. Our gracious God spreads His Word to everyone, sinner and saint alike. What we do with His Word is our choice.

> *Some people are like seed along the path, where the word is sown. As soon as they hear it, Satan comes and takes away the word that was sown in them* (Mark 4:15).

Why is satan allowed to steal the Word? Because we fail to defend against the theft; we do not search the Word of God for the appropriate defense against satan. We leave ourselves open for random robbery.

Remember that satan is the thief. It is his job to steal. Yet we *can* keep him out! Give me a few paragraphs in which to build for you a wall of defense that will keep the thief from stealing the Word out of your heart.

Let me start by giving you a hint: The enemy gets to steal because we steal.

The first "soil sample" Jesus discusses is first for a reason. Being the "first" is important in Scripture: the *firstborn* and *first fruits*, for example, are the strongest of seeds, symbolically. You'll recall that Jericho was the very first battle in the Promised Land—the first city the Israelites would take and their first access to non-desert-smelling spoils!

> *The seventh time around, when the priests sounded the trumpet blast, Joshua commanded the people, "Shout! For the Lord has given you the city!"* (Joshua 6:16)

How exciting it is to hear that God has given you the city! It's yours! (This, for us, signifies living in the unseen world.) God has pulled victory from Israel's future and given it to them, but they have to engage a battle to close the deal. Not only that, but God has given them an important stipulation: *"The city and all that is in it are to be devoted to the Lord..."* (Josh. 6:17).

"Hey, wait just a minute," you wonder, "I thought it was ours."

You're paying attention. That's good! But keep reading: "...*Only Rahab the prostitute and all who are with her in her house shall be spared, because she hid the spies we sent"* (Josh. 6:17).

Imagine this one on *Nancy Grace.* "Let me get this straight, Mr. Nunson. Are you suggesting these so-called 'spies' stayed at a house of prostitution? And now you want to save the chief prostitute and all those in her house, whom I assume would be *more* prostitutes? For what purpose, I might ask?"

Religious folks would not have condoned this course of action; but our God is not religious. He is faithful and merciful. In fact, Rahab, the prostitute, is named in the lineage of Christ. She was saved by her faith in God (see Heb. 11:31). She married into the tribe of Judah and had a son named Boaz (see Matt. 1:5) who married Ruth (see Ruth 4:13), who had a son named Obed, who had a son named Jesse, who had a son named David—yeah, king David (see Matt. 1:5-6). God uses the most unlikely of candidates. Ouch.

Here comes the stipulation about the spoils:

> *But keep away from the devoted things, so that you will not bring about your own destruction by taking any of them. Otherwise you will make the camp of Israel liable to destruction and bring trouble on it. All the silver and gold and the articles of bronze and iron are sacred to the Lord and must go into His treasury* (Joshua 6:18-19).

Hold on. The Israelites fight, but don't get any spoils...land...anything. They are not allowed to touch the goodies. In fact, they burn the city and are forbidden to rebuild it. It was a nice city, I'm sure some would have wanted to stay.

After 40 years of waiting, finally entering the Promised Land, and fighting their first battle, where is the pay-off on all God's talk about cities they did not build? Israel just took Jericho—but for what? Nothing. Zip. Nada. They don't get to keep any of it. Why?

Here's a clue: Jericho means "moon."[1] *"The highest heavens belong to the Lord, but the earth He has given to man"* (Ps. 115:16).

Jericho is a picture of the moon, which is located in the heavens. This is a symbol that the first fruit of the Promised Land belongs to God. The earth is ours, the heavens belong to God. Jericho is off-limits because it is the Lord's.

If you are wondering what happens when you touch something that is God's, look no further than the story of Achan in Joshua 7. After the battle of Jericho, Achan buries some of the devoted things in his tent. Joshua doesn't know what he did and proceeds to send a small force up to a place called Ai to take some more territory.

Ai is a weak little place; Joshua and company see it as a territory-taking slam-dunk. Unfortunately, Ai defeats Joshua's army.

Stunned, Joshua cries out to God, who reveals the fact that someone kept some of the devoted things. You see, no more land can be taken as long as Achan has these things. When we steal from the Lord, we stunt our own growth and find ourselves defeated.

Achan was not the first to make this mistake. When Adam touched the fruit of the tree of the knowledge of good and evil, he disobeyed God's command (see Gen. 3:3) and was cast out of The Garden to work for the land. God made nothing evil in The Garden. He hand-planted it! He simply put one tree in there that was labeled, "No touchy." After he and Eve ate from the tree, they found themselves in slavery to this world. The Garden dwellers were back in Egypt.

What else is not to be touched? The answer is in the Book of Malachi, which describes a specific kind of robbery: *"Will a man rob God? Yet you rob Me. But you ask, 'How do we rob You?' 'In tithes and offerings…'"* (Mal. 3:8).

Yes, I remember now. The tithe is the Lord's. It belongs to Him and is not to be touched. God is giving you a beautiful, wonderful new life in the Promised Land. Part of the deal enables Him to finance the expansion of the Kingdom of God by dispersing his Word to the world. He gets 10 percent of your increase. This makes you and God partners. (What's yours is His, and what's His is yours.) If this angers you, then check your heart. Are you like Achan?

We must develop in ourselves a willingness to give, or we will find ourselves unable to take any more land. It is ridiculous and selfish not to be able to give the Lord your tithe of all that He has given you. In fact, the best part is that the tithe will save you from Promised Land Enemy No. 2 (to be discussed later).

The tithe is important to God. Under the Old Covenant not tithing produced a curse: *"You are under a curse—the whole nation of you—because you are robbing Me"* (Mal. 3:9).

Jesus broke the curse off of us. You are not under a curse if you do not tithe. Further, the blessing came before the tithe and the blessing is within you. God always gives first: He loved first and He gave His Son first. The first thing He did after creating mankind was to bless them. Then He introduced and set aside the "don't eat me" tree.

When Isaac laid his hands on Jacob, he blessed him. It was later that Jacob made a vow to tithe to the Lord. The blessing came first. Abraham was blessed before he gave 10 percent of all that he had to Melchizedek. Tithing doesn't enable you to have the blessing; yet you must tithe in order to experience the blessing.

Keep reading! *"Bring the whole tithe into the storehouse, that there may be food in My house…"* (Mal. 3:10).

OK, you can't pay partial tithes to the Lord and call it good. Interesting. It's like paying half your electric bill and hoping they don't shut off the power. Of course, God doesn't shut off the power. The purpose of the tithe? That there might be food in His house. Remember that the Church is the dispensation system for the water and food of God—the Word. You go to church and someone is preaching, teaching, and planting God's Word in the people. The people need the seed to grow.

Any church that is in God's purpose will dispense spiritual food. How about your church? Does it preach the Word of God? If so, your church is in His purpose and your tithe supports its mission. Some think the tithe is designed to help the church paint a rundown neighborhood. New paint on someone's house will add a smile, but God's Word can change a life.

The primary purpose of the Church is to supply spiritual food! The Church is the storehouse. I'm not talking about the church building, but about the people who are being fitted together to become a dwelling for the name of the Lord (see Eph. 2:22). Deuteronomy 14:23 tells us to tithe at the place where the Lord's name dwells. It says we are to eat our tithe. Not only do we give our 10 percent, but we must listen to the seed that goes forth. Why protect the seed if there is no seed to protect!

> *"... Test Me in this," says the Lord Almighty, "and see if I will not throw open the floodgates of heaven and pour out so much blessing that you will not have room enough for it"* (Malachi 3:10).

The blessing is not in the tithe. I've heard it said that you cannot be blessed if you don't tithe. That isn't exactly true. The wording is wrong. God's blessing is free to you—it comes by faith in Him. Jesus died so that the blessing given to Abraham would be yours. Not tithing keeps us from experiencing the physical manifestation of the blessing. Like Israel, we cannot take more land until we deal with Achan, the thief inside our own camp.

Achan might be living inside of us. He's the guy who doesn't want to give. He is a stumbling block to our progress; we *must* deal with him. Joshua dealt harshly with Achan. After that, Israel went back to taking the territory successfully. The tithe is important, because the condition of our hearts is important!

The passage from Malachi 3 is not one-sided. In fact, there is a reward for tithing: the windows of Heaven are poured out to us. Remember, the blessing is already within you; tithing involves the physical manifestation of the blessing. This is a kind of bonus reward promised here:

> *I will prevent pests from devouring your crops, and the vines in your fields will not cast their fruit," says the Lord Almighty* (Malachi 3:11).

That is an outstanding promise. Take a moment to soak in it, because we are finally getting to my point, which involves the soil. In the parable of the sower and the seed, Jesus said that for some the devil comes and steals the seed, in a very specific way: *"As he [the sower] was scattering the seed, some fell along the path, and the birds came and ate it up"* (Mark 4:4).

Birds are pests when it comes to devouring crops. There is a pest in our fields, too, and here the mystery of his identity is revealed (drum roll, please): satan is the pest. In the New King James Version of Malachi 3:11, he is described as the devourer: *"I will rebuke the devourer for your sakes, so that he will not destroy the fruit of your ground...."*

Yeah, that is him—the devourer. God will rebuke satan. We are not asked in the Bible to rebuke satan. We are asked to resist him (see James 4:7; 1 Pet. 5:9). God is the one who rebukes satan; and He is better at doing it, too.

The Promised Land is a place of sowing and reaping. If you sow theft as Achan did, you will reap the same—cornstalk for cornstalk. When you rob God, the devil gets to rob you. God does not rob you; it is not in His nature. The trouble is that He cannot protect you, because what you have sown you will reap.

Christians generally associate tithing with protecting their finances, and rightly so. But there is a much more powerful seed than money, and it needs protecting, too. It is the seed of God's Word in your heart. If the devil is allowed to steal the Word, he has stolen your ability to grow and take more of the Promised Land. The devil literally steals wisdom, which is far more valuable than gold.

This is what Jesus teaches us in the parable of the sower and the seed: We need to keep that pesky bird far away from the ground of the heart.

As for the booty won at Jericho...the tithe: God's word on these is "No touchy!"

Now, let's look at the next type of non-fruit-producing ground.

Ground Type No. 2: The Soil Is Shallow

When I want to plant flowers at our house, I run up to Wal-Mart and purchase plants in small plastic pots. You know the kind I'm talking about; you can get six of them for about three bucks.

When I plant these flowers, I plant them pot and all. That's right. I leave the flower in the pot. I've seen resorts do this, and I am guessing they do it for the same reason as I do. I call it "flower laziness." That little flower doesn't live very long. If I leave it in the pot, I can switch it out with a new flower lickity-split.

Let's pretend that the little flower pot is your heart. If you plant a seed in there, it will produce life quickly, but that life will only go so far. A tree couldn't survive in that tiny pot. The roots could never get deep enough to support a tree.

Whatever you plant in that tiny piece of ground will be susceptible to the elements. Once it gets hot out, the plant soon dies.

> *Others, like seed sown on rocky places, hear the word and at once receive it with joy. But since they have no root, they last only a short time. When trouble or persecution comes because of the word, they quickly fall away* (Mark 4:16-17).

The key identifier of the individual with this kind of heart seems to be that they receive the Word "at once" and "with joy." Well that seems to be the correct way to receive God's Word, doesn't it? Yet Jesus is citing this soil condition as a problem.

When I teach the Word of God, I want people to receive what I'm saying. Hey, I've been studying hard, I did the math, I prayed, I sought God, now please get what I'm saying. At the end of the teaching, I want someone to chase me down (not that I'm running) and say, "Wow, that changed my *life*!!"

Or while I'm teaching someone will say, "Yes—*yes*. That is the word I needed to hear!"

This sounds great, but according to the parable in Mark 4, a response like this could indicate shallow soil. If so, it is incapable of producing deep roots. I wouldn't say that everyone who receives the Word with joy is having this problem, but the potential is there.

Why? Well, let's say our friend Jimmy has shallow soil. He hears the Word of God that says he is supposed to be blessed. He receives it and shouts, "Amen!" Soon, the ground heats up. Jimmy loses his job and life gets harder. Jimmy asks God, "Hey, wait, why aren't You blessing me?"

Unless there is some depth of soil in Jimmy's heart, he gives up on the Word he heard and received with joy. The same can happen to a cancer patient who has been praying and believing God for healing. If a bad report comes, the fact that she is tired and disappointed might cause her to give up on the Word of God.

Marriages are also susceptible to shallow soil. The honeymoon period is great, but years later, the marriage is requiring some work. The ground is heating up and the picture doesn't look as rosy anymore. Unable to sustain root growth in the soil of their hearts, they call it quits.

Faith is not needed when life is perfect. Anyone can believe in God's Word when the pressure is off. Faith is a tool designed for *overcoming* mountains, problems, and storms. Jesus used faith to save lives and calm winds and waves.

The Word of God growing in our lives produces greater faith. But this same Word is attacked by the trials of life. Natural circumstances can make it hard to keep believing. However, a deep-rooted word from God will force the circumstance to change and be reconciled to God's promise. Shallow roots cannot accomplish this. Instead, we end up finding reconciliation shortcuts—it's still a plant, but it's withered.

Shallow soil cannot anchor growth. If you were to install a professional basketball hoop at your home, you would want to anchor the pole several feet into the soil to keep the hoop from falling over. God wants His people anchored, grounded, and not easily tossed to and fro by every wind and wave of doctrine. He wants the soil of their hearts to be deep.

When God came to Moses in the burning bush and asked him to lead the Israelites out of slavery, Moses' response was surprising. He told God to find someone else. He did not receive the Word immediately with joy. Moses did not say, "Amen! Yes. I have been waiting for this!"

Moses had a deep desire to bring the people out of slavery and, in fact, to be their ruler. He showed this early on when he murdered an Egyptian for abusing an Israelite (see Exod. 2:11-12). An Israelite questioned Moses at the time asking, *"Who made you ruler...over us?"* (Exod. 2:14).

The irony is that, 40 years later, God would make Moses ruler over the Israelites. When he killed the Egyptian, Moses had gotten ahead of God. He was out of season and it created a mess from which he had to flee. Yet, when God asks Moses to step into his destiny, He literally has to talk Moses into it (see Exod. 3:11-4:17).

If a burning bush started talking to me, I would probably listen and do whatever it tells me to do. This is God speaking, after all! So why didn't God choose a guy who would just shout, "Yes! I receive that! Thank You"?

God knew that getting Moses on board with His plan would be tough; He also knew that once Moses started this thing, he wouldn't quit. God was right. When the ground started getting hot and Pharaoh told Moses to take a hike, Moses didn't quit. When the Israelites were trapped between the Red Sea and the Pharaoh's army, he didn't quit. When the people grumbled against him and wanted him dead, he didn't quit. Moses anchored that word deep in the soil of his heart and became immovable.

Moses was not easily swayed. This is a strength. A person who knows where they are going and what they are doing is not easily changed. They have deep soil. An opportunity may come along that is good, but because they are not easily swayed, they stay focused on the target at hand. Many Christians are tossed around by mountains *and* by opportunities. When a mountain gets in the way of the goal, the shallow-soil Christian decides that it must not have been God's will. When a new opportunity comes along, this believer is too quick to believe that it is an open door from God.

This is the door myth.

Walking through any door that opens and accepting every door that closes seems like godly behavior. It isn't so in the Bible, though. If you are going toward a God-given goal and a door slams shut, then you are to break that door down and keep going!

People say, "I'm just waiting for God to open doors and then I will follow His lead."

If I were the devil (which I'm not), I would open and close doors just to get people off track. Satan has to be pretty excited about a person who will walk through any open door. He can easily lead that person away from God's foreordained destiny.

Satan can use people to get us off course. When someone says all the right things, we tend to assume there is a divine connection. Yet, satan can use such encounters to distract us. Of course, he can only have his way if we allow ourselves to be deterred.

A salesman says, "You need this car."

"I do? Yeah I guess I do."

We can be easy marks for smooth talkers, multilevel marketing schemes, and work-from-home-and-make-a-billion-in-two-weeks distractions. We walk into new friendships that look like divine appointments and we find ourselves giving all our money into an investment we know nothing about. "Well, he looks like a nice guy," we reason.

Oops.

Meanwhile the devil gloats, "Watch this. I open this door and—wait for it, wait for it—yes! In he comes."

Deep soil means having a clear sense of where you are going. When you have that settled, you become practically immovable. It would take a burning bush and voice of God to change your direction, but even then it might take some coercing by God.

When you are focused on accomplishing in excellence the task at hand, you will mow down the doors satan has closed as though they were made of balsa wood. The more you do this, the deeper your resolve and your soil will become.

God wants deeper soil operating as we learn, too. We should plant and digest the Word slowly. (Remember from Chapter 4, that the Passover lamb was roasted over the fire.) Sheep graze and digest slowly. In order to grow in the heart, we must enlarge and refine our capacity for wisdom.

Now let's look at the third type of nonproducing soil from Jesus' parable in Mark 4.

Ground Type No. 3: Thorns Choke the Word

In Arizona, we have to plant winter grass every October. This might seem like a pain in the neck, but hey, we don't have to shovel snow.

The best grass in Arizona is the winter variety. It is greener, easier to keep, and nicer to play on during the cooler weather. In summertime, playing outside is a challenge, especially because you might burst into flames.

One year I picked up a bag of grass seed that was on sale. Winter grass on a budget, you could say. My soil is soft and deep and good for growing grass. Yet, as my discount seed germinated, so did a whole mess of weeds. Apparently, the seed I purchased was on sale for a reason.

From reading the bag, I learned that all grass seed has a certain amount of weed seed mixed in. Cheap seed has a lot of weed seed. I'm guessing maybe 50 percent. This was a problem. I had weed species sprout up that I had never seen before. I am pretty sure one of the species tried to eat my 12-year-old at one point. He is still emotionally scarred from the attack.

The weeds were so strong that they kept the grass from growing. So I spent my winter mowing the weeds. I'm not sure why God created weeds.

Maybe they are just spinoffs of good plants that have been corrupted by the Fall of Man. In any case, weeds are unsightly. They grow up really fast and they suck away all the water from the good plants.

Maybe God created weeds as an example of Jesus' parable about the four types of ground. We learn from experience that, to kill a weed, you have to pull it up by its roots. If you just mow it down, it will grow back with a vengeance.

Let's see what the Bible says about the type of heart ground that yields the wrong stuff:

> *Still others, like seed sown among thorns, hear the word; but the worries of this life, the deceitfulness of wealth and the desires for others things come in and choke the word, making it unfruitful* (Mark 4:18-19).

Thorns are the Ites in our lives. It is not a coincidence that Numbers 33 referred to the Ites as thorns, or that *thorn* and *sin* are synonymous terms. Or, for that matter, that Jesus here calls the weeds *thorns.* God is speaking to us clearly about how these terms are connected.

Ites are thorns. They are the people inhabiting the Promised Land, and the Israelites must remove them. They are the territories in your heart that must be taken. They include worry, the deceitfulness of wealth, and ungodly desire.

In Mark 4:18-19, Jesus breaks down our Ites into three major groups. The first is *worry.* Jesus tells us in Matthew 6 not to worry about the things of this life (what we will eat and what we will wear). Worry is the beginning of fear, which is a direct contradiction of faith. Low-self esteem—the feeling that you are not valuable—lives in this category. So does a lack of confidence. These issues are fear's relatives.

The next Ite Jesus mentions is *the deceitfulness of wealth.* (This happens to be Promised Land Enemy No. 2, which we will discuss at length later.) This is the strongest of enemies. It is no wonder that the truth of it is distorted by some in order to support the false belief that God wants us to be poor. (Those who advocate "poorsterity"—yes, I made up that word—are repeating the same argument the ten spies offered to Moses.)

The deceitfulness of wealth is the idea that money will solve your problems and make your life happy. If that were true I wouldn't spend so much time mentoring wealthy people who are struggling to find fulfillment.

The last Ite named in Mark 4:18-19 is the one that covers many miscellaneous Ites. It is the *desire of other things.* What do we desire? Does it match up with what God desires? If not, we get into areas where perversion, laziness, overeating, envy, jealousy, selfish ambition, or other Ites might live.

Jesus gives us these three groups of Ites to help us identify anything in our hearts that is contrary to the Word of God—whether we planted them or inherited them from our ancestors. (That's right. There are prebaked Ites and they are especially tough to handle.)

Based on Jesus' description of Ites, I am confident that listening to old Def Leppard records is not among them. Religion tends to make up its own Ites. Man-made rules are not good; let's stick to God-made rules. Check out this passage:

> *Since you died with Christ to the basic principles of this world, why, as though you still belonged to it, do you submit to its rules: "Do not handle! Do not taste! Do not touch!"? These are all destined to perish with use, because they are based on human commands and teachings. Such regulations indeed have an appearance of wisdom, with their self-imposed worship, their false humility and their harsh treatment of the body, but they lack any value in restraining sensual indulgence* (Colossians 2:20-23).

That's a really long way of saying that we need to allow the Lord to help us attack the Ites *He* targets. Religious rules like "Don't date" or "Don't wear make-up" or whatever else, might sound like wisdom, but they are based on human commands.

This is not a free pass to sin, either. A kid once shared with me his belief that the Bible doesn't say not to smoke pot. True. Marijuana is not named in the Bible. The real question is whether his parents are OK with him smoking pot. He needs to honor and obey his parents, according to Scripture.

Furthermore, is it against the law of the land to smoke pot? Oops. According to Scripture, he needs to obey the law of the land. And doesn't the Word teach us not to be drunkards? Isn't being high equivalent to being drunk? Let me say this: if you want to find loopholes in the Bible in order to condone your sin, there is a much deeper problem at hand.

Meanwhile, let God reveal your Ites. If you ask the Holy Spirit which piece of land you are to take next, He will show you which Ite is up for eviction. By the way, asking your spouse is often helpful, too.

Ite Behavioral Science

Exactly how do Ites choke out the Word and keep it from being fruitful?

Remember God's warning that the people who remain in the land will become thorns in your side and barbs in your eyes (see Num. 33:55). Ites remove your ability to see the unseen world, which is precisely what God needs you to see. They also distract you something terrible.

Let's say that a man has a lust tree in his heart. This is probably generational. If you are one of the very, *very* few men who did not have to deal with this tree in your teenage years, consider yourself blessed. You get to skip over a very tough battle.

Our fathers and grandfathers probably had lust, too. This can make the battle tougher. For some men, this lust converts into a healthy desire for their spouse. Great. God wants you to desire your wife, so go get her.

Some men, however, have allowed lust to grow up into perversion or coveting. Let's say you get married. Your overall happiness hinges in large part on your relationship with your other half. It is no secret that having a great relationship with your spouse enhances your ability to enjoy your life and mature with a big ol' smile on your face.

This is God's will for your life. Now let's assume for the sake of this argument that coveting drives you to check out other women. You are distracted and unable to give all of yourself to your wife. Guess what? That is not a Kingdom marriage. The promises God has for you cannot be fruitful until you kick out this group of Ites and take the territory.

Unless and until you deal with this thorn, you will ensure that fulfillment in life is diminished for both of you. Suddenly, she will feel as though you don't love her. Before you know it, everything starts slipping—your relationship, your work, your children, your future.

Let's say you are a single man who deals with perversion. You long for your soul mate, that perfect someone created just for you. You need this person in your life and God wants you to have her, but why would He bring her into your junk? If you marry her, you just might end up cheating on her. Even if you do meet her, the perversion you hide will repel her, because the Spirit inside her tells her to run away!

Do you see how Ites function to squelch your life?

Sin Consciousness

If you get to this part of the book, but your life is still stuck in the Wilderness, then go back a few chapters and take another look at grace. Remember that God is your partner here in the Promised Land. He is giving you victory over these thorns. Thorns do not separate you from Him. God is only saying, "Hey, let's get these weeds out of here so we can really have a nice garden."

God isn't mad about your weeds. He wants to help you with them. He loves you. Remember that He loved us while we were yet sinners. Remember that Jesus died so that these weeds would be powerless to separate us from God. Just as He is there to help Joshua overcome the peoples in the Promised Land, He is helping us.

You need to know that it is not healthy for you to take a sin inventory of your life every day. God knows which weeds to deal with, and in which order. Of course there are some weeds to deal with. Relax and give it into His hands.

Cleaning up this garden is the part of the journey we are on now. We left Egypt, changed influences, grew stronger, learned to serve, fathomed grace, dared to believe God and cross the Jordan. We studied circumcision, gave our first fruits to the Lord at Jericho, and now we are ready to take the territory.

All of this is leading us into the Lord's rest. Remember that we must learn the Lord's ways to enter. That means getting the Word of God to grow in our heart and produce fruit. Removing the weeds may seem like we are focusing on sin, but we really aren't. We are just tending to the part of the journey we are on.

When crises happens in our lives, we have to be willing to look in the mirror and say, "You did this. And I know which part of you did it. Now I'm going to march around the mess, blow the trumpets, fast and pray, and partner with God. I will do whatever it takes, but this thing is defeated! It's going down. It is not going to happen again. I've been struggling with this for 15 years and I'm done. Today the Jebusites (or whichever Ites) are going to die. God has given you into my hands! You'll never produce fruit in my life again. I curse you at the root!"

Now you are making leaps and bounds. That's how you take territory. Wimpy Christian attitudes will keep you marching around the city an eighth time. I say, "No dice. Be strong, get your sword, get your God, and go!"

Fruitless Trees Waiting to Produce Fruit

Getting free of Ites is my favorite part. When you beat one, the Word of God that has seemed dormant in your heart suddenly springs to life. The weed is no longer choking it; your growth in wisdom, blessings, and territory will be much like that of the Israelites as they took the land.

After a war, they had more valuables and rewards than they could carry. They received wells they did not dig, harvests they did not plant, and cities that they did not build! When you finally get up and defeat an Ite with the overcoming attitude and tenacity that is required, your life will come alive like a fruit tree in season.

This, my friend, is the path to rest. If you refer back to our map on page 116, you will see that we are still following the original command of God to subdue the earth. The earth you subdue first is the earth in your heart. Until you do this, you are not quite ready for the authority God has in store for you. For now, you must keep pulling up any weeds growing in the soil of your heart.

You *cannot* skip this step.

The Parable in a Nutshell

You have a good grasp on the parable of the sower and the seed. Let's cap things off with a simple, but graphic illustration of the three types of soil.

We know that the seed represents the Word and the soil is the ground of our hearts, but let's imagine that the seed is money. In the first type of soil, a person who is not a tither invests the money. This seed has fallen along the path; therefore, the devil can come and steal the investment. As a result, the individual never realizes the blessing. It doesn't mean that they aren't blessed (empowered to prosper); they simply did not experience the blessing. Keep in mind that sometimes the devil doesn't always steal the seed right away. Sometimes he waits until your investment gets bigger, and then he steals it.

The second situation involves a person with shallow soil. He receives every investment idea immediately with joy and puts his money on the line. He sees every door of opportunity as being Heaven sent. Once again, the investment is devoured. He failed to "chew on" the investment. He should have meditated it, studied it, and allowed the Spirit to lead him, thereby deepening the soil.

In the third scenario, a person sets out to invest, but worry, addictions, and the desire for other things keep the person from achieving the goal. This individual is worried about losing the money on a bad investment, so they keep spending their investment on stuff they don't need. That darn Starbucks addiction keeps eating their seed. The deceitfulness of wealth drives them into debt. And—well, you can imagine the rest of the story.

In all three cases, there was seed and there was ground, but nothing ever grew. Of course, the seed of God is far more valuable than money. It is God's wisdom. We need to receive the seed by reading the Word of God and hearing it preached. We have to retain the Word, by taking notes, studying the Word, and meditating on it.

If we persevere, we will produce a crop called *wisdom.*

Chapter 17

Don't Throw Me in the Briar Patch

As a kid I never could understand the need for the self-destruct button used in action stories. Do you remember when all the superheroes from Superman to Aquaman got together? They were called the Justice League—a group of the strongest superheroes in the world. They had an amazing high-tech facility where they organized to save the world.

As a kid, I remember one episode in which I learned that the base had a self-destruct button. That was hard for me to fathom. It seemed like an admission that, at some point, we might have to blow up all this good stuff.

You and I have a self-destruct button—and we are designed by God with more power than any superhero. Our self-destruct button comes in the form of some kind of Ite. The devil needs only one thorn in your life, just one weed that he can grow and grow until it becomes powerful enough to destroy everything good in your life.

Think of it: he only needs you to believe one lie. That is how satan operates; he steals, kills, and destroys. He never takes a break or a nap. No. He is always plotting to destroy. His problem is that he has no power over you. But he is clever. He figures out ways to get you to destroy yourself.

Let me give you an example of how he works. A person deals with low self-esteem. They call it *humility*, but it is not godly humility. It is a misconception of a godly trait. People with low self-esteem shun glory and run from the limelight. They do not want their names to be made great, since they believe it would make them seem prideful.

Mind you, an individual with low self-esteem can be walking in the Promised Land and taking territory. The promises of God begin to manifest and he or she will start to experience tremendous success. (After all, God has promised to make our names great.)

Here's the hitch: once the level of success exceeds this person's perceived value of *self*, he or she will subconsciously self-destruct at least enough to ratchet back the success level to a place commensurate with diminished self-esteem.

This person does not value self the way God values them. Remember this: Your level of success cannot be sustained beyond where you see yourself. So the individual gives back the territory that has been taken, and chooses to live a more "comfortable" life that, unfortunately, short-circuits God-given destiny. I have met people who are self-destructing. I can literally see the light blinking red just behind their eyeballs, about to implode everything they and God have built, all unintentionally.

You will notice that I haven't detailed a bunch of different Ites given specific instructions on how to beat each of them. Only God has a specific plan for dealing with yours. My responsibility here is to reveal the concept of taking the territory. Let God give you the details you need.

We are about to take another look at the Ites to find further understanding. In particular, we are going to follow three paths that will reveal the outcome of an Ite that is left to mature. Joshua, Samson, and Paul will help fill in the story.

Subdue

The word *subdue* sounds gentle to the untrained ear, but it is a powerful word that reveals a strong course of action *"So Joshua subdued the whole region..."* (Josh. 10:40).

Subdue the whole region—in fact, the whole earth. That is where we are supposed to be headed. We discover in Joshua 13 that Joshua and the Israelites did not subdue the entire Promised Land. They let some Ites hold onto territories God had promised to them. In other words, they forfeited parts of the promise.

Joshua did, however, subdue significant areas, as described in Joshua 10. Subduing territory is a process of subduing people. If you want to subdue somebody, you must first chase them down and capture them. If you are engaged in subduing something, it indicates that you are not currently in charge of it, but are in the process of taking charge.

With Adam and Eve, with Joshua, and now with you, God's theme is the same. *You have not subdued yet, but I want you to.*

Notice that it is not a question, but a command. It works the same way with "Honor your parents." God has not asked us to do this; He has commanded us to honor our parents. Subduing the earth and driving out your Ites are not just promises from God, but commands. These are things we *must* do in order to experience the fullness of our destinies.

Let's take a fresh look at the Ites. Don't gloss over this, because we have not yet squeezed out all of the wisdom in it yet.

> *But if you do not drive out the inhabitants of the land, those you allow to remain will become barbs in your eyes and thorns in your sides...* (Numbers 33:55).

Ites distract us and make it impossible for us to see. When we walk in the promises of God and begin taking territory, we become targets. Satan says, "Uh-oh" and realizes that we have reached a place most Christians do not reach. We seem to be headed toward light, dominion, authority, success, prosperity, and rest. That is contrary to satan's game plan. So, he will try to get you to destroy yourself.

How? He looks for one weakness—one lie that he can get you to believe...one thorn that has been left in your heart that he can use as a gate to come in and steal. Just one. That is all he needs.

The word *remain* in Numbers 13:55 indicates that we have some time to take the land. God is patient with us as we take the territory. His mercy guards us from destruction so that we can address one territory at a time. If we allow one to remain in enemy hands long enough (I don't know how long that is, but in my opinion, it would mean completely ignoring the thorn and choosing to live it), then the devil will start to work overtime.

The self-destruct button will have been pressed. It happened to Samson.

Samson Likes the Women

Samson is one of the judges of Israel, a leader over them as they lay in servitude to the Philistines. He is a powerful man anointed by God to start the deliverance of the people.

"One day Samson went to Gaza, where he saw a prostitute. He went in to spend the night with her" (Judg. 16:1). Gaza is a long way away, about 40 miles. Without a car, that is quite a trip. Furthermore, Gaza is the Philistine capital at this time. Samson is somewhere the Israelites wouldn't be. It is the Las Vegas of Israel—you know, "What happens in Gaza...."

Samson is not exercising a great deal of restraint, which gives us insight into his life: Samson digs the ladies. He has an Ite called *lust*. Like most people, he probably thinks he can hide this thorn. Samson is wrong. His secret life was exposed and documented for all eternity.

Samson is a Nazarite, someone who makes a stringent vow: no haircuts; no wine or grapes in any form; no getting near a dead body, not even when a loved one dies. This vow is part of the person's being separated for the Lord's service (see Num. 6).

Yet, Samson is driven by desire. It caused him to seek out a prostitute, an act out of line with what he was supposed to be doing. He was distracted by a woman.

> *The people of Gaza were told, "Samson is here!" So they surrounded the place and lay in wait for him all night at the city gate. They made no move during the night, saying, "At dawn we'll kill him." But Samson lay there only until the middle of the night. Then he got up and took hold of the doors of the city gate, together with the two posts, and tore them loose, bar and all. He lifted them to his shoulders and carried them to the top of the hill that faces Hebron* (Judges 16:2-3).

Samson escapes. His escape is a picture of Christ being crucified. Jesus, of course, did not sleep with a prostitute, but He took the sins of the world upon Himself when He died on the cross. He carried the cross (with some help) up to the top of a hill and hung on it until He died.

In Matthew 16:18 Jesus said, *"On this rock I will build My church, and the gates of Hades will not overcome it."* The gate at Gaza in Judges 16 represents the gates of hell. Satan wants to keep his gate in your life so he can come and go and destroy things whenever he likes. It's his gate, and he wants to maintain unhindered access to it.

However, Jesus destroyed the gates of hell, symbolizing the destruction of the power of darkness and sin over mankind. Samson's story foreshadows Jesus' sacrifice. Just as Jesus carried His cross, Samson carries the gates and posts to the top of the hill. His problem with women almost gets him killed, but Samson escapes—this time.

The Ite, however, "remains." God, in His mercy, allows Samson to serve Him, despite his sin. Yes, Samson likes the women. We will see shortly how much it would cost him.

Joshua's Treaty With the Gibeonites

In Joshua 9 is a story about a particular group of Ites, the Gibeonites. Joshua and Israel have defeated Jericho and Ai. They are taking territory and gaining a reputation in the neighborhood. In their travels, they run into the Gibeonites, who are actually Hivites from a city called Gibeon.

The Gibeonites appear to have traveled a great distance to meet with Joshua. They are carrying old wine skins and moldy bread. Unfortunately, it is a ruse. These are actually local Ites, living nearby in the Promised Land. They don't want to be on the wrong side of the Israelites, so they tell Joshua, "We are from a distant land. We want a treaty with you because we hear your God is super strong and we don't want to die" (see Josh. 9:6-11).

The Israelites check out the Ites' provisions and are duped. Joshua 9:14 reveals Israel did not check out the travelers' story with the Lord, they simply looked to see if it appeared that these people had traveled from a distant land. So they made the treaty and the leaders of the assembly ratified it by an oath.

The first warning sign should have been the fact that God had specifically instructed Moses never to make a treaty with anyone in the Promised Land (see Exod. 34:12). Yet, Joshua does so. Soon, he discovers that the visitors live up the road. But it's too late. The Israelites have committed allegiance to a bunch of Ites.

What does this story mean to us? It is about the treaties we make with our Gibeonites. These are the thorns we allow to stay in our ground. It is that thing with which you are contending. You know the thing. You decided to live with it and now it is a mature thorn. Eventually, it will become a barb in your eye. Yes, you have some time to deal with it, but not a lifetime.

This particular Ite is key because it is a great deception. The Gibeonites deceive the Israelites, and now the Ites are allowed to remain forever in the land. This was unacceptable to God. He said to drive the Ites out. He knew the Ites would lead His people into idol worship and a mess of other stuff.

The Ites

I must remind you now of something I mentioned before; the peoples inhabiting the land of Canaan represent thorns we may be dealing with For instance, The Hittites represent fear and terror and worry. The Canaanites represent perversion and lust. The Amorites hold a strong position among Christians representing selfish ambition, jealousy, envy, and gossip. The Perrizites and Hivites are village dwellers, indicating extreme poverty. People who have poverty in their hearts will repel wealth and opportunity, even if they are believing God for it. It is a thorn that chokes out the word of prosperity. The name *Jebusite* indicates something worthless, having no value. Many people accomplish very little in their lives because they just don't think they can do anything. There are many more that do this also.

Which Ite is your Gibeonite? Which one will cause you to leave territory unconquered, as in Joshua's case?

> *When Joshua was old and well advanced in years, the Lord said to him, "You are very old, and there are still very large areas of land to be taken over"* (Joshua 13:1).

Joshua did not get the job completely done. Joshua did not lead the people into rest. *"For if Joshua had given them rest, God would not have spoken later about another day"* (Heb. 4:8). Joshua made a treaty with Gibeon.

It is true that the Israelites from this day on would leave God, then return, then leave. They would fall back into slavery and destruction over and over again, led by these other peoples to worship other gods, turning away from the Lord.

> *The angel of the Lord went up from Gilgal to Bokim and said, "I brought you up out of Egypt and led you into the land that I swore to give to your forefathers. I said, 'I will never break My covenant with you, and you shall not make a covenant with the people of this land, but you shall break down their altars.' Yet you have disobeyed Me. Why have you done this? Now therefore I tell you that I will not drive them out before you; they will*

> *be [thorns] in your sides and their gods will be a snare to you"* (Judges 2:1-3).

This outcome is a picture that should motivate us greatly. Don't be discouraged by Israel's failure; instead, be motivated and freed by the truth. The Gibeonite deception was a good one. It was well planned. We face the same kind of enemy. We can be deceived into thinking that everything that happens is just part of who we are. We begin to justify the particular Ite and find ways to define it as something other than sin.

That is what Samson did. It looked like he had escaped the consequences of his Ite, but let's return to his story to see how he is faring with his Gibeonite treaty.

On the surface, Samson has done a good job with his Nazarite vow. He has cherry-picked the portions of his vow that he will obey; he isn't drinking or cutting his hair. Yet, he is missing the larger point. He's been sleeping with a prostitute.

In Judges 16:4, just after his trip to Gaza, Samson *"...fell in love with a woman...whose name was Delilah."* This is not the same girl as the one from the song. This girl is seriously bad news. The devil is now going to exploit Samson's weakness in order to destroy him.

The Philistine rulers offer Delilah 1,100 shekels of silver from each of them if she will help them find the secret to his strength. That is 28 pounds of silver,[1] or just over $6,700 (on the basis of silver trading at $15 per ounce).

We don't know how many Philistines offer Delilah this bounty; we do know that she agreed to their demands. The exact word they used for capturing Samson is *subdue.* Here is where things get confusing. Samson appears to lose his ability to think. *"So Delilah said to Samson, 'Tell me the secret of your great strength and how you can be tied up and subdued'"* (Judg. 16:6).

Samson lies to her, saying: *"If anyone ties me with seven fresh thongs that have not been dried, I'll become as weak as any other man"* (Judg. 16:7).

Delilah hides the Philistine rulers in the room, ties him up, and then yells, *"Samson, the Philistines are upon you"* (Judg. 16:9).

Samson breaks free. Yet, he is so blinded by desire for this woman that he doesn't leave. I can tell you that if the woman I loved were recently caught trying to kill me, I would probably leave. Not Samson. She continues to set him up—twice, then three times. He lies to her each time. On the fourth go-round, Samson explains his Nazirite vows and reveals the importance of his hair. In direct violation of his vows, Delilah cuts Samson's hair.

Samson rendered himself vulnerable, but before we get to the ending of his story, consider Judges 14:5-6. That is when Samson approached some vineyards. This is a picture of drawing near to sin because, for Samson, grapes are forbidden fruit. There a roaring lion attacks him; Samson kills the lion by tearing it apart with his bare hands.

Sometime later, Samson happens by the lion's rotting carcass and finds honey inside it. He proceeds (this is really gross) to scoop honey out of the carcass and eat it (see Judg. 14:6-9). Remember, a Nazarite vows three simple things: no haircuts, no grapes or grape juice or wine, and no being around dead stuff. Eating honey out of a corpse qualifies as a direct violation of the Nazarite vow. Eating honey is the equivalent of cutting your hair.

My point is this: The haircut is not what cost Samson his strength. It was not the violation of the Nazarite vow. If it were, then grapes or being near a dead body would have produced the same results: no strength.

In a moment I will show you in the Scripture what finished off Samson. First let me show you the trap. The devil first tried to kill Samson head to head via the lion attack. Remember that the devil creeps about like a roaring lion, seeking whom he may devour (see 1 Pet. 5:8).

The roaring lion that attacked Samson was defeated. So the devil set a less obvious trap. He thought, "If I can't kill him with a lion, maybe I can destroy him with temptation."

You will remember that honey is a symbol of physical pleasures. God sent us to a land flowing with milk and honey. He wants us to enjoy this earth, but on His terms and according to His principles.

The honey was in the lion's carcass. Samson found the honey, dug it out, and ate it. That was when the devil learned how he could destroy Samson. He learned that Samson could be led into sin by the temptations of sensual pleasure. Samson wasn't supposed to go near dead stuff, but could be lured into it when tempted by something sweet.

In Proverbs 5:3, Solomon describes the adulteress as a woman whose lips drip with honey. This is how satan formulated his trap for Samson. The prostitute thing failed; but Delilah scored. Now hold that thought; we will return to the exciting conclusion of Samson's story in a moment.

First, let's introduce our third character, Paul.

Paul's Journey

Paul was the apostle chosen by God to preach the Gospel to the Gentiles. The man was a radical Jew who killed Christians. That is, until he had a radical encounter with Jesus Christ on the road to Damascus (see Acts 9). Paul (originally named Saul) became a truly radical Christian.

Paul had a journey just like you and me. He was a slave to the law, which can be compared to being in Egypt. He accepted Jesus as the Son of God and was born again in one life-changing moment. Still, Paul had to go through the same steps as the Israelites leaving Egypt.

He was blinded and had to learn to trust solely in God for direction, just as the Israelites had to follow the cloud by day and the pillar of fire by night. Paul couldn't hang out with his old Christian-killing friends anymore. He had to leave them all behind.

Paul had to learn about faith and grace and the wisdom of God, just like we do. He goes out to heal the sick, teach the ways of God, and learn how to serve the Lord. This is his journey. God gives him tremendous revelation—why? Because he is out there doing it. He is walking in his purpose, pulling the Spirit of God upon him in power through the anointing. Paul is making a difference.

You see, it's not so much about what you don't do; it's about what you do! Paul was an amazing man, yet he was still an imperfect vessel. Aren't we all? With that in mind, Paul has something he wants to share with us now; it is a confession.

> *To keep me from becoming conceited because of these surpassingly great revelations, there was given me a thorn in my flesh, a messenger of Satan, to torment me* (2 Corinthians 12:7).

What is this thorn in Paul's flesh? What is he admitting? It is sin; it is an "Ite."

> *Three times I pleaded with the Lord to take it away from me. But He said to me, "My grace is sufficient for you, for My power is made perfect in weakness"...* (2 Corinthians 12:8-9).

There is a great deal of speculation among Christians about Paul's thorn. Is it a sickness? A crippled hand? Bad vision?

Do you want to know what I think? Well, here goes: Paul uses the word *thorn.* God is consistent in His use of metaphors. God's Word is food, bread, manna. The Holy Spirit is fire. Seven days is completion. A thorn is sin.

The apostle Paul, by inspiration of the Holy Spirit, uses the word *thorn* to describe his weakness. He even identifies the delivery method as a being "a messenger of satan." If you are still unsure about this, sit tight. I will explain.

If a person has a headache, what kind of medicine does he take? Advil, maybe Tylenol, or aspirin—headache medicine. It is the right prescription for the ailment. You would obviously not rub Bengay on your elbows if your head were hurting.

God has prescriptions for our needs. Many speculate that Paul's thorn was his eyesight. He couldn't see well. But let's consider God's prescription. God responded to Paul's thorn by saying that His *"grace is sufficient"* (2 Cor. 12:9).

Does God prescribe grace for a sickness? No. God's prescription for sickness is healing. Jesus' prescription for a blind man was to restore his sight. That is *healing.* Grace is a prescription for what? For *sin.*

Everywhere else in the Bible where you see a prescription for sin, it is grace. What was Jesus' prescription for the woman caught in adultery? Grace. Forgiveness.

That makes perfect sense. When Paul talks about his struggle with sin in Romans 7, he described it as something that he didn't want to do, yet kept on doing. *"For what I do is not the good I want to do; no, the evil I do not want to do—this I keep on doing"* (Rom. 7:19).

Paul had such a deep revelation of grace because he was dealing with it firsthand. Why should we be surprised that Paul had sin? Don't we all have sin? Should we think any differently about Paul just because he sinned? Of course not. He was bold enough to put his hand in the air and say, "Hey, I'm working on something right now, not everything is perfect. I have a sin. I know about it."

> *...Therefore I will boast all the more gladly about my weaknesses, so that Christ's power may rest on me. That is why, for Christ's sake, I delight in weaknesses, in insults, in hardships, in persecutions, in difficulties. For when I am weak, then I am strong* (2 Corinthians 12:9-10).

At this moment, we are not looking at the insults, hardships, persecutions, or difficulties, we are looking at the "weakness." And the remedy for this weakness (which is sin in Paul's life) is that Christ will be strong in it. That is the perfect prescription.

We have to partner with Christ, God, the Holy Spirit, as we battle our Ites. We cannot fight them alone through abstinence; instead we battle them with Christ, who sets us free from the desire. The weed is destroyed. So let me engage you with a startling question: Did God allow Paul to serve Him in ministry, to heal the sick, to write much of the Holy Spirit-inspired Word of God while he had sin in his life?

Yes. Of course He did. If God can only use perfect people, then He will get nothing done. But remember that we have been made perfect and holy in Christ! Many Christians are waiting to get their lives cleaned up so they can serve God. Stop waiting. God's grace is sufficient for you!

Are you ready to return to Joshua's story?

Justifying Your Gibeonite

OK. So Joshua and the Israelites have been deceived into making a treaty with a certain group of Ites.

> *Then Joshua summoned the Gibeonites and said, "Why did you deceive us by saying, 'We live a long way from you,' while actually you live near us? You are now under a curse: You will never cease to serve as woodcutters and water carriers for the house of my God"* (Joshua 9:22-23).

This is what we do when we make a treaty with that one special "Ite." We try to find a way for our addiction to serve us. We say, "My anger actually makes me stronger, it motivates me to be better."

When I do this I go beyond mere justification. Instead, I'm rooting the Ite deeper in my heart by giving it a position of service in my life. It's my woodcutter and water carrier. "My pornography addiction actually takes the sexual pressure off of my marriage and my wife, so my marriage is better with this addiction."

"My drinking helps me to relax and get ready for tomorrow's successes." When we go beyond justification and begin identifying with and making room for our Ites, we have reached the second step on our path of destruction. We have found a way that our sin is now benefiting us (but not really).

"I get so jealous because I love her. If I didn't love her, there would be no jealousy." We want to believe the Ite is serving us.

Step two is two-thirds of the way to destruction. The third step is when you live long enough with your Ite that you lose all common sense. You are so blinded by the Ite that you can't see how out of whack things are. You become self-consumed and thoughtless as the desire pushes you past the point of no return.

The devil is no dummy. He knows he only needs one thorn (one Ite) to *remain* long enough in the land to *become* the destroying force. Satan needs it to become a consuming tree of the knowledge of good and evil, so that you will eventually eat of its fruit.

Checkmate.

The devil has patience. He takes his time. He will even help you keep the sin concealed without having any real consequences for as long as possible. He's not out to make a small splash; he wants the whole enchilada.

Which brings us back to Samson.

Samson's Self-Destruct

Delilah fails three times to get Samson to reveal his Nazarite vow. Finally, she lulls him to sleep and has his head shaved (see Judg. 16:19). Then with a room full of Philistine rulers (and 28 pounds of silver per ruler)...

> *She called, "Samson, the Philistines are upon you!" He awoke from his sleep and thought, "I'll go out as before and shake myself free." But he did not know that the Lord had left him* (Judges 16:20).

Samson thinks nothing has changed. He will just do what he always does; shake himself free. Samson himself did not believe that the haircut would make a difference, because it was nothing to do with his hair.

Samson's Ite has finally grown into destruction. Samson had begun to believe in himself instead of God. He was utterly blinded by the Ite. He was not serving the Lord. He was not fighting Philistines. It appears he was just lying around a lot, fooling around with his girlfriend. Utterly distracted, off course, out of service, out of purpose—yet feeling invincible.

Now the Philistines can subdue him.

When David sinned with Bathsheba his response was to plead, *"Do not take Your Holy Spirit from me"* (Ps. 51:11). By contrast, Samson had become so numb to God that he didn't even realize God had left him.

The Philistine rulers gouged out his eyes and took him to Gaza (see Judg. 16:21). Samson had one final act of strength. The Lord returned to him and he tore down the pillars of a building, killing a thousand Philistine rulers (see Judg. 16:30). Still, this was not God's ending for Samson's life. This was not God's plan. Samson's eyes were gouged out because his sin had become a barb in his eye. He couldn't see or produce the unseen anymore. He was immersed in his Ite, producing no fruit for the Lord.

This is a perfect metaphor of bringing the unseen, spiritual realm into the seen, physical realm. In this case though, he moved the tree of destruction from his heart and into the physical world.

Wasn't God's grace sufficient? Yes. God's grace means that He loves us despite our sin. God's mercy is different. God gives mercy to whom He gives mercy (see Exod. 33:19). Mercy is God's allowing you to continue to serve despite your sin. Mercy can run out, my friend.

> *Land that drinks in the rain often falling on it and that produces a crop useful to those for whom it is farmed receives the blessing of God. But land that produces thorns and thistles is worthless and is in danger of being cursed. In the end it will be burned* (Hebrews 6:7-8).

Being burned here doesn't refer to hell or eternal damnation. A field is burned in order to restore it to productivity. The burning means everything that you have grown will be lost. A man with lust is finally consumed with it and caught. His wife divorces him. Fifteen years of marriage and his children will be kissed to bed at night by another man. The things that are important to happiness are gone.

And for what? Some desire you let take hold of your heart and blind you. All that you built has been burned to the ground, in the hopes that you may yet find a way to become productive.

We need some happiness about now, so let's get back to Paul.

Paul Gets Free

> *For the grace of God that brings salvation has appeared to all men. It teaches us to say "No" to ungodliness and worldly passions, and to live self-controlled, upright and godly lives in this present age...* (Titus 2:11-12).

Paul wrote this letter to Titus later in life. I do not know exactly how old he was. Most Bible scholars agree that it was within a few years of his death.

Just before 64 A.D. Paul overcame his Ite and he now shares the key of wisdom from the other side of the struggle. It was exactly what God had shared with him earlier when God said, "My grace is sufficient...."

Paul explains that grace is the teacher. It teaches us to say, "No" to ungodliness and worldly passions. Ungodliness is to live in lack. But when we live in godliness, our days are full of life and resources. God's supply does not run out.

So how does grace teach us? Well, it is another way of saying what I already said. Grace is the realization that sin cannot separate us from God. As a result, we employ the power of God to help us overcome sinful desires.

You might say, "Yeah, but God left Samson over his sin." Sure, but there are important differences between his covenant and ours. The Spirit of the Lord that was *upon* Samson left him. We have the Spirit *in* us. God has now promised, because of Christ's sacrifice, that He will never leave us nor forsake us. You can have the Spirit upon you as you pull the power down through your purpose to serve God. If you are just lying around sleeping with your girlfriend, you aren't walking in any purpose at all.

Also, make no mistake, a fully mature and unopposed thorn in your life can consume you and bring you to destruction. If we ignore the teacher (grace) long enough, that is our fate.

There are many prominent Christian leaders who were accomplishing great things for the Lord, but whose lives ended in destruction. All that they had built was burned. God's blessing and favor remained on them as they produced fruit, but over time, the thorn that remained became a barb in the eye.

The self-destruct button fired.

Then, when the minister falls, the whole world says, "See, Christianity doesn't work. These people are all fakes."

No. They are just people, like you and me. King David, a man after God's own heart, committed adultery and murder. Solomon entered the rest of the Lord, but his wives led him into worshiping other gods. Both of these people made substantial contributions to God's Word. They were mighty men of God—good people, trying to deal with sin. But we have a new teacher, one called grace!

Allow grace to teach you. Employ God. Don't make a treaty with an Ite. Ever.

Defeating Gibeonites

Do you want to be free of your Ite, but feel you are losing the battle? Do some of the stories we have discussed resonate with your life? If so, listen carefully: If you continue your alliance with your Gibeonite, you will have your field slashed and burned. God cannot be mocked; sowing and reaping are in effect in the Promised Land. He is most merciful. Sin, however, has consequences.

Be smarter than satan. He will help you hide sin so that he can spring the consequences upon you when they can do the most damage. So, how do you defeat his strategy? Here are some effective ways to head him off:

1. Let your motto be: *"Lead* [me] *not into temptation"* and ask the Lord to do exactly what Jesus told us to pray: *"deliver us from evil"* (Matt. 6:13). Remove all temptation from your life and realize that asking the Lord's help is necessary. You cannot defeat it, but He can. Remember that the power of grace is going to be key, so don't let your sin separate you from God. That is why the Israelites needed the Lord with them to win the battles in the Promised Land. Shine the light on sin: Tell Jesus about your struggle. Get it out in the open. Sin has power as long as we hide it. Every time the thought comes up let it remind you to pray to God for deliverance. Then tell your body NO.

2. Fast: Fasting breaks the strongholds of the enemy in your flesh by reminding the flesh who is actually in charge. Skip some meals. When Jesus went into the Wilderness to be tempted by satan, He fasted. Some of the temptations in your life were in place at your birth. They came from an ancestor—a dad or grandfather, etc. That's right, we get traits such as hair color, height, eye color, talents, and abilities from parents and—oh, yes—we also get their sins. In fact, sin increases from generation to generation. Scripture tells us, for instance, that the sin of the Amorites had not yet reached its full measure in Abraham's day (see Gen. 15:16). Science shows us time and again that kids who have never met their alcoholic parents often end up as alcoholics. Weird. This goes back to your "motto," above: if you can break the temptation off of your life, your kids will not have to deal with it. Identify the Ite that you and God are attacking; then go on a fast.

3. "Eat" your daily bread: Being in the Word a little bit every day can be the influence you need to make it past your temptation for the entire day. Remember that some of what you are struggling

with is a "habit." Defeating a habit means not engaging in it for 21 to 40 days. Church every week and the Bible every day can be just the trick to making it past that habit-breaking landmark.

Chapter 18

Using Your Good Ol'-Fashioned Horse Cents

GOD'S WORD IS WAITING to produce fruit in you. As you take more territory, that Word has more opportunity to grow and produce in your life.

The Promised Land and fighting; this is our current location, but not our destination. Our destination is to enter the rest of Lord; to subdue the earth; to find ourselves in the position to administer justice as rulers.

For now, we are still in the fight to defeat the Ites.

Promised Land Enemy No. 2

In Chapter 16, we briefly touched on the most important and strongest of all the traps satan sets for us:

> *...the deceitfulness of wealth and the desires for other things come in and choke the word, making it unfruitful"* (Mark 4:19).

Now we are ready to fully expose and defeat this formidable enemy. Remember that Promised Land Enemy No. 1 is the enemy within: the Ites. This second enemy undermines our beliefs about provision. It is the primary argument supporting the fallacy that God does not want us to be wealthy or even to take the Promised Land.

This enemy has triumphed over Christians too often. It has kept them wandering in the Wilderness, believing that the Promised Land must not be from God. The argument is, "Well, look what the place does to people. You get your hands bloodied in the Promised Land. That can't be God." The name of this enemy: Greed.

So, how do we beat this enemy in our thinking?

Let's go back to when Moses first prepared to enter the Promised Land, before the 40 years of wandering in the Wilderness. The Tabernacle had just been completed and Israel is celebrating the Passover Feast. This is the year after they left Egypt and Moses has sent in spies to check out the land (see Num. 13). There were 12 spies in all: one from each tribe.

The spies return with a bad report of the land advising the Israelites not to cross over. They admit it is a great land flowing with milk and honey, but feel it is too scary to try and take it. Here is an excerpt of their report:

> *And they spread among the Israelites a bad report about the land they had explored. They said, "The land we explored devours those living in it..."* (Numbers 13:32).

The key clause is: *"The land we explored devours those living in it."* According to 10 of the 12 spies, the land—the good land God promised them—is devouring people. The Promised Land itself has become the trap. I've seen it happen in Christianity way too often. Throughout the Book of Judges, the Israelites show us the pattern for Trap No. 2 in the Promised Land. Here is how it goes:

1. God blesses the Israelites; they get wealthy.

2. They leave God and start worshiping Molech (or some other god).

3. Everything falls apart for them and another nation begins to rule them.

4. A godly leader comes along; the people repent and turn back to God.

5. Rinse and repeat. The cycle starts all over again.

The land devours those living in it. Israel eventually found herself locked into this cycle. God had warned about it during Israel's Wilderness days:

> *And the Lord said to Moses: "You are going to rest with your fathers, and these people will soon prostitute themselves to the foreign gods of the land they are entering. They will forsake Me and break the covenant I made with them"* (Deuteronomy 31:16).

God knew that once they got into the Promised Land they would leave Him. He had Moses prepare a song for the people as a witness to them. In the song is a better description of why they would leave:

> *He* [God] *made him* [Israel] *ride on the heights of the land and fed him with the fruit of the fields. He nourished him with honey from the rock, and with oil from the flinty crag, with curds and milk from herd and flock and with fattened lambs and goats, with choice rams of Bashan and the finest kernels of wheat. You drank the foaming blood of the grape. Jeshurun* [Israel] *grew fat and kicked; filled with food, he became heavy and sleek. He abandoned the God who made him and rejected the Rock his Savior* (Deuteronomy 32:13-15).

The blessings of the land devoured the people. They did not have the advantage we have; Jesus had not yet defeated the power of darkness. We have the benefit of the finished work of the cross; we should be able to break this pattern, but it remains rooted in Christianity.

I teach the message of the promises at my home church. My theme is: The inheritance is for you. I can tell you firsthand that scores of Christians receive the blessing and are suddenly gone from church. A few years later, I hear the awful story of how they were broken and destroyed.

The land devours some of those who inhabit it. Wealth, which should bless, becomes a dangerous tool of the enemy. It becomes a counterfeit for trusting in God. Wealthy people can purchase their way out of many problems and crises. They can sleep through the storms, not because they assert their authority over them, but because they can afford to ride out storms with big, quiet boats and earplugs.

If someone gets sick, the wealthy can get the best doctors. Wealth becomes something in which you invest your faith. People typically seek God because they need Him. In the Promised Land, as life gets better and better, and the promises become more and more activated in our lives, that need seems less pressing. Those fervent prayers start to disappear. Time in the Word becomes a distant memory. We miss church because we are traveling again.

The blessings themselves can become the trap that lures you into drifting from the Lord.

Most Christians who stand at the edge of the Wilderness and peer into the amazing Promised Land will say, "Not me, Jason. I won't lose sight of God as He blesses me. I won't leave Him."

Yeah, that's what Peter said to Jesus when He prophesied the scattering of His disciples during the crucifixion. He foretold how Peter would deny even knowing Christ three times before the rooster crowed (see Matt. 26:31-34).

"Not me Jesus. I won't leave You," vowed Peter (see Matt. 26:35). Sure, our intentions are good, but we need to have more than good intentions; we need to prepare ourselves to avoid this trap. We need to understand it, and have a strategy so that we don't end up shipwrecked on the island of "IdontneedGodatos." (Yes, I made that up.)

We've all heard stories about lottery winners. Take the man who is struggling to make ends meet; he's a good husband and father, maybe even a Christian. One day, he buys a lottery ticket. And ya-hoo, he wins millions of dollars.

What is the rest of the story? What is the happy ending of this man's life? Often, he goes broke and loses his family. Don't get me wrong: the promises of God are not like Lotto. They are inherited through faith and patience, which means they are fulfilled over a span of time.

If you have a rich grandfather who is going to leave you everything when he dies, you may be torn. Do you want Grandpa to live? Of course you do. Are you excited about all that moola? Heck, yeah.

Well, God has a lot more wealth than Grandpa does and you don't have to wait for God to die. In the Bible days, a son could receive his inheritance before his father's death. Jesus said this is like the Kingdom of God. He tells a story about a son who gets his inheritance from his father, who is alive and well:

> *Jesus continued: "There was a man who had two sons. The younger one said to his father, 'Father, give me my share of the estate.' So he divided his property between them"* (Luke 15:11-12).

A couple of kids are living with Dad, and one of them asks for his inheritance now. This is a picture of what is available to us. Many Christians wait until they die, but we don't have to wait. It is available now. God, in fact, would rather you receive it now so that you will use your authority and fulfill your destiny in the earth.

You approach God by grace (which says that you qualify) and faith (which is your belief that God can and wants to bless you). This is how you ask the Lord for your inheritance. By faith you receive the promises of God into your life. They are planted in your heart so they will grow up and produce fruit. When that fruit is eaten, the promises will manifest physically as divine health, a Kingdom marriage, and more money than you need so that you can bless others and accomplish whatever tasks God has placed in front of you.

The story of the two sons gives clues about our lives. Know this: we don't have to do what the first son did. In his story, the inheritance seemed to include only money. Your inheritance is not, of course, just money, although money is part of it.

> *Not long after that, the younger son got together all he had, set off for a distant country and there squandered his wealth in wild living* (Luke 15:13).

You will notice that the younger son hung out with his dad for a bit. This is God's plan. We do not receive our inheritance just so we can move out. We are encouraged to stay. In fact, this son's departure is a picture of his leaving a godly life. He leaves the will of the Lord and the purpose for which God created him.

What caused him to leave? The money. The inheritance. Some might say, "Well then, God isn't going to give you your inheritance if you are just going to go use it to sin."

Yes He is. God desires to bless you. He doesn't want these blessings to be a snare to you, although they might be. That part is your responsibility. The blessings can either help you accomplish the things of God or usher you headlong into selfish desires. You choose.

Of course God blesses you. Blessing is the free gift granted to a child of the king. It is a gift, not something you earn.

Yet, the very blessing of God can devour you if your heart is not right. The young son in the parable does what the Israelites do. When he is broken and defeated he returns to God humbled. And God says, "Hey, too late Bozo. You blew it."

Right?

Wrong. That isn't our God. The young man's father throws a party the day his son returns. Then he gives him another inheritance. That is a picture of our heavenly Father. So, does that mean that you should go and sin some more? Well, you can try that approach out if you want to. Let me know how that works out for you. (Smile.)

Here is my advice: don't ever use God's principles or blessings to mock Him.

Resources for You and for Others

The inheritance is a resource for you. Resources are tools. When life is good, the marriage is rocking, finances are ticking upward, your energy and health are humming along, you find yourself ready to serve with diligence and skill.

If Moses had been sick in bed, how would he have led anyone anywhere? If you believe God put you in the hospital to minister to someone who was dying, then you do not understand God's ways. You can go to the hospital and minister to the sick without being sick. They have visiting hours.

When you are feeling great and your bills are paid and success and favor are everywhere, you are in a great position to serve—but only if you avoid the deceitfulness of riches. That trap tells you that you don't need the Word today. You skip the daily bread that helped get you to the Promised Land. You're no longer hungry for God. You don't need Him this week.

That is the ultimate trap!

It is amazing to see how all of us cry out to God when crisis hits. Oh, yeah, now we need Him. We will strip our lives down to what matters and lay broken before Him. That is good, but misses God's larger point. You see, Promised Land dwelling is a learning process with a mission. There we discover that God is not just for me, He is for others.

If our inheritance is just for us, then we are already in the trap, ensnared by the devouring force. I have a Bible that is about denying self and empowering others. In the Wilderness, we don't have enough to help anyone but ourselves. In the Promised Land, we have more than we can contain.

What are you to do with the overflow? Who is it for? God told Abraham he would be a blessing to others (see Gen. 12:2). This is the path toward subduing the earth. We have plenty of rulers who are motivated by self. God is seeking a rulership that is motivated to help others, bring justice to the land, rule with God's principles, and bring His will onto the earth.

Me, Me, Mine

The promises of God can start to look like me, mine, and more for me. Spoiled brat syndrome. It's like some rich kids who had everything all their lives. For some reason, some of them feel as though everyone owes them something.

All of this can lead right into greed. Greed is when I hurt others to help myself. Greed means believing not only that the promises of God are for me, but that other peoples' promises are mine, too. "Hey, invest in my business. It will be good for both of us…I think."

I'm becoming the enemy. I hide it from myself through justification, reasoning that others will be blessed through me. Greed is the exact opposite of the promises of God. It is using other people's resources to benefit myself. I can still sleep at night because I pretend it is for them as well. I see a Dooney and Bourke purse attached to a person. Instead of focusing on the person, I'm targeting her dollars.

Yes, Christians live here as well.

Wealth Warnings

Much of the Christian world frowns upon wealth. Of course, so do Hitler and communism. A disdain for personal wealth is a fundamental tenet of socialism.

The reason these views exist is because wealth destroys many people and some wealthy people are greedy. That is fact. Yet, man's perversion of God's promises does not negate the truth of Scripture. Money is not evil. It is incapable of being evil. *"The* ***love of money*** *is a root of all kinds of evil"* (1 Tim. 6:10). Money itself is not evil. Money is a tool. Loving it, however, is a serious problem. I eat food to stay healthy, but I do not love my fork and plate. They are just tools.

I'm going to introduce some Scriptures that caution us in regard to wealth. I want to make sure you are aware that you cannot use one Scripture to negate another Scripture. All Scripture is true. The Bible is incapable of contradicting itself. If there appears to be a contradiction, it is because we do not understand the Word.

> *If anyone teaches false doctrines and does not agree to the sound instruction of our Lord Jesus Christ and to godly teaching, he is conceited and understands nothing. He has an unhealthy interest in controversies and quarrels about words that result in envy, strife, malicious talk, evil suspicions and constant friction between men of corrupt mind, who have been robbed of the truth and* ***who think that godliness is a means to financial gain*** (1 Timothy 6:3-5).

The corrupt person uses godliness as a tool to get wealthy, instead of using the blessings of wealth as tools to expand the Kingdom. Godliness is not a tool! Wealth is not a goal!

Again we must ask ourselves the *why* behind our actions. There is certainly nothing wrong with godliness. We are to be imitators of God, who is wealthy. Yet, the street outside my house is paved with asphalt, the cheapest possible drivable surface. Why is the cheapest material used? Because it takes a lot of asphalt to pave a road.

What does God use for roads? Gold. In religion, that is a waste. The religious person will complain that the gold should have been used to help the poor. That reasoning almost seems to make sense. Yet, the problem God is pointing out in our passage from First Timothy 6 is that godliness can be misused for the sole purpose of becoming wealthy. It's a problem of me... me...and mine.

The purpose of the blessing is Kingdom expansion here on earth and destiny fulfillment for God's people. Blessing positions us to influence this world, conqueror nations, and administer justice.

Paul goes on to say:

> *Godliness with contentment is great gain. For we brought nothing into the world, and we can take nothing out of it. But if we have food and clothing, we will be content with that. People who want to get rich fall into temptation and a trap and into many foolish and harmful desires that plunge men into ruin and destruction* (1 Timothy 6:6-9).

Godliness will bring you wealth, but we must add that wealth to contentment. Contentment will allow me to keep wealth in check and treat it as a tool. Jesus told me not to store up wealth in a barn or to store things where moth and rust destroy (see Matt. 6:19). What kind of stuff do we have that we don't need?

After a teaching, a man asked me whether having ATVs for him and his family to ride once in a while qualifies as an example of a stash that moth and rust will destroy. The answer is *no*. He is using the quads as tools to build memories with his family. He is raising his kids and spending time with them. This is not storing. That is giving.

The key to Paul's caution begins with the idea of storing something that is not being used. Next it is the kind of item that loses value over time. Moth and rust are eating it. Sell it on craigslist and give the money to the Church and the poor.

Here in First Timothy we learn that we can't take our toys into eternity with us. We need to put our wealth and resources to work here on earth. It's like the parable of talents. The one who buried the money got in trouble; the ones who put the talents to work were commended. We should not strive to work for money, but instead put money to work for us.

I'm not saying that everyone has to be wealthy to accomplish his or her destiny. Just know that money is a resource and resources are not inherently evil. Instead, they are the result of godliness. God wants you to have the resources you need to accomplish your God-given destiny. John the Baptist is not a sinner for not being rich; neither is Abraham a sinner for being wealthy. The purpose of your resources dictates the outcome in your life.

Now let's go back in our minds to our time in the Wilderness. Remember that God was looking for people who were willing to serve and willing to give in order to build His house. Their experience was designed to develop in them the strength to resist the temptation to abuse their wealth. Their story teaches us the same lesson.

You might recall that their participation in building the Tabernacle was not a requirement. Although all were encouraged to learn the lesson, not everyone did. God did not command them to give to His house; it was a free choice. When we make the choice to give into God's house, it develops in our hearts increased strength to defend against the deceitfulness of wealth.

Greed and Idolatry

The ten spies noticed that the Promised Land devoured the people living there. God warned that the blessings would lead them to worship other gods, which was considered by God to be a form of spiritual prostitution.

In Deuteronomy 31:16, God said that the Israelites would soon prostitute themselves to other gods. He said they would sell themselves to become part of these other gods. Worship here indicates an intimacy at the sexual level, which is the highest form of intimacy. That's why he used the word "prostitute" as an adjective to describe what the Israelites would do.

Sex can be emotional, physical, and intellectual. In a Kingdom marriage, it is all three. The highest form of intimacy also indicates the highest form of trust. The giving of oneself to another is predicated on trust. I have to trust you before I can take off all of my clothes and turn down the lights. Without my clothes, I feel vulnerable.

Idolatry is our worship, and therefore our trust, in something other than God. Money is a great false idol, because people trust in it for answers to their problems. Money is just a tool that God gives us, but people can lose sight of money's source and see the money itself as their source.

Colossians 3:5 states clearly that evil desires and greed are the sin of idolatry. You don't have to have a golden calf; your idol can be your brokerage firm or the business you build. You can go to bed at night thinking of more ways to gain wealth for yourself. It is perfectly OK for you and the Lord to work on ways to bring in more money for the Kingdom; but if you are only seeking more for yourself, then you may be worshiping the mighty dollar.

Even the dollar bill is smarter than that. Look on the back of it. What does it say?

"In God We *Trust*."

If a nation as morally whacked out as ours recognizes who is worthy of our trust, shouldn't we?

Defeating Greed

Tithes and offerings to the Lord are for the purpose of building the Kingdom of God. Troubling as it may sound, you can tithe and give offerings with the purpose of gaining wealth and therefore remain in greed.

There is a fine line I must walk as I discuss this. We should expect our tithing and giving of offerings to produce wealth in our lives. This is our faith in God's Word. He promised it and we believe the promise.

However, if I am using the principles of God just so I can get more stuff, I am using godliness as a means for selfish financial gain. I need to change my heart, but how?

In Luke 11, Jesus gives us the same clue He gives many times when dealing with greed. Here He addresses the Pharisees who are *"full of greed and wickedness"* (Luke 11:39). In verse 42, He does note though that the

Pharisees are tithers. Yet, they are greedy. They are using godliness as a means to gain wealth. Jesus' solution for the Pharisees is this: *"Give what is inside the dish [what you have] to the poor, and everything will be clean for you"* (Luke 11:41).

Jesus' remedy for greed is to give it all to the poor. To the rich man in Mark 10, Jesus said, *"Sell it all. Give some to the poor. Then follow Me"* (see Mark 10:21).

The greedy man will despise the poor in his heart. Giving to the poor is a direct attack against that attitude. Greed cannot live if you have given it all away.

All of this giving may sound like a high price, but what will a man give in exchange for his soul? This doesn't mean that a person is eternally damned to fire for not giving. It simply means that the act of giving can free you of greed.

Here is another question to ask yourself: Would you be content if you had nothing, materially speaking? You sure would have to trust in the Lord, wouldn't you? You would be left with God and only God. It would feel a lot like being nailed to the cross. This is a difficult thing to do. When Jesus told the rich man to sell everything and give the money away, the man walked away from Jesus saddened. He made his decision. Yet, I wonder how much more wealth he might have acquired had he followed Jesus' instruction.

The difference between this man and us is the fact that he was not yet saved. We are born again. He was rich without God's blessing. The hole in an unsaved rich person's heart can be medicated; but it will not be healed. There will always be a lack of fulfillment, an emptiness within because resources are not being used for their intended purpose: to bring God's will in the earth.

Blessings are tools to help us subdue the earth. Jesus asked the rich man to put his money to work on behalf of the Kingdom of God. He received a personal invitation to follow Christ. He was shown the value of a willingness to give!

Many people will see the exchange between Jesus and the rich man and conclude that God is anti-wealth. That is impossible. If that were true then God is confused, and we know that God is not confused. His Word is true. Remember: Anytime it seems that God's Word is contradicting itself, then we are misunderstanding something. It would be the equivalent of saying that anyone who wants healing must wash himself in the Jordan River seven times. That was the solution for one man (see 2 Kings 5:10). Jesus only asked certain people to give away their material wealth. (Of course, if God is calling you to give it all away and you obey Him, then you are going to end up with a lot more than you ever had!)

Jesus asked those who were dealing with greed to part with their wealth. It is a picture of the solution we need when greed creeps into our hearts.

The Right Attitude of Wealth

We have been dealing with the subject of wealth in this book for some time now. I keep reminding you that the promises of God are resources. They are tools to assist in achieving your destiny, which is to subdue the earth and be a just, selfless, and loving ruler who influences the world and expands the Kingdom of God according to His will. (Whew, say that in one breath.)

We have now identified a great trap called *greed.* Identifying the trap disarms its power. Focusing on the problem, however, is not God's plan. So let me show you a better way.

We are all familiar with Matthew 6:33 which talks about seeking first the Kingdom of God and His righteousness and having all the other "stuff" added to us because we sought Him first.

The caution here is: Don't seek first the Kingdom of God so that you get the other things. Seek first the Kingdom of God because it is your destiny in Christ and it will bring you true fulfillment.

For example, a person who struggles in tithing has misunderstood his relationship with God. He does not understand the purpose of this life or

God's purpose for mankind. Hopefully, he will obey regardless of this understanding, because obedience will help him grow in this area of wisdom.

Remember that we don't want to be sin conscious, always focused on what we shouldn't do. Instead, we need to focus on what we should do. That is the posture of looking toward the finish line. David, a man after God's own heart, understood this. If you can get your head around this concept, you will avoid the trap of greed altogether and find yourself stepping into the fourth phase of our journey which is the rest of the Lord.

Hear what David said: *"For the sake of the house of the Lord our God, I will seek your prosperity"* (Ps. 122:9).

King David was raising money so that his son could build the house of the Lord. David wasn't afraid to seek prosperity because he understood its purpose. He wasn't lying awake at night trying to figure out how to get more money, because the money was not for him, it was for God.

David believed that the house of the Lord should be a great and awesome house. At that time other nations made tremendous temples for their gods and filled them with treasures. David had much more in mind for the living God.

> *David said, "My son Solomon is young and inexperienced, and the house to be built for the Lord should be of great magnificence and fame and splendor in the sight of all the nations. Therefore I will make preparations for it"...* (1 Chronicles 22:5).

If you have ever walked into a church and thought to yourself, "They should not have spent so much money on making this place look nice," then you have some weeds to uproot. David is showing us the better way: to desire that the house of the Lord be magnificent. It needs to be spreading the Word to the world.

I was at the main office of NBC Universal, the media and communications giant that owns a large percentage of the music and movie industry. The place was enormous and beautiful, fully staffed, and seemingly fully funded. NBC Universal brings its message to the entire world every day.

That message is not the Word of God. We are the Church. The Word of God is our message.

Still, the Body of Christ does not have the funding to accomplish our calling—at least not yet (grin). If we want to change America, we have to change Americans. Only the Church has the tools to do this. We are the dispensation system for the Word of God.

David recognized this in his lifetime; he knew that his focus on building the Kingdom of God could change the world—not only influencing the people of Israel, but the other nations that would see the Lord's splendor and fame. What was the result? After the building of the Temple, Israel reached its golden age. It was Israel's wealthiest and most influential period in history. Peace reigned. Kings traveled from afar to listen to Solomon. Silver was so common that it had no value. David reaped what he sowed. David took the Promised Land. From the time he became king until the day he handed the kingdom to Solomon, he more than tripled the size of the nation of Israel. Yes, David took territory and gave money. He was seeking prosperity for the sake of the House of the Lord:

> *King David dedicated these articles to the Lord, as he had done with the silver and gold he had taken from all these nations: Edom and Moab, the Ammonites and the Philistines, and Amalek* (1 Chronicles 18:11).

As David took the territory he gave to the Lord not just the spoils from the first nation he subdued, but five nations. David was on a mission to build the Kingdom of God. He was battled, risked his life, and then gave all of the gold, silver, and bronze to the Lord. Battle after battle, victory after victory, David took territory for the expansion of the Kingdom of God—and gave to God from his personal treasury as well.

> *Besides, in my devotion to the temple of my God I now give my personal treasures of gold and silver for the temple of my God, over and above everything I have provided for this holy temple: three thousand talents of gold (gold of Ophir) and seven thousand talents of refined silver, for the overlaying of the walls of the*

> *buildings, for the gold work and the silver work, and for all the work to be done by the craftsmen. Now, who is willing to consecrate himself today to the Lord?* (1 Chronicles 29:3-5)

Let me put this into today's dollars. It was 100 tons of gold and 260 tons of silver. There are 32,000 ounces in a ton. At the time I write this gold goes for $925.44 per ounce and silver is $13.14 per ounce. The total dollar value today is $3,070,732,800. More than $3 billion! Was David blessed? Did he probably have a nice palace? Dress nicely? Own a nice chariot? All these things the Lord gave him, blessing him with more than he could contain.

This is God's promise for you as well.

The blessing is a free gift, and what you do with it is a free choice. Your choice determines your future. Choose wisely.

Part 4

The Rest

Chapter 19

Holding on to Win With Both Hands

Some are quick to point the finger at God and say, "How can I serve a God who allows so much death and suffering?"

The truth of the matter is that we are not stewarding His creation the way He expects us to do. He has left us in charge; He asked us to subdue and tend this planet.

"Huh?" you ask. Well, don't shout me down just yet. Let me finish my thought: *"The heaven, even the heavens, are the Lord's: but the earth hath He given to the children of men"* (Ps. 115:16 KJV).

God has done a fabulous job of managing the heavens. Streets are clean and shiny. The earth is a bit messier. This is not God's fault. God has given us the earth to manage. We are accountable for the mess in this world and we have the authority and power in Jesus' name to fix it! We cannot blame God.

Here's how this stewardship thing works. The other day, my son mentioned to me that his room was a mess. I can just see him discussing this with his friends.

"Hey, Ted, my room is a mess. Why would my dad let my room get so dang messy? My socks are on the floor. My bed isn't made. It's starting to smell and everything. To tell you the truth, Ted, I don't know if I want to know a dad who would let my room get into this condition. Maybe my dad doesn't even exist."

You can see how ludicrous this argument sounds. When my son said his room was messy, I told him to go and clean it up! Of course, he can ask me to help him do it, but it's his room. The house is mine and everything in the house is mine, but I have given that room to my son. If it is falling apart, he is the responsible party.

We live in a world that points its finger at God whenever destruction occurs. Mankind gives itself credit for the world's successes, yet blames God for its failures. It is God's desire for us to have a clean world. It is His will and He is the ultimate authority, He is almighty, but has delegated roles to us. He needs us to help get His will done! We need to step up to our places as rulers and influencers.

Obviously, He is God. If we don't do our part—well, He can even raise up the rocks and stones to do His will. But God has created a system in which we are so very important, even necessary. If He didn't need a man to lead the Israelites out of Egypt, He would not have commissioned Moses.

We need to allow the life of Christ that is in us to bring us to the place of influence we were created to occupy. That life must become the light that drives back the darkness. God has asked us to put our light on a hill! We need to take godly influence to the high places in this world so that our voices can be heard. Then we can accomplish God's will with more force, bringing the earth in line with the way it is in Heaven. We are on our way to doing this, but we have much to learn. We've been from Egypt, through the Wilderness, and into the Promised Land. Now what? Well we better pull out the old map and see.

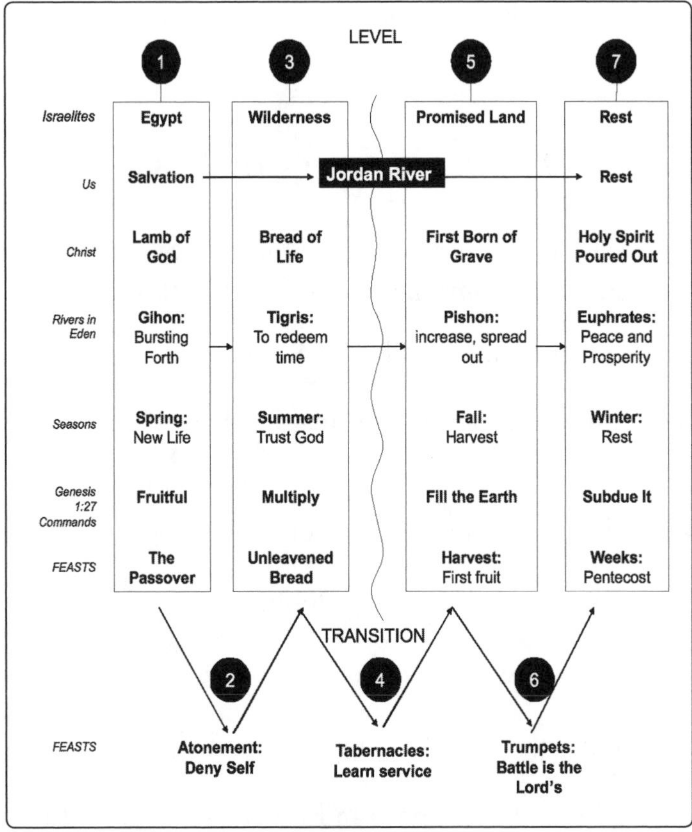

[Figure 1]

We are now entering the fourth stage (and seventh step) of the Christian life. On the seventh day, the Lord rested (see Gen. 2:2). We cannot skip the earlier steps and waltz into the rest. It has been a process of preparing our hearts for the fullness of God's promise.

Notice on the map that during Pentecost the Holy Spirit came upon the 120 people in the Upper Room. In the Place of Rest, you realize that when you walk in the purposes of the Lord, the Holy Spirit is upon you constantly. It is no mystery that very few make it to this place, even though it is attainable by all.

Notice, also, that we are in the winter season of our Christianity—the time when the farmer rests and the barn is full of food. The coinciding river in the Garden of Eden is the Euphrates, which means peace and prosperity. Peace is rest.

The Attributes of Rest

What are some other characteristics of rest? Let's explore the following attributes as exhibited in someone who has reached this stage.

The person experiencing the Place of Rest:

1. Engages in the cycles of planting and harvest in the things of God.
2. Exemplifies strong, immovable faith and is highly focused.
3. Understands God's ways and exhibits great wisdom.
4. Realizes that blessings are tools for expanding God's Kingdom.
5. Is demonstrably blessed in many areas of life.
6. Is living his or her purpose and experiencing glory (his or her name is great).
7. Rules the territory justly and is a respected influencer of many people.

It is rare to find these seven attributes active in someone's life. They are our destination, and I believe you and I will get there!

Transition to the Seventh Step

To get from the Promised Land to the Place of Rest we must take the transitional sixth step, the Feast of Trumpets, commanded by God of the Israelites.

> *The Lord said to Moses, "Say to the Israelites: 'On the first day of the seventh month you are to have a day of rest, a sacred assembly commemorated with trumpet blasts. Do no regular work, but present an offering made to the Lord by fire'"* (Leviticus 23:23-25).

It is the seventh month and we are approaching our seventh step. This is the day of rest, as mentioned in Hebrews. The Lord calls the day of rest *today* (see Heb. 3).

Let's search out the details.

The significance of trumpets to the Israelites is important. What do trumpets mean to us? A high school band? Football game? The song played after someone dies in a Bugs Bunny cartoon?

To the Israelites, the trumpet was a war cry. If a nation attacked or any kind of war was fought, they would blow a trumpet. It was the signal to assemble the army from your town. They didn't have a draft or email reminders; there was no intercom system, either. Trumpets worked nicely, however, to call out the troops.

Trumpets were important to Israel's warriors, even the reluctant ones.

Gideon

Gideon was just such a warrior. He answered the call, but wondered what God saw in him. Before we study his battle fully, let's glance at the battle's aftermath.

Israel had been attacked by Midian and suffered seven years of Midianite oppression. God did an awesome work to free His people. After Gideon's victorious campaign, Israel enjoyed peace:

> *Thus Midian was subdued before the Israelites and did not raise its head again. During Gideon's lifetime, the land enjoyed peace forty years* (Judges 8:28).

Forty years of peace seems to be the going rate. This is exactly how long King Solomon enjoyed peace. Peace is rest from your enemies. It is *shalom,* which means rest and prosperity, nothing missing and nothing broken.

Unlike Joshua, Gideon had just one battle to fight (and yes, trumpets were involved). Looking back over the journey, we find a pattern of generations going from Egypt to rest. We know that Moses' father was a slave in Egypt, but Moses led the people to the Wilderness. Joshua was Moses' assistant and later led the people to the Promised Land, the place of warfare. Gideon was the one who showed us the picture of rest. Another pattern shown to us later, King Saul was a picture of the Wilderness; he was under the law. When Saul disobeyed God, the kingdom was ripped from his hands and given to David. King David's reign was a picture of the Promised Land and warfare. David took a great deal of territory for the kingdom. Even when David sinned, God forgave him. He was operating in mercy. Solomon, then, was the picture of Rest. Do you see the pattern?

Now Gideon will lead the people to the Place of Rest. This part of the journey was later represented by King Solomon who reigned in peace after his father ruled through war.

Just how did Gideon lead Israel into rest and what does this story mean to us? To answer that question, we must first understand the challenges Israel faced.

> *Now all the Midianites, Amalekites and other eastern peoples joined forces and crossed over the Jordan and camped in the Valley of Jezreel. Then the Spirit of the Lord came upon Gideon, and he blew a trumpet, summoning the Abiezrites to follow him* (Judges 6:33-34).

I love this passage because it waters so many of the things we have already discussed. The Spirit of the Lord comes upon Gideon and Gideon blows a trumpet (representing the Feast of Trumpets). His battle is a symbol of our battle to enter into God's rest. It is a new kind of battle and we are transitioning into it.

Many nations are coming against Israel. It does not appear to be a fair fight. The Midianites have lorded it over Israel for seven years, but it is time for the Israelites to break free. Whenever we prepare to break free, the enemy joins forces with other "nations" to attack us.

The mention of seven years of oppression is not a coincidental number. It is indicative of completion, the time to enter the resting place of God. As Gideon prepares a large army for a huge battle, God speaks to him.

> *The Lord said to Gideon, "You have too many men for Me to deliver Midian into their hands. In order that Israel may not boast against Me that her own strength has saved her, announce now to the people, 'Anyone who trembles with fear may turn back and leave Mount Gilead.'" So twenty-two thousand men left, while ten thousand remained* (Judges 7:2-3).

Too many men? Seriously? Two-thirds of Gideon's army leaves (not your typical preparation for war). Do you think the remaining soldiers are happy about this?

"Hey, where's everyone going? Are you going to let us fight alone?"

God cannot take people into rest who are still dealing with worry and fear. To enter rest, the last regime of fear must die. Any remaining worry-thorns in your heart must be uprooted. There is no room for fear where we are going. That's what these troop reductions are all about. Shrinking your army in a time of war directly attacks any fear lurking in your heart. It brings you to the laser-focused question: Whom do I trust?

Gideon does not question God.

> *But the Lord said to Gideon, "There are still too many men. Take them down to the water, and I will sift them for you there. If I say, 'This one shall go with you,' he shall go; but if I say, 'This one shall not go with you,' he shall not go"* (Judges 7:4).

The men go down to the water to drink; three hundred who lap up the water (the way a dog would) get to stay and fight. So out of 32,000 men we have 300 left. Three hundred men are going to fight all these nations.

God's Word Does the Work

For any storm that comes your way, God has a word for you. There is a word for sickness, a word for poverty, a word for bondage, a word for blindness. God has already given you His Word.

After whittling down the army, Gideon is struggling with a bit of fear, and as you know, fear will not be helpful in battle. He must be fearless to succeed. So God sends him down to the enemy camp to hear what they were saying. God is giving Gideon a word for this battle.

> *Gideon arrived just as a man was telling a friend his dream. "I had a dream," he was saying. "A round loaf of barley bread came tumbling into the Midianite camp. It struck the tent with such force that the tent overturned and collapsed." His friend responded, "This can be nothing other than the sword of Gideon son of Joash, the Israelite. God has given the Midianites and the whole camp into his hands"* (Judges 7:13-14).

This is a strange dream. It's like a Dr. Seuss book. If I dreamt about a loaf of bread doing something, I would chalk it up to bad pizza the night before.

So what does this dream mean? The Word of God is often symbolized by bread. Here the bread is tumbling, indicating momentum. God's Word is always moving, always at work. God spoke creation over 6,000 years ago, and it is still working today. Everything in the universe is held together by His most powerful Word.

When Jesus spoke the word, "Let's go to the other side" (see Mark 4:35), that word had the power to carry them through a fierce storm to the other side. The Word is alive and active (see Heb. 4:12). Jesus never feared the storm. It was incapable of stopping the word that had been spoken.

So what is going to give Gideon victory? The Word of God. It is described as the sword of Gideon. The Word is a sword. It is the sword of the Spirit. In Gideon's case the Spirit was upon him. The Spirit is *in* you and can be upon you as you learn to do things for the Lord, serving Him and expanding His Kingdom. The Spirit within you wields the sword. The victory is obtained without even fighting the fight.

The Battle Is the Lord's

Gideon hears about the dream and gets his men up. He divides them into three camps, each of 100 men. Then he gives each man a trumpet and a jar with a torch inside. They travel to the battlefield.

> *The Midianites, the Amalekites and all the other eastern peoples had settled in the valley, thick as locusts. Their camels could no more be counted than the sand on the seashore* (Judges 7:12).

Remember, there are only 300 Israelites about to battle a sea of people. On cue they break their jars, hold their torches high with the left hand, blow the trumpets and yell, *"A sword of the Lord and of Gideon"* (Judg. 7:19 NKJV).

At this the enemy troops begin to attack their own ranks. There is fleeing and running and killing. The Israelites win.

Let's take a closer look. The trumpets were held in the soldiers' right hands, the torches in the left. Imagine the sound as they chant, *"A sword of the Lord and of Gideon."* Now picture the trumpets being raised slightly—and the torches, too. Each man gives his trumpet and his torch a shake.

It's a powerful image, with much symbolism. The right represents the strength and might of the Lord (see Exod. 15:6). The trumpet indicates that the battle is the Lord's. When the Israelites blew the trumpet during peace times it was a call for all of Israel to come together as an army and fight, war was at hand.

Here, though, the trumpet is the sword of God, it is His army you are calling. It is at the sounding of the Lord's sword that the enemy defeats itself.

Suddenly 300 men would seem like plenty of power, since the Lord's army was the one fighting.

In the left hand is a torch. The fire here represents the Holy Spirit (see Matt. 3:11). Also, a torch needs oil for fuel. The oil represents the anointing. When Samuel anointed the shepherd boy David to be king, he anointed him with oil. The torch itself is made of wood, symbolizing the cross. The torch and the cross are pictures of your purpose. When you accept that torch, the flames come alive.

What am I getting at? We have to accept that we do what we do for the Lord; His assignment is our purpose. It becomes a sword for us, but also a torch. The oil of the Holy Spirit fuels our fire to accomplish the supernatural. It doesn't always mean changing what we do, but instead changing why we do it. It is all for the Lord. Because it is God's assignment, then it is God's responsibility to assure us the victory. And let me tell you—God likes to win big.

What does the fire of the torch teach us?

It involves the next feast. Let's go there now.

The Feast of Pentecost

> *Now to each one the manifestation of the Spirit is given for the common good. To one there is given through the Spirit the message of wisdom, to another the message of knowledge by means of the same Spirit, to another faith by the same Spirit, to another gifts of healing by that one Spirit, to another miraculous powers, to another prophecy, to another distinguishing between spirits, to another speaking in different kinds of tongues, and to still another the interpretation of tongues. All these are the work of one and the same Spirit, and He gives them to each one, just as He determines* (1 Corinthians 12:7-11).

Gifts of the Spirit are just that, gifts. The power for miracles is available to us even before we receive Christ. Many who were healed by Jesus did not know who Jesus was. They were healed before they believed.

Gifts are not fruit. They are not something you must bear. Instead, we are instructed to use them in accordance with our measure of faith. As Christians, seeing God perform miracles and save lives is not an "alien" experience. For the lost, these signs and wonders validate the message of Christ.

As you mature in your Christianity (in your imitation of Christ), you will see increasing consistency in having the miraculous come to pass. Nevertheless, it is so important to know that the power is available to you *wherever* you are in your journey. If a brand-new Christian is diagnosed with cancer, it would make no sense for that person to say, "Well, I don't have enough wisdom to be healed. I'm not mature enough." Healing is a free gift. Brand-new Christians have the same Spirit that raised Christ from the dead.

Sometimes I pray for a common cold and nothing happens. If I pray about it and stand in faith, it will be gone in about seven days. Of course, that is when it would be gone anyway. I see it as an exercise in faith. As we mature, our consistency in the miraculous grows. We are learning to plant faith and grow the fruit of faithfulness.

When my daughter was born, she didn't breathe. She turned blue. The doctors and nurses rushed equipment into the room and began to work on her. I grabbed my wife's hand and said a very simple prayer. I couldn't trust doctors to save the life of my child, but I could trust God to do it. I just said, "Breathe, in the name of Jesus."

That was all. Life is in the name of Jesus! She cried out at the name of Jesus and began to breathe. Now I can't get her to stop talking.

The Feast of Pentecost. The final feast. Let's look to the feast to see what God associates with His rest. Jesus had predicted the Pentecost event. The reason we call it Pentecost is because it happened on the day of the traditional Hebrew feast of the same name.

> *...He appeared to them over a period of forty days and spoke about the kingdom of God. On one occasion, while He was eating with them, He gave them this command: "Do not leave Jerusalem, but wait for the gift My Father promised, which you have heard Me speak about. For John baptized with water, but in a few days you will be baptized with the Holy Spirit"* (Acts 1:3-5).

Being baptized in the Holy Spirit is not to be confused with receiving the Spirit within us. When you receive Christ you receive the Spirit inside you. Remember that the Spirit can be in us, among us, and on us. Baptism in the Holy Spirit is immersion in the Spirit. This is when the gifts begin to manifest the miraculous.

> *When the day of Pentecost came, they were all together in one place. Suddenly a sound like the blowing of a violent wind came from heaven and filled the whole house where they were sitting. They saw what seemed to be tongues of fire that separated and came to rest on each of them. All of them were filled with the Holy Spirit and began to speak in other tongues as the Spirit enabled them* (Acts 2:1-4).

Today's definition of the word translated "filled" does not paint the complete picture here. The Greek word used is *pimplēmi,* which is sometimes translated "completed," "fulfilled," and "accomplished"[1] (see also Luke 1:23; 2:6; 2:21-22).

According to *Thayer's Lexicon* the word indicates that "what wholly *takes possession* of the mind is said to *fill* it."[2] So here the Holy Spirit completed, fulfilled, and accomplished the work by baptizing this group.

What Changed?

Of all of the gifts of the Spirit mentioned, which gifts resulted from Christ's sacrifice? Had anyone ever been healed before Christ came? Well yes. Sure, Abraham, Samuel, Elijah prayed for healing, to name a few. Had anyone ever prophesied before? Well, yes. There are books of prophecies, such as Isaiah and Daniel. Was there wisdom? Yeah, Solomon had plenty of it.

So what is new here? Well, two things. First, the gift of speaking in tongues is new. This had never happened before. So why now? In the days of Babylon, God confused the language of the people to create division (see Gen. 11:9). Now at Pentecost, He wishes to unite us, so He gives us a common language, a spiritual language.

If this is weirding you out, well you need to eat all of Jesus (go back to the chapter on the Passover lamb). If you have not asked the Lord for this baptism, you need to. It is not something weird; it is a biblical principle. I will admit that not all Christians are comfortable speaking in tongues. Yet, the Scripture is not vague about it. It is called a gift. Paul claims to pray in the Spirit more than anyone (see 1 Cor. 14:18). This shows us that it is a most powerful prayer tool.

I encourage you to study it out for yourself. I'm not saying it doesn't seem weird to unbelievers. Paul admitted as much. Some things have not changed. In high school my friends came to our church. Someone nearby was speaking in tongues really loud. My friends looked at me like I was in a cult or something. Nevertheless, I have heard many testimonies of Bible teachers speaking in one language and being understood in other languages. That's nothing short of a miracle.

The second "new thing" after Christ is that this outpouring of the Spirit is available to all who will believe. All. Anyone. Take a look.

> *In the last days, God says, I will pour out My Spirit on all people. Your sons and daughters will prophesy, your young men will see visions, your old men will dream dreams. Even on My servants, both men and women, I will pour out My Spirit in those days...* (Acts 2:17-18).

All. Everyone. Even women. (I'm being funny.) Daughters prophesying? Uh-oh.

Now in this book I have mentioned three ways the Spirit interacts with us. The Spirit is in us from the moment we receive Christ. The Spirit is among us when we commit to the building of the house of the Lord. This last one I want to explain a bit more, since I have only mentioned it in passing until now.

The Spirit Upon Us

The Spirit is upon me when I am acting in my purpose and my assignment. What is your assignment?

Samson was called to fight Philistines, so when he fought them the Spirit would come upon him. The Spirit of the Lord came upon Gideon when he went to battle. Jesus said it this way:

> *The **Spirit** of the **Lord is** on **Me,** because He has anointed Me to preach good news to the poor…* (Luke 4:18).

This was the beginning of Jesus' ministry. He said that the Spirit was upon Him *because* He was anointed to do some stuff, and that is what He was about to do.

When we step into what God has called us to do, the Spirit is upon us. So before I preach I always call it into existence; "The Spirit of the Lord is upon me because He has anointed me to…." Then I say what it is that I am about to do.

How do you know if the Spirit is upon you? It can be easily identified because when you act in it, the supernatural becomes natural. Average is done away with. Mediocrity has no place. This is glory; it is victory propelled by the eternal power of God.

Like the apostles at Pentecost, God wants us to operate in all three: the Spirit in us, upon us, and among us. This is necessary to our entering the rest God has prepared.

Are you ready?

Chapter 20

How to Take a Load Off

In September 2008, while RE:ZOUND was playing concerts, we traveled up to Denver to play at Orchard Road Christian Center. We played a concert on Friday night and stayed over to lead worship at the weekend services.

After the gig on Friday, we went back to the green room and the senior pastor, Reece Bowling, stopped in. Pastor Reece Bowling is an awesome guy. He asked, "Hey Jason, do you want to go jogging tomorrow?"

Now there are only two possible answers here—*yes* and *no.* Keep in mind that I do not jog. I work out, but cardio is way down on the list for me. Yes, I want to spend time with Pastor Reece. We have a good time talking; he makes me laugh. We have a lot in common—the ministry, family, stuff like that. But no, I do not want to jog. Not because I don't like jogging, but because I am a man with an ego. I don't want my lack of lung development to become a source of embarrassment.

I remember watching Joel Osteen tell a story once in which he said, with his Oklahoma accent and famous smile, "I wuz out jo-ggeeng…."

I thought to myself, "You *would* jog." You know the type: perfect smile, up early every day, and jogs to boot. (I love Joel, by the way.)

A gal at the church told me once that she was organizing a group to run a marathon. You know how when a bunch of people are doing something, you think, "Oh, I should do that too."

Not me. Not if it's jogging. And definitely not if it's a marathon. Still, it seemed like everyone was talking about jogging all of a sudden. Maybe the Holy Spirit had been preparing for this moment with Reece. All of these things raced through my mind in just a moment of time as Reece awaited my answer. (I think someone even had a dream where they saw a loaf of bread chasing me, and I was wearing jogging shorts, now that I think about it.)

So Reece asked me and I replied, "Yes," although I replied slowly, almost like a question. Reece stared for a moment, his eyes darting around the room in the awkward silence. Then he turned to leave.

"Great, I'll pick you up at the hotel at seven," he piped with a head nod that made it just through the doorway.

The guys in the band all looked at me like I had just swallowed rat poison. "You jog?"

Of course I don't jog. I walk around onstage a lot while I sing. That should help. Now I knew that Pastor Reece runs marathons all around the country. He is a serious runner. This concerned me.

Still, I was really excited about spending time talking and conversing with him—you know, really sharing and sparking each other's interests. What I didn't realize is that when I'm jogging I am incapable of talking. The only time my mouth opens is to suck air. Please keep in mind that we are in Denver. If you know anything about atmospheric pressure, you know that there is no air left in Denver. It is too high. If you travel to there, you'd better bring oxygen.

Lord, why not take me jogging in San Diego?

Early the next morning, I drove to the jogging area. I did in fact bring workout clothes for the hotel gym, and Reece was kind enough to lend me his wife's windbreaker (it wasn't pink or anything). There was a nip in the air. The landscape was beautiful. Denver has built within its city limits an amazing surfaced jogging trail that takes you right through God's country. The trees were all colors and shapes and sizes, spots of grass sprinkled the ground as far as the eye could see. Scores of people were gathered in the area, pulling their ankles to stretch, grabbing shoulders, and doing that quick little run in place thing followed by the head going back and forth.

These were serious joggers. I soon discovered that there is a code of etiquette and a fashion ethic among joggers. As in any sport, the veterans can quickly identify the guy who doesn't belong. Because I do not believe the male body was ever intended for tight short shorts, I was quite comfortable in my sweat shorts. They were nice and baggy and went just past my knees. Even with the grand mountains gray and ominous in the distance, I guess I stuck out like a nun in a Pentecostal church.

Reece patted me lightly on the back, and staring blankly off into the horizon he said, "I was thinking we'd do an easier run" (here he made a stretching groan), "just a mile and a half up and then back."

Do the math; that's three miles. I have never in my whole life run three miles. I ran one mile, like 20 years ago. I've driven three miles. Still, I made up my mind that I was going to complete this run; I was not going to quit.

Turns out, it was a lot of fun. Reece had a great conversation while I—well—breathed. It took us 33 minutes to run, which is not all that fast. It's actually about the speed of a normal walk. We just bounced up and down to look like we were keeping up a jog pace. I finished the run (not that quitting was much of an option).

If you ever look forward to a good rest, it is always after a period of exertion. Who wants to rest after a day of doing nothing? After that jog, I just wanted to put my feet up. (Where's that footstool? Praise God for the person who invented it. If it weren't invented yet, I'd invent it myself.)

Entering the Lord's rest only works on the heels of one heck of a fight. Many Christians get frustrated because not *all* the promises of God are instant. We want a microwaveable inheritance. Later in this chapter, we will discuss the footstool. We will revisit one more detail from the story of Gideon and tie it in with our inheritance as rulers. We'll talk about what the qualifications are. We are also going to find out that not everything is a gift.

Rats.

Joint Heirs With Christ

With all this talk about inheritance, let's take a look at it under the magnifying glass.

> *If we are children [of God], then we are heirs—heirs of God and co-heirs with Christ, if indeed we share in His sufferings in order that we may also share in His glory* (Romans 8:17).

We are co-heirs with Christ. This makes great sense, since we are in covenant with Christ. We are, after all, His Bride. What's His is ours, and what's ours is His. (Suddenly it seems so obvious that we would give the Body of Christ at least 10 percent of our finances.)

Anyway, to be a co-heir means we share the inheritance. This inheritance is infinite; there isn't less for me and more for you. With that in mind, I want to give you a glimpse of Christ's inheritance.

> *I will proclaim the decree of the Lord: He said to me, "You are My Son; today I have become Your Father. Ask of Me, and I will make the nations Your inheritance, the ends of the earth Your possession. You will rule them with an iron scepter; You will dash them to pieces like pottery." Therefore, you kings, be wise; be warned, you rulers of the earth* (Psalms 2:7-10).

Here Christ's inheritance is the nations and the ends of the earth. This only happens after Christ dies. Therefore, the promise is in the future tense. "Ask of Me and I *will give* you..." It is only after Jesus became a man that He had access to the ownership of the earth, which had been given to man. According to God, the earth was to be ruled by man.

In practice, authority is held by what- or whomever is obeyed. When we obey God we give Him authority in our lives. When we obey satan, we give him authority. Adam ate the fruit because it was desirable. When man obeyed the fleshly desire, which was made of the dust of the ground, he placed that dust (the earth) in authority over him. The fruit had been produced by the earth, and Adam obeyed the earth.

He also gave satan power at that time, resulting in God's cursing satan and the earth so as to bring balance to the power that had just been handed over (see Gen. 3:14-15). Notice when you read the Genesis account that God did not curse the man or the woman. He only cursed the earth and the serpent: *"Cursed is the ground because of you; through painful toil you will eat of it all the days of your life"* (Gen. 3:17).

Man was designed to be in charge of the earth, so that the earth would serve man. But because of sin, he was now going to work for the earth. His life would require painful toil. As each human being was born, the sin of Adam was born in that child, because every child was in Adam when Adam fell.

Jesus was not born into Adam's sin, because He did not descend from man. Jesus did not obey the flesh; therefore He had immediate authority over the earth again. After Jesus rose from the dead, He announced that all authority has been given to Him and He charged us to disciple all nations (see Matt. 28:18-19). His inheritance of all authority happened after He died on the cross, having defeated the powers of darkness completely through His death and resurrection.

Jesus had to become a man to access this authority. He was born as a man and called to subdue the earth (in the future tense). By the time of His resurrection, He had subdued the earth. He walked in that dominion during

His ministry on earth. However, the promise of Psalms 2 came to pass after He died.

That glory required a sacrifice. Now the inheritance is within you as a free gift. The blessing is a free gift. You did not earn it; you were not good enough for it. Here's the kicker, though: for the inheritance to manifest into your physical world, you will need to abide by some stipulations in God's Word. Remember, God's Word does not contradict itself, so we need to gain some understanding of His ways. Through these next few chapters I will show you what I mean.

Christ's inheritance (according to Psalms 2) is to rule the nations and the earth with an iron scepter. We are co-heirs with Christ, so this passage is for us as well. What? This might seem a hard bridge to cross at first. Something within you may already be screaming "I'm not worthy!"

You are not only worthy of this calling, but God needs you here and Jesus paid the price. Rulers are influencers, and God wants His people doing the influencing. The nations have developed places of high influence. Our education system would certainly be an example. So would our government and the media. God intends for you to rule. He made you co-heir with Christ, and then gave Christ the authority that He promised Him in Psalms chapter 2.

Because you are in Christ, this passage is speaking to you. Put your name in there when God says, "You are my son (or daughter), ask of Me and I will make the nations your inheritance, the ends of the earth your possession."

Now let's read from Romans 8:

> *The Spirit Himself testifies with our spirit that we are God's children. Now if we are children, then we are heirs—heirs of God and co-heirs with Christ, if indeed we share in His sufferings in order that we may also share in His glory* (Romans 8:16-17).

You see, we are God's children. Now look at the stipulation: "if." Uh-oh. An *if* clause. I know the inheritance is a gift, which means there is no stipulation. Therefore, disregarding the stipulation cannot remove the inheritance. What it can do is keep you from experiencing the inheritance in your time here on earth. Like the prodigal son, the inheritance will be squandered away to destruction instead of glory. God has a destiny for you, but you can choose not to live it. He has blessings for you, but you can choose not to experience them.

The Romans passage says, "If indeed." The term *indeed* indicates a deed you must be in. There is an action that must happen in this stipulation. What deed must you do? You must share in His sufferings in order that you may also share in His glory. There now is the explanation of the stipulation. *If* relates to the ability to experience the inheritance in terms of glory. Glory only happens in victory, perfect victory that is. Glory will be the result of your accomplishing what God has you here to do. It comes when you skillfully complete your assignment.

You cannot accomplish His will without His inheritance. When the victory happens there is glory. Now you might still be saying, "I'm not worthy" (cue the *Wayne's World* visual). If you believe that, then you will not accomplish God's destiny for your life.

First Peter 5:4 explains that those who serve God will be crowned with glory. A crown indicates authority. You are a royal priesthood. God promised Abraham that He would make Abraham's name great. That same promise is now yours. Why would God promise to make your name great if it weren't part of His will?

People who shun glory will fail. People who seek glory, making their own name great, will have a whole other mess of destruction. But those who follow the path of God and destiny will have their name made great, crowned with glory, and placed in a high position to rule and influence, bringing God's will here to earth.

Ladies and gentlemen, now is the time for this process to start. The Church is ready to take its place in authority now.

Suffering

Experiencing the inheritance in your life is a process of sharing in Christ's sufferings. God has promised us milk and honey...wait—that doesn't sound like suffering, does it?

Let's define suffering now. "Suffering" here comes from the Greek word *sympascho,* which means "to suffer or feel pain together, to suffer evils (troubles, persecutions)...with one another."[1] Some might be too quick to say that we need to die as martyrs, like Christ. This would be defeating the way that Christ has set us up for victory.

Paul recognized that he needed to stay alive and continue the work of the Lord, bearing fruit for the sake of God's people (see, for example, 2 Cor. 5:1-13), even though, in God's timing, Paul did die as a martyr. You do not need to die on the cross; Jesus already did that. He did not leave any unfinished work where defeating death is concerned.

Others might mistakenly believe that our shared suffering means living in lack with barely enough to get by. Or maybe bashing your head with stone tablets. These are the beliefs of Wilderness dwellers who have decided that if they suffer now, they can reap a reward when they die.

This is not true or biblical. Living in lack is where the enemy wants you—he can keep you needy so that you are incapable of giving. Where is the reward in that?

The suffering God is talking about in Romans 8 is the work and sweat, the painful toil associated with carrying our cross, which is our purpose. I discussed this briefly in Chapter 5. Jesus asked us to take up our cross. Jesus' cross was His purpose. You do not need to bear His cross; you need to bear yours. Bearing your cross tomorrow might mean that after a long, hard day you play with the kids, help with homework, clean up the kitchen, and have a quality conversation with your spouse—instead of vegging out on the couch the way you'd like to. I know the drill: When you are tired and you need a moment to yourself, it feels like doing the right thing is another nail through your wrist. (Well, not quite.)

It is, however, denying yourself and your selfish needs so that you can live for others. At the end of suffering is the rest God wants you to enter. Your enemies cannot bother you there. Crises can't get all over you there.

Yet, even rest doesn't mean you do nothing. Some Christians get stuck here, on the couch, trusting God. Jesus kept going. He was living above the circumstances, but He was at work. He was moving. He did more in three and a half years than we do in a lifetime.

There are going to be difficult times associated with your purpose. This is your part in going through the cross. On the other side of your suffering is glory. You can experience glory while en route:

> *I have brought You glory on earth by completing the work You gave Me to do. And now, Father, glorify Me in Your presence with the glory I had with You before the world began* (John 17:4-5).

Remember that Christ has asked you to take up your cross and follow Him. The cross is your course. Your assignment is part of your course. At the end of your course is glory, which is the victory produced in your work that creates influence. That course is preparing you and drawing you closer to your destiny. Jesus here is asking for glory. You are a joint heir with Christ, so don't be afraid of glory; receive it, because you are purposed for glory.

Yes. You are purposed for glory.

Jesus was not afraid to ask for glory. He asked God straight up, *"... Glorify Me..."* (John 17:5). There is an interesting point here to note. Jesus' request for glory rested upon the following statement: *"I have brought You glory on earth by completing the work You gave Me to do"* (John 17:4).

Now please realize Jesus had not yet completed the work. He had not yet died or risen from the dead when He prayed this. But Jesus would argue that faith sees things completed. In the unseen world, Jesus had died and risen from the dead long ago. It was written in great detail in Psalms 22. When you start on your assignment and begin down the path of glory, you are already due the glorification and inheritance. These are resources that help you reach the finish line in victory. They are your resources to win!

Salvation is a free gift. Glory is not free.

You can experience the inheritance manifested in your life. Ask a business owner if there was sweat and blood involved in building the business. Ask them. They will tell you about sleepless nights, 90-hour workweeks, no vacations, and often no pay. What is on the other side? Glory. Inheritance. Victory.

Ask Jesus about the cross. Was it hard? Did You sweat? Now ask Him what was on the other side. He would tell you it was glory.

We must be willing to go through the cross in the pursuit of our purpose. We will suffer persecution. Have you noticed that not everyone rejoices in your course to victory? It's true. Many will hate us and say all kinds of bad things about us. People will come against us. We will suffer evils, meaning we will experience thorns in our hearts that we will need to overcome and be delivered of. We will suffer trouble. The enemy and the world will present us with mountains to overcome. Storms will blow in. I'm not telling you to believe for trouble, evil, and persecution. I'm warning you to be prepared for the battle.

> *I consider that our present sufferings are not worth comparing with the glory that will be revealed in us. The creation waits in eager expectation for the sons of God to be revealed* (Romans 8:18-19).

You may remember from Psalms 19:1 that creation itself screams of God's glory. The work God's hands has produced says something about Him. It speaks, and it creates influence.

The works of our hands partnering with God should reveal something as well. The same creation that communicates all of this glory is waiting eagerly for you and me to be revealed in glory. It is waiting for glory to be revealed in us. It is waiting for us to step into our roles, accept our assignments from the Lord, and allow the work of our hands to create influence through victory!

Not only has God called you to produce victory in your destiny that will result in glorious influence, but creation is also waiting for you to do it. If you have kids you know what it is to wait for everyone to get in the car. "Come on, hurry up!" You are eagerly waiting for the kids to get settled in the car!

Today you are that child climbing into the back seat of the car of glory while creation waits so that all of us can go on to the next age. Our present sufferings are not worth whining about when we will stick it out on the path the Lord has for us.

The Footstool

God invented the footstool long before the La-Z-Boy. Remember we were made in God's likeness and image, and apparently He likes to put His feet up when He's resting.

First Chronicles 28:2 says, *"King David rose to his feet and said: 'Listen to me, my brothers and my people. I had it in my heart to build a house as a place of rest for the ark of the covenant of the Lord, for the footstool of our God...."'*

David rose to his feet; he was working in order that God might rest. David is a picture of the taking of the territory through battle, even though we want to eventually find ourselves entering the rest. Here David makes an association between the Lord's rest and the footstool. Let's take a closer look at this.

A footstool holds up the weight of your feet, under which it is placed. Your feet are the lowest part of your body, meaning that whatever is under your feet is completely under your authority. The intent of this authority or purpose is to bring you rest.

The footstool positions you, not for battle, but for rest. You cannot fight with your feet propped up. That is the point. Your feet are propped up by your enemies, that is, by all rulers and authorities. This means that the enemies have become your tools. The same evil that was meant to harm you has now been turned to good use.

The voice of the media brings a flood of negative influences to the world, but when you take your position at the helm (those who are called to rule the media nation), you turn this tool to good use. Evil is when we take something that is meant for good and make it good for nothing. Evil is the absence of God. To remove godliness from something makes it evil.

God has created all authorities, they are by Him, and they are for Him, but they are not all serving Him. These nations created by God and for God may now be under evil rule. So then evil has built up cities and dug wells in this world. These are part of God's plan. The devil wants to take good things and make them evil. God wants to take evil and turn it to good. This is the age-long battle. We have authority on this planet to serve God or oppose Him. *But, ultimately, all will be given to the just.*

The Lord spoke to Moses about this as part of the inheritance of the Promised Land:

> *The Lord your God* [will bring] *you into the land He swore to your fathers, to Abraham, Isaac and Jacob, to give you—a land with large, flourishing cities you did not build, houses filled with all kinds of good things you did not provide, wells you did not dig, and vineyards and olive groves you did not plant...* (Deuteronomy 6:10-11).

As we take the territory in our hearts, we advance our physical world. First we take it in the spiritual realm, then in the physical. Spoils from the territories you possess in your heart that were once used for evil now find their way into your life and physically manifest as benefits to the Kingdom. The addiction you overcome is used as a testimony for good. The greed you overcame allows you to experience wealth. The sickness you overcame makes way for health. These tools then become useful to others, but over time. Weeds grow fast. Trees grow slowly. Yet, surely and steadily the worldly influencers are overcome. Eventually, the platforms the enemy built for them to spew evil, becomes your platform to voice godliness.

It becomes your footstool. Let's review the passage once more before taking another step.

> *I will proclaim the decree of the Lord: He said to Me, "You are My Son; today I have become Your Father. Ask of Me, and I will make the nations Your inheritance, the ends of the earth Your possession* (Psalms 2:7-8).

God makes a statement of fact: "You are my Son...." He reminds us because we are so often forgetting that the Creator of all and the Supreme Authority of all has adopted us as sons and daughters. We are nobility. The son of the king lives in the palace and has authority by association. We need to be continually reminded of this fact.

He asks us to "ask" of Him. This demands agreement. He is saying, "I want to give this to you, but you must also want it." What is it? Glory. We don't seek glory, we seek God, but we are not ashamed of the glory that He desires to reveal in us. Like Christ, we imitate Him, and are not afraid to "ask," as Jesus did, "Glorify Me, Father."

I stepped on your toes just then, didn't I? Look, this is not about your glory! It's about the resulting godly influence you attain, the ability to bring Heaven's order to earth. God is asking you to ask Him for it, so why would this conclusion be surprising? We are joint heirs, remember?

You are not God. You are not the only-begotten Son. You are an adopted son. You must clearly know your place and purpose to find your way to this part of the journey. Your place is to subdue the earth and influence it. Your purpose is simply to bring God's will here to earth.

I have much more to say about this, but first, let's continue building the case:

> *The Lord says to my Lord: "Sit at My right hand until I make Your enemies a footstool for Your feet." The Lord will extend Your mighty scepter from Zion; You will rule in the midst of Your enemies* (Psalms 110:1-2).

Looking again to Jesus' inheritance; we are joint heirs with Him. Here God introduces the footstool. God's right hand is His strength. David wrote: "The Lord says to my Lord…."

Jesus later explains it to the Pharisees:

> *While the Pharisees were gathered together, Jesus asked them, "What do you think about the Christ? Whose son is He?" "The son of David," they replied. He said to them, "How is it then that David, speaking by the Spirit, calls Him 'Lord'? For he says, 'The Lord said to my Lord: "Sit at My right hand until I put Your enemies under Your feet."' If then David calls Him 'Lord,' how can He be his son?"* (Matthew 22:41-45)

Christ is identifying that He Himself is the recipient of this Scripture. He is the "My Lord" that David referred to. God is promising to place the enemy under Jesus' feet. We are co-heirs. So then *your* enemy becomes your footstool, fully under your authority and subdued. The spoils are the wells you did not dig and the cities you did not build. The evil things of this world have been laid up for the just, to be our footstools…tools for rest…tools for doing the bidding of the Lord so that we might be converting all that is in the world for good.

Sit Down

In Psalms 110:1, the command from the Lord to our Lord Jesus Christ is "Sit." God is telling His Son not only to *ask* but also to *sit.*

Sit down.

Have you ever gone into a meeting with the Big Guy and He motions to the chair, "Sit."

This time He is asking you to sit next to Him, behind the desk, to help Him rule. You see, this is the command. Now recognize its timing. This is after Christ has gone through the cross and fought the battle. It is after the Ites are defeated. Now He is told to sit.

Just as is explained in the Book of Hebrews then, God has invited us to enter His rest. Let's be sure none of us falls short of doing so.

His invitation is clear: "Sit down. Take a load off. Put your feet up."

The Mighty Scepter

Both in Psalms 2:9 and Psalms 110:2, we see a mighty scepter. It is described as iron. It is the rod with which you will rule. This scepter is the sword of the Spirit; we conquer with the sword and we rule with the scepter. This is God's Word.

As rulers we are to impart to the rest of the world justice. What is wrong with our education, our media, our governments? They are laden with misconceptions and corruption. There are misconceptions about morality, love, goodness, and the things of God. There is corruption that allows justice to be purchased from our rulers.

A ruler who abides in God and takes the journey God has placed in front of him will be mature. Therefore, corruption will not be tempting. Greed? Heck, we beat that several chapters ago. Now godliness becomes the only way and we implement rulership with truth and justice. (Now you sound like Superman.)

It is the Word of God that will dash the rulers to pieces like pottery (see Ps. 2:9).

Let's revisit that.

Psalms 2:9 says, *"You will rule them with an iron scepter; You will dash them to pieces like pottery."*

When were we talking about breaking pottery last? Oh, yes, it was Gideon's battle. His one and only battle. Gideon is a picture of the moment we enter rest. In his battle the men *"blew their trumpets and broke the jars that were in their hands"* (Judg. 16:19).

The jars they broke symbolized the rulers who were to be defeated. Why broken? God is not interested in destroying those who are currently ruling the nations (the ungodly voices that influence our world). He is interested in breaking them just like you were broken. This is a breaking of the will and a bringing into submission to God's will. If they will not break, they must be removed. Like King Saul, who would not break and was removed.

Man is a clay vessel; the Word of God is breaking man so that there can be a rebuilding. Ask a drug addict when it was that she finally turned to the Lord. She will answer, "When I hit bottom." That is being broken.

Ask a Christian in the Promised Land how he got in; it was when he broke down and realized his sinfulness and knew that Christ loved him anyway and even died for his sins. Once clay has dried, it cannot be reshaped without breaking it.

God is speaking to rulers: "Break or be removed." What is the Lord waiting for? He is waiting for us to get in position. He is waiting for us to climb up to help Moses build the Tabernacle, to help Joshua defeat Jericho, to climb the mountain with Gideon and blow our trumpets, to raise a sword in one hand and a torch in the other, having broken the vessel and allowed the Spirit of God out to fight our wars! To bring victory.

God is maturing Christians who will be just. We are made righteous because of Christ's sacrifice. We are justified. This does not make us just. Imagine a world in which all of the influencers were just. Remember that finding a place of influence requires victory—glorious victory.

You can get there! Just do things God's way. The world is coming undone. Our economy is controlled by greed. It is the Babylonian system that is based on getting as much as you can. Operate in God's economy, which is based on giving as much as you can. See the difference? Can you envision the outcome?

The wealth of the wicked is laid up for the just...not the justified.

You must be justified in order to mature and become just. Being justified is the starting line. Being a ruler means that your decisions affect people's lives. When you are a ruler, you can hurt people with an unjust decision. You might be in a position to hire, fire, give raises, and bonuses. You might be the one who decides whether someone should go to prison. You may be tasked with determining what is said on the news about an individual. Your decision may result in thousands of jobs being lost.

Being in authority will not make you popular. Being just will definitely place you under tremendous persecution. Moses didn't make the popular decision when he had the golden calf destroyed. It was Aaron who made the popular decision. Being just rarely lines up with what the people ask for, but it does what is best for the people and is never self-seeking.

Just rulers are always persecuted. Just ask Abraham Lincoln, a man who split a nation over doing what was right.

Overcome

> *Here I am! I stand at the door and knock. If anyone hears My voice and opens the door, I will come in and eat with him, and he with Me. To him who overcomes, I will give the right to sit with Me on My throne, just as I overcame and sat down with My Father on His throne* (Revelation 3:20-21).

This is the kicker. To him who overcomes. Overcoming is the right to sit. This Scripture is tying everything we have covered in this chapter into one final destination. Most of God's promises are gifts earned by what Christ accomplished on the cross. They come by faith. Yet, this Scripture does not say "to him who believes." Instead, it says, *"To him who **overcomes**...."*

Overcoming indicates a battle, a strenuous assignment, sweat equity, enduring troubles, stubborn evils, and suffering. The promise is experienced by the one who overcomes. The promise was available all along, but could not be experienced until the place of overcoming was reached.

This is not for those who have quit. Why not?

When you first become a Christian, you are not in a position to rule. You are not ready. You will mess it up. There is no fast track to management here. The journey outlined in the Word is the only way and it could take most of a lifetime. Those who overcome have found love, wisdom, perseverance, self-control, faith, and more.

Not many find this overcoming. Still, it starts with faith. Faith is the activating element of your journey. You are saved by faith, you enter the Promised Land by faith, and you overcome through faith. Hebrews 11 mentions the Bible's heroes of faith, people like Abraham, Moses, and others who "*…through faith conquered kingdoms, administered justice, and gained what was promised…*" (Heb. 11:33).

Overcoming does not happen *by* faith, it happens *through* faith, working, and waiting.

Overcoming = Faith + Suffering Indeed + Patience

Now we "gain" what was promised, meaning we experience the promises. Our feet are propped up. These kingdoms are defeated. Why? Ah, yes…so that we can administer justice!

Overcomers are invited to sit with Christ on His throne. If you were concerned earlier that I was overstepping my bounds in regards to our being joint heirs with Christ, make no mistake now; Christ wants you on that throne. Imagine this, Jesus, King of kings, Lord of lords, asking you to sit on His throne! The question, once again, demands agreement. You must agree to sit on the throne.

This will require you to "feel" worthy. You will have to avoid that self-destruct button at all costs. Here your enemies are made your footstool, you are ruling with an iron scepter, and you are administering justice. You are chairman of the board at Harvard, and you are beginning to change the way people are educated. Welcome to the nation you rule.

Be just. Christ qualified His remarks in Revelation 3:20 saying, *"If anyone hears My voice…."* What is His voice saying?

Psalms 2:7: *"You are My Son…."*

Romans 8:16: *"The Spirit Himself testifies with our spirit that we are God's children."*

Jesus comes up from being baptized in the Jordan and the voice of the Lord is heard saying, *"This is My Son…"* (Matt. 3:17).

Are you hearing the voice? The cornerstone passage of this journey, Hebrews 3:7-8 says, *"…Today, if you hear His voice, do not harden your hearts…."*

Are you a son of God? Well then, what are you waiting for? *Ask* Him. Then sit down. You are an overcomer! Jesus said, *"…In this world you will have trouble. But take heart! I have* ***overcome*** *the world"* (John 16:33).

Chapter 21

I Got the Need, the Need for Seed

We have not talked at length about the gifts of the Spirit in these chapters. This is a hugely important subject, but not one that this book can cover in great detail.

It is imperative to say this, however: the gifts were not just active in the early days of the Church; they are active *now.* I have witnessed miracles in which the deaf hear, the blind see, the lame walk. You can find videos online of amazing signs and wonders. These are for the unbeliever. Give an evangelist a field full of the lost, and let the signs and wonders begin!

These are gifts, you cannot earn them. The gifts of the Spirit are not the same as the fruit of the Spirit. Gifts are free. Fruit is something we must bear. The word *bear* connotes the intricacies of childbirth. For the mother, this means carrying, birthing, and nurturing her. Ask any mother about bearing children. It is a process.

The Seed

Be fruitful. This was the first command of God to man (see Gen. 1:22). It is where our journey began. Leaving Egypt, we began to immerse ourselves in the Word. The idea was to grow up in the things of God, things like learning to control our will and enhance our self-control. We have been becoming fruitful ever since that first step. Now the fruit is maturing and it is time for us to discuss it.

How are seed and rest related in our journey? Entering the rest of the Lord means that the seed of God that was planted is now producing mature fruit—fruit that lasts. We must always start with seed. Seed production involves toil—painful toil. Initially, only painful toil will force the earth to produce for us.

As mentioned earlier, entering the Lord's rest is about the heart's production. Which seed is planted, and what does the fruit look like? What is the process? These questions all have infinite answers, because the things of God are infinite. The seed itself contains the power of infinity and the fruit contains the seed.

To get us started, let's break down two passages of Scripture in which we find an overview of our journey from God. The first deals with seed; the second, fruit (we will focus on the seed for now):

> *For this very reason, make every effort to add to your faith goodness; and to goodness, knowledge; and to knowledge, self-control; and to self-control, perseverance; and to perseverance, godliness; and to godliness, brotherly kindness; and to brotherly kindness, love. For if you possess these qualities in increasing measure, they will keep you from being ineffective and unproductive in your knowledge of our Lord Jesus Christ* (2 Peter 1:5-8).

> *The fruit of the Spirit is love, joy, peace, patience, kindness, goodness, faithfulness, gentleness and self-control. Against such things there is no law* (Galatians 5:22-23).

Second Peter 1 outlines the steps of growth; it is an overview of our journey encapsulated in one passage of Scripture! Just as our map has seven parts and creation has seven days, so also this first passage lists seven items or seeds that move us toward God. Fittingly, the eighth item on our list is love. God is love.

We need to pay attention to and carefully plant each item along the way: faith, goodness, knowledge, self-control, perseverance, godliness, brotherly kindness, and love. They are building blocks in life, each one important for the next. Skipping steps would be counterproductive, because your life will eventually crumble back to the step you omitted.

Like farmers planting seed, we have work to do. The steps are not automatic or free. In fact, we are commanded to add something fresh and new to each one. We start with faith and then add goodness, to which we add knowledge, and so on, all the way to love.

As we consider this planting process and briefly describe the genius behind the order, remember that each Christian is entitled to the same promises, regardless of which step they are at. Once we start the steps, with faith, then the promises are available. This is true even for the prodigal son, who gained his inheritance with poor intentions. His missteps cost him the fullness of the promises, yet he is not disqualified from growth. None of us earns the promises; they are gifts we receive by faith.

The following Scripture explains the same principle I described earlier in a different way: *"Grace and peace be yours in abundance through the knowledge of God and of Jesus our Lord"* (2 Pet. 1:2).

This peace is rest. It is the spiritual "place" where the promises of God are active in your life; nothing is missing and nothing is broken. The promises come by faith, but through the *knowledge* of God. This Scripture implies that many will have difficulty realizing the promises because they do not have knowledge of God.

> *For if you possess these qualities in increasing measure, they will keep you from being ineffective and unproductive in your* ***knowledge*** *of our Lord Jesus Christ* (2 Peter 1:8).

Peter is referring here to the seven steps to love. Notice that the qualities do not have to be matured and finished, but just need to be growing. You have to be trying. All along the journey, from Egypt all the way to the Place of Rest from your enemies (your "footstool rest"), you must exert effort. That means you must be growing and persevering. Growth ends when we lose patience and quit.

Peter warns us that stopping will cause you to become *"ineffective and unproductive in your* ***knowledge*** *of our Lord...."* Remember that the promises come by faith and through our knowledge of the Lord. When we stop trying we become unproductive. This is the Christian who has lost hope in all this Promised Land jazz. "It just didn't work...I tried it."

Unproductive. Ineffective. It isn't that people in this condition don't believe in God anymore or even that they don't believe they qualify for the blessing. They simply stopped growing on this seed-planting path.

The Ites have to be continually uprooted so our seeds can take root, flourish, and produce abundant fruit. All along our journey, we have been hearing the Word and planting seeds. Yet, we *really* started seeing some production once we entered the Promised Land and took some territory.

All of this activity is an expression of our divine nature and assignment in the earth. Peter explains it nicely:

> *His divine power has given us everything we need for life and godliness through our knowledge of Him who called us by His own glory and goodness. Through these He has given us His very great and precious promises, so that through them you may participate in the divine nature and escape the corruption in the world caused by evil desires* (2 Peter 1:3-4).

God has used His power to give us life (the absence of death in every area of our existence) and godliness. This comes through knowledge, but by faith. In this passage from Second Peter, we see that the promises of God allow us to participate in God's divine nature.

How? When you have the abundance of God available to you, you are in a position to bless others. You are also in a position to create. These are the ways of God. These blessings also help us escape the corruption caused by evil desires. These desires are key in our discussion.

The list provided in Second Peter 1:5-8 is a roadmap, even a formula that will change any ungodly desires. Let's take a look at the first step in the list.

Step One: Faith

This is the starting place. Jesus describes our starting place as a gate:

> *Enter through the narrow gate. For wide is the gate and broad is the road that leads to destruction, and many enter through it. But small is the gate and narrow the road that leads to life, and only a few find it* (Matthew 7:13-14).

Entering this narrow gate requires faith in Jesus. Jesus is the gate; the only way to the Father is through Him. It is popular today to say that those who are "good enough" or well-intended, or who worship *a god,* will find their way to Heaven. This is not what the Bible says. Scripture tells us there is *one* way, and that is Christ. That is it.

Jesus is available to anyone who seeks. Remember that King David knew Christ before Christ walked the earth. He referred to him as "My Lord" in Psalms 2. Faith is the starting point. We enter that narrow gate with faith in Christ. The narrow gate, once entered, leads to life. It opens up into a vast world of possibilities, to the supernatural. Freedom lives here. The narrow gate opens up into the infinite. Picture a "V"; at the bottom of it is the gate. Once you go through the gate, your world expands. Everything exists in this open space. The opposite is true for those who enter the big gate. It is wide at first and seems freeing, but the road narrows to a single destination—destruction.

When you plant seed, you get fruit. When you plant the seed called *faith,* you bear the fruit of the Spirit called *faithfulness* (listed in Galatians 5:22).

The fruit of faithfulness will not be a man-made interpretation, but an exact pattern of God's faithfulness.

For now, it is the seed you plant, and it takes work to nurture it. It will require you to go against what comes naturally, even in the midst of a storm. Fear is a natural reaction to a storm. So is doubt. You will learn to defeat fear and doubt as you persevere and watch the Lord reveal His faithfulness. Little by little, you become an imitator of that faithfulness and, in time, the corresponding fruit of the Spirit is born.

Before I go too far into the fruit, let's move on to the next seed.

Step Two: Goodness

According to Second Peter 1:5, I must add to my faith *goodness.* Goodness is the desire to do what is right. It comes right before knowledge and well before godliness. Christians who fail to develop goodness will try to gain godliness for themselves instead of for others; they will attempt to manipulate God's promises for selfish gain. Still others will find goodness but not find faith. They are good people, trying to do the right thing, but either don't believe in God or choose not to seek.

For those who have faith in God, goodness is seen when you desire to do the right thing and obey God even when you don't understand what He is asking of you. That is why it comes before knowledge. It's saying "I don't know all the rules yet, but I want to do right." Goodness is where the fear of the Lord lives. Many Christians wait until they understand a command from God before they will commit to obeying it. *"The fear of the Lord is the beginning of knowledge…"* (Prov. 1:7).

Without goodness, we will not be able to get to the next step, knowledge. Solomon was saying in this very first proverb, "OK. Before I can teach you anything else, you need to know this, fear God. If you don't get this one, you won't understand any of them."

Step Three: Knowledge...and Beyond

Add to your goodness, *knowledge*. Continued growth will require you to continue learning. You want to do what is right, but then, what is right? So we have to learn the knowledge of God's ways.

To make this process a reality, you must be hearing and reading God's Word. As you do so, you are planting knowledge that will, in turn, grow wisdom. So, you hear with your ears, then you take what you have heard to the Spirit of God, who helps you refine that Word. Then, you plant it deep in your heart.

This is how you "grow" the things of God. We first believe in Christ, which is *faith*. Then we decide to obey His will, which is *goodness*. Next we learn what His will is, which is, to us, *knowledge*. With knowledge in hand, we need the *self-control* it will take to do what God is asking. Of course, we must develop *perseverance*, so that we can continue to do the Lord's will when doing it becomes difficult.

Are you getting the idea? This takes work. You are planting the seeds of God, tilling the soil, and continually uprooting the Ites.

Speaking of Ites, self-control is involved when dealing with these weeds. You are busy watering and growing your fruit. This is like carrying your cross. You experience some defeats and victories. What you do with each will determine whether you continue on. It will take self-control to respond in the right way.

And without perseverance, you cannot complete a step. You keep starting, stopping, and starting over again. This cycle will wear you out. At best, it will keep you stuck. At worst, it will have you moving backward.

After perseverance is working, you begin to tap into the blessing. Perseverance also seems to be the transition point into a new type of seed. *Godliness* is when you realize that nothing is supposed to be missing or broken in your life. This is also where you begin to experience the reality of that level of wholeness. You are imitating God and His ways, and God is not short of anything. He has more than enough. Wisdom lives here, too. You are in a position to bless others because you have more than you need.

People who do not develop perseverance and self-control will not be able to remain in godliness. Some will try to use godliness as a means to financial gain or self-aggrandizement. This will end in destruction. Greed cannot cohabitate with godliness.

After godliness we move to *brotherly kindness.* When we are in a position to bless others we should; brotherly kindness is the action of blessing others with the blessing you have, especially the wisdom of God. This is the greatest gift you give. God has shown you so much and given you so much; you must share it so that someone else can grow. All of this is part of the work of seed planting.

Finally, we reach the destination in seed planting, the sowing of love. This is not love the way the world understands it. It is a seed that is produced as you experience how much God loves you. Because you are loved, you can plant this seed so that it grows, not only in your heart, but outward to others.

Seed Summary

You are full of seed and ready to plant more! Before we get on to the fruit of the Spirit, let's take a final look at our seed, the building blocks of our Christianity from Second Peter 1:5-7:

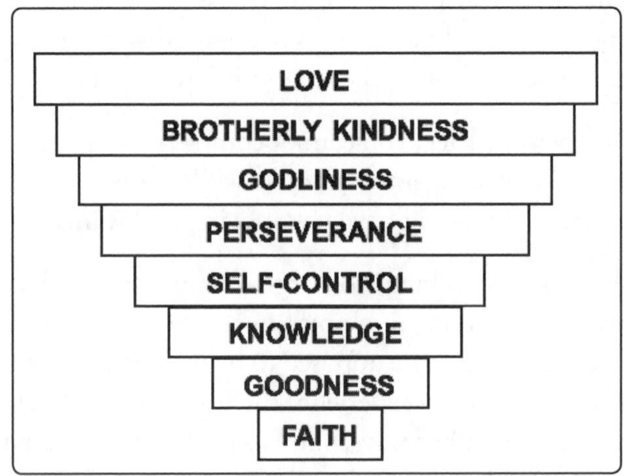

[Figure 5]

Faith is the narrow gate through which we enter. As we grow, the infinite things of God open up to us more and more! Faith is not only about salvation. As I have said before, faith must grow in order for us to make transitions throughout our growth. As we continue, each of these blocks increases in its measure.

Just as Christ is the chief cornerstone, faith is the foundational block for change. Now about that fruit mentioned in Galatians. That's for the next chapter.

Chapter 22

Fruity or Fruitful?

In the prior chapter we discussed the seed we plant, but what are we growing? Let's look at our "fruit" Scripture again:

> *The fruit of the Spirit is love, joy, peace, patience, kindness, goodness, faithfulness, gentleness and self-control. Against such things there is no law* (Galatians 5:22-23).

The fruit of the Spirit are produced in your heart; but to have fruit you must grow a tree. Each fruit of the Spirit is unique; they each come from separate trees, which, in turn, come from separate seeds.

For example, the kindness tree produces kindness fruit. For the sake of demonstration, let's see them as one tree that functions like the Church, in which we are the branches and Christ is the vine. The trunk of the tree pulls from the nutrients in the heart. These nutrients started with the seed of faith, that narrow gate which is Christ. This grows up in us and matures to the point of producing fruit.

Figure 6 is an illustration of the fruit, listed in the same order God lists them in Galatians 5:22-23.

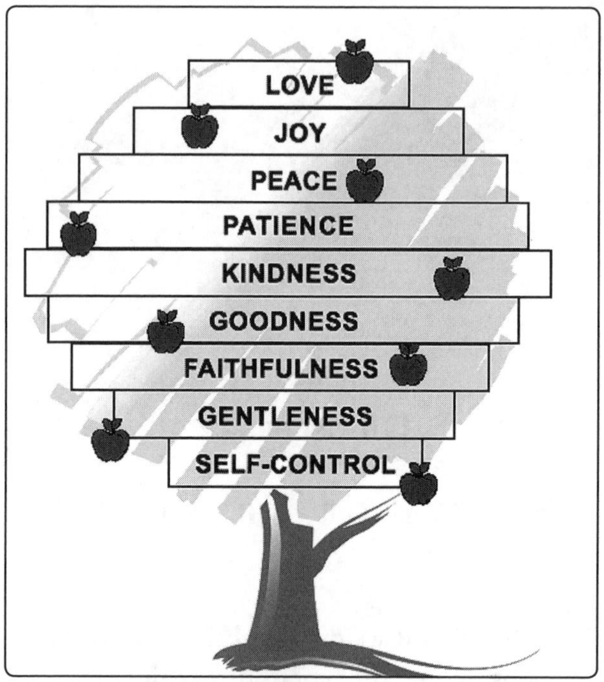

[Figure 6]

Each seed that we plant from the list provided in Second Peter 1:5-8 is a building block of our Christianity that is designed to produce fruit. We plant them in the order shown us in the Scripture; however, that is not the same order in which they grow.

This is important to understand. If you are tempted to be overwhelmed right now, I would encourage you to persevere. Reread this section if you need to. Then check out Figure 7. It is a list of all the seeds and the fruit each produces.

Remember that the planting order and the growing order are not the same. The chart is arranged in the order of planting. Note also that the seed of knowledge is not listed here, because knowledge is necessary for all of the fruit to grow and facilitates growth in wisdom in each area. We must apply the knowledge of our Lord to all we do. Remember that Adam *knew* Eve and she produced a son. We must not only believe in God, but *know* Him so that we can produce fruit.

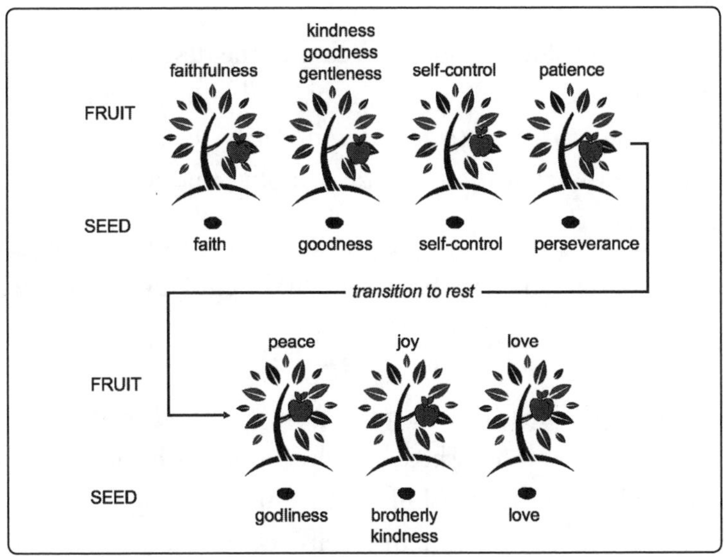

[Figure 7]

Figure 7 is designed to clarify the relationship between each seed and the fruit it produces, while Figure 8 enables us to view both seed and fruit in their original orders, side by side. This illustration also links fruit with their corresponding seeds and shows how knowledge works in nurturing all of the fruit.

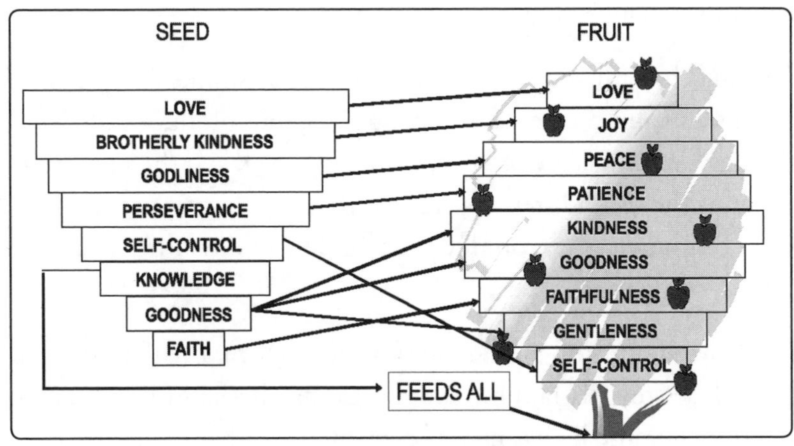

[Figure 8]

We start our planting with the seed called *faith,* but faithfulness is not the first fruit of the Spirit to grow. The first fruit that shows up is self-control, the lowest-hanging fruit on the tree.

Notice that both illustrations show love as the destination. But a change occurs when the seed of perseverance is planted and the fruit of patience is borne. This is the transition to rest. I will clarify this idea in the next two chapters, because this transition is critical to our journey.

First, let's get some understanding as to why the fruit are not growing in the order of planting. God has His reasons, and we need to understand them.

Ready?

Self-control is the first fruit we must grow. No other fruit will grow until we grow this one. This is a flashback to our bouts with the Ites. The weeds in our hearts will keep the Word of God from becoming fruitful. We must first learn to control self. We have to crucify self with Christ. This fruit, self-control, is your conquering of the Ites. You are taking the territory.

I have met many Christians who have great knowledge of the Lord. Some can read Hebrew and Greek; they can quote the Bible like nobody else; yet they are living in the Wilderness. They continue to make bad decisions. They have planted plenty of seed and have vast knowledge, but it never seems to translate into a changed life.

What are they missing? The answer may be as simple as *self-control.* The Word is in them and can be discussed, but it cannot produce fruit. The battle with the Ites has not been won. First comes the seed, and then the fruit. Fruit production is the second step toward manifesting the promises in this physical realm. But how can we produce faithfulness or any other fruit if we still have no self-control?

Without self-control, a man will find himself in an affair with another woman and destroy his family. Another cannot be faithful to show up for work on time because he has no self-control.

The Seed of Transition

The planting of perseverance is the first of three phases that transition us into rest. Phase two occurs as we grow that perseverance into patience. Phase three happens as we eat the fruit of patience in our hearts and see the promises manifest in the form of godliness (seed) and peace (fruit).

We will explore all three phases shortly. Know this in the meantime: both the seeds and the fruit beyond perseverance and patience manifest as activated promises of God that are experienced in the physical realm.

Godliness is your first harvest of God's promises. It is the first time you have more than you need. Still, you must plant this seed and remember that your first harvest goes to God. You give it to the expansion of His Kingdom. In this, you demonstrate that God's goal is more important than your need for a fast car.

This is where many make a mess of things. They decide to invest the money in a business or a big house, thinking they will earn even more for God. But the first portion always belongs to God. It is devoted. No touchy!

Planting godliness in the Kingdom will grow peace. Do not use godliness as a means for financial gain! Once you plant godliness and grow the fruit of peace, the tree now has the ability to continue to produce after its kind, and so the cycle begins. Now, you can have that fast car and build God's Kingdom simultaneously. Remember, Solomon had one heck of a chariot (and some kind of house), but he built the Temple first. Solomon had peace for 40 years—this is the rest!

Phases of Transition

All of this starts with the first phase, which is the planting of perseverance. This is where we learn to persevere for the sole reason that God has asked us to. You might want to quit at times, feeling that your investment is going to exceed your expected return. But if you will press on in obedience anyway, then the supernatural must balance with the investment you have given and God is employed to reward you, because hope does not disappoint.

Suffering without quitting is what teaches this perseverance:

> *Not only so, but we also rejoice in our sufferings, because we know that suffering produces perseverance; perseverance, character; and character, hope. And hope does not disappoint us, because God has poured out His love into our hearts by the Holy Spirit, whom He has given us* (Romans 5:3-5).

Remember that hope is the younger brother of faith. In time, hope converts into faith. Then perseverance expands your faith and enables you to continue moving forward into larger and larger territories.

We only quit when the road seems too hard in relation to the reward we believe we will receive. If I'm searching the couch for a nickel, I won't search long. If I'm searching the couch for a million dollars, I will tear that sofa to pieces, if necessary. I won't quit. The expected reward will keep me going!

Now here's a key for you to digest: If I persevere beyond the expected reward, I will develop character, in the form of patience. Patience reproduces hope, which feeds faith and does not disappoint. This means that no matter how hard you try or how much you suffer, the Lord Himself will make sure the reward exceeds your investment—but only if you don't quit.

Hope will not disappoint. Unfortunately, we often quit early and set ourselves up for unnecessary disappointments that have nothing to do with God. Too many people throw in the towel on marriage early and never experience the reward that was ahead. Of course, marriage is just one example of something people quit on, but I think you get the point: Obedience to God needs to happen even when the reward seems inadequate. That is character.

You cannot fail if you haven't quit trying yet.

The second phase of this transition into the promises is to convert the seed of perseverance into the fruit of patience abounding from your heart.

The planting of the seed takes work, but the fruit of the Spirit, including the fruit of patience, come naturally to us. Instead of requiring work, the fruit yields pleasure. We will see this in more detail later—in fact, it is the premise of this entire chapter.

With the fruit of patience being borne, we enter the third phase of this transition when patience produces a physical manifestation of the promises. We are now eating the fruit of patience in a place where the promises of God produce without hindrance; they are neither stolen nor able to produce destruction.

We will complete the discussion of the fruits peace, joy, and love in the following chapters. Before we go there, however, we need to look at how the fruit of the Spirit changes you. Also, I want to make sure you understand that planting is a continual process. We don't plant one seed at a time and wait for the fruit to show up before we plant another seed. Instead, like farmers, we are always scattering seed in our hearts. It happens automatically as we hear and meditate on God's Word.

What Does Fruit Do?

How does the production of the fruit of the Spirit lead us to rest? How does it change us? As the fruit of the Spirit begin to produce in our lives we move ever closer to experiencing the *rest* that God has promised us.

Here is the principle at work:

> *So I say, live by the Spirit, and you will not gratify the desires of the sinful nature. For the sinful nature desires what is contrary to the Spirit, and the Spirit what is contrary to the sinful nature. They are in conflict with each other, so that you do not do what you want. But if you are led by the Spirit, you are not under law* (Galatians 5:16-18).

Now that we understand both the seed and the fruit we can see more clearly what God is communicating in this passage. Self, the sinful nature, is at war with what the Spirit wants. Whoever has more trees growing in your heart wins. If self has trees of lust growing in the heart, you will make the wrong choice in regard to abstinence, even though you know what is right. Or, if you chose to abstain you will be miserable. This is a lose-lose scenario.

God offers us the power to turn the same situation into a win all around. The key word here is *desire.* Your desire will be determined by the fruit growing in your heart. As the Ites are defeated, the fruit of the Spirit grow and take hold of desire. A tree of goodness will produce the fruit of goodness and you will desire to do good.

When you do good, it produces the fulfillment of doing what God wanted. Therefore, resisting good makes you miserable. Do you see the dynamics of change that are at work when the fruit take root?

The seed of goodness produces gentleness, goodness, and kindness (all fruit of the Spirit). These promote the desire for godly actions. If this desire goes unfulfilled, you will feel empty. This is the flip side of what you experienced when sin ruled your life. Back then, you either indulged your sinful desires in order to find fulfillment, or you abstained and were left empty. Neither choice created fulfillment.

This is a classic trap of the enemy. Here's the antidote: Joy happens when we are doing what we desire to do. (Again, desire is at the heart of the matter.) God's kind of joy causes us to enjoy even the sacrifices we make. This means the fruit have grown up in us; they are producing the desire to make the sacrifice. The suffering associated with the sacrifice produces joy and fulfillment. Jesus, *"...who for the joy set before Him, endured the cross..."* (Heb. 12:2).

Now put this into perspective: Jesus is full of the fruit of the Spirit. When the storm hits (see Mark 4), the peace within Him produces the desire to be at rest, knowing that God is His shield. That knowledge of God's faithfulness, combined with the fruit of peace, is the reason the disciples find Jesus fast asleep in the stern of the boat.

Getting back to lust: With the sinful nature in charge, lust has a good chance of winning. With the fruit of the Spirit growing in your life, lust has no chance. In fact, lust makes you miserable, because your desire is to love others with God's love. Gentleness, kindness, and self-control are producing the desire to do what is right; therefore fulfillment happens in your obedience.

This is the heart condition of someone who is controlled by the Spirit. This is where you are finally doing what you want to do! The fruit of the Spirit transforms your desires and controls your will. This is how we escape the corruption of this world that is mentioned in Second Peter 1:4.

Before we move on, let me leave you with this thought. We take the Promised Land spiritually first and in the physical realm after that. It is a process, not an event. The goal is to continue on and press in, remaining productive and effective in our faith.

Our hearts have been in a state of unrest, caught in a battle between the sinful nature and the spirit of man. This unrest goes back to the beginning of the journey. Developing the fruit of the Spirit is the only way to reconcile this battle. This is where we truly begin to do what we want to do and unrest becomes a thing of the past. This peace begins in the heart and manifests in the physical realm afterward.

As the battle calms down in your heart, it is getting ready to calm down on the earth as well.

Chapter 23

How to Wait at a Green Light

THE NEXT TWO CHAPTERS are the stadium-of-life grand slam we have been building toward. This is the game-winning at-bat.

I say this in all humility. It isn't me; it is the Word of God that is going to lace up the journey. We started out in Hebrews discussing the idea of entering His rest. Now we will return to where we started and do a run-through of the entire journey, pausing with great detail on the seed of transition and the final three fruit of the Spirit.

If you have been searching this book for the key to entering the Lord's rest, get ready, because it is revealed here. Of course, without the foundation presented in previous chapters, knowing the key will not help. You won't know which door to open with it.

Let's go all the way back to our man, Abraham. There is more that his life is about to reveal:

> *The Lord appeared to Abraham near the great trees of Mamre while he was sitting at the entrance to his tent in the heat of the day* (Genesis 18:1).

What is Abraham doing? Nothing. It is hot out. It might be afternoon and Abraham has nothing pressing that he has to do. No crisis in the flock today. Nephew hasn't been taken hostage. Everything is smooth. Yet, what is ahead is anything but run of the mill. Abraham is going to meet the Lord and learn that his promised son, Isaac, is coming soon!

Abraham is one of the few guys in the Bible who lived the journey from beginning to end. He received the promises of God and is resting in the entrance to his tent. Moses got out of Egypt, but never reached the Promised Land. Joshua started at the threshold of the Promised Land, but never achieved rest for the people. Jesus obviously entered the rest, but few others in the Bible did. Even among those Bible characters we highly regard, how many started in Egypt, finished in the Promised Land, and arrived at the place of rest?

Abraham did. Here he is, kicking back, enjoying a nice view of the trees—and the Lord shows up. The Lord has taken a bodily form for the occasion and Abraham gets to walk and talk with Him.

In human terms, Abraham does not appear to have done much in the way of great things. He wasn't an evangelist. He didn't write any great books of prophecy. He didn't lead a great nation. In my initial search for Abraham's accomplishments, I found that he really didn't *do* much.

I say that recognizing that I was looking for the wrong things. What I see as godly greatness is not what God credits as greatness. God's Word regards highly the great patriarch, Abraham, the father of many nations. We sing about him in children's church. "Right hand, left hand, father Abraham, had many sons...." He is mentioned throughout the New Testament. He is the man through whom God chose to bless all peoples. The inheritance of God refers to the promises Abraham received. Jesus died so that the blessing given to Abraham would be ours.

So what exactly did Abraham do? Why is he so highly regarded in the Lord's eyes? The answer is simple, but will take a great deal of explanation.

When I looked more deeply into the life of Abraham, I was astonished at what I found. Abraham's sterling achievement was this: Abraham received the promises (see Rom. 4:13; Heb. 11:11). That is it.

It may seem like a small deal to us that Abraham is great in God's eyes simply because he received the blessing—not, mind you, because God gave him the blessing, but because he received and experienced the blessing.

This forces us to examine the basics of faith again. We receive the promises by what? Faith. Without faith we cannot please God (see Heb. 11:6). But let's go a step further and look at the flip side of this: why was God angry with the Israelites?

Let's revisit God's explanation:

> *Who were they who heard and rebelled? Were they not all those Moses led out of Egypt? And with whom was He angry for forty years? Was it not with those who sinned, whose bodies fell in the desert? And to whom did God swear that they would never enter His rest if not to those who disobeyed? So we see that they were not able to enter, because of their unbelief* (Hebrews 3:16-19).

God was angry because they did not receive what was promised them. He was angry because they were not willing to receive all that He had given. The first thing God did for man was to bless him. After the Fall, God gave His only Son so that we would have access to this blessing again. He has spent a great deal to get us blessed.

Funny as it may seem, God is not asking us to receive the blessing; He is commanding it. It is our *responsibility* to be sure none of us fall short of it: "*...Let us be careful that none of you be found to have fallen short of* [His rest]" (Heb. 4:1).

As you can see from this book so far, it is no small feat to receive the promises of God. The gift is free, but experiencing the promises in the absence of destruction takes some maturing. Our sinful nature is a formidable opponent to this experience of the blessing. Sin does not separate us from the blessing; our guilt does. This guilt is one of the repercussions of sin in our lives. There are other side effects. Try robbing a bank and see what happens.

Abraham is highly regarded in God's sight because he in fact received the blessing, which means reconnection to the original plan. Again, why does God want us blessed? Answer: So that we have the resources to reach our destinies; reach glorious victory; rule with influence while administering justice; and bring God's will to earth as it is in Heaven.

What is His will? Answer: That none would perish, but all would come to the saving knowledge of Christ (see 2 Pet. 3:9). Christ regained the authority and returned it to us in His name so that we could disciple all nations. Remember that the nations are the high places of influence in our world. Abraham had this influence in his world. When Abraham came to town, the king would take notice. I've traveled to many nations and have yet to have the king show up at the airport to greet me. I'm not there yet. Abraham was.

When I look at Abraham's life, I see the simplicity of the journey. It is the kind of life that inspired me to write this book. God visits Abraham just like He did Moses and the Israelites and tells him to leave and go to a new land. Both his journey and the Israelite's 40-year trek started with a promise. I don't know how many other men God may have asked to do this, but Abraham did it.

It appears Abraham's father was on his way to Canaan, but got hung up along the way. I wonder what the story is there.

> *Terah took his son Abram, his grandson Lot son of Haran, and his daughter-in-law Sarai, the wife of his son Abram, and together they set out from Ur of the Chaldeans to go to Canaan. But when they came to Haran, they settled there* (Genesis 11:31).

Terah parked in Haran, but Abraham obeyed and went to Canaan.

There are distinct similarities between the journey of Abraham and that of the Israelites. Both went down to Egypt, through the Wilderness, and into the Promised Land. The same land was promised to both; in fact, it's the same promise.

When Abraham arrived, God made a covenant with him (see Gen. 12:7). This covenant was confirmed later with circumcision (see Gen. 17:11). Abraham's covenant of circumcision was the first time a man was in covenant with God through circumcision.

Remember Joshua in Gilgal? When the Israelites arrived in the Promised Land they went to Gilgal for the covenant of circumcision (see Josh. 5:2).

Abraham then had to fight a battle, just like Joshua fought his first battle at Jericho. If you'll remember, Jericho was a picture of the tithe and was not to be touched. All the spoils went to the house of the Lord.

Right after his battle, Abraham tithes to the high priest Melchizedek, who is a picture of Jesus Christ (see Gen. 14:20) and is referred to as the King of Salem (*salem* means "peace").[1] Christ, of course, is the Prince of Peace.

Melchizedek is a man with no lineage, beginning, or end (see Heb. 7:3). This High Priest and King of Salem receives the tithe, a tenth of all that Abraham has, and blesses him. Abraham refused to touch any of the spoils from the battle he had won. This is the first time in the Bible that a man tithes to the Lord. There were offerings mentioned, but never a specific tenth. God did not ask Abraham to give him a tenth, he just did it. It was not a tenth of what he had earned that week, month, or year. It was a tenth of all that he had.

Many Christians question tithing because they aren't positive that it is a command of God to us. Some reason that the tithe was dispelled with the advent of the New Covenant. But, here we see the true heart of one who follows God. He needs no command to give to God. He wants to do it.

Without prompting, Abraham is beginning to define God's characteristics. How does he do this? He has an understanding of God; Abraham knew God's ways. He knew by divine revelation.

Later, I want to show that Abraham enters the rest of the Lord, but first, what are some of the other things Abraham does? He is the first man on earth to meet Christ (the Priest Melchizedek). He is the first man described as coming face to face with the Lord at the great trees of Mamre. He is the first man to be renamed. (God renames all of us when we receive Him.) Abraham is the first man mentioned by God in the Scripture as a prophet. The first prophet? When did Abraham ever prophesy? *"Now return the man's wife, for he is a prophet, and he will pray for you and you will live…"* (Gen. 20:7).

God may define the word *prophet* a little differently than you and I. This is because we are still learning God's ways. God was saying, "When Abraham speaks, I will do it." This is what God did when Jesus spoke to the storm (see Mark 4:39). They are examples for us; we are to imitate God and call things *"that are not as though they were"* (Rom. 4:17).

This is prophecy. God would do what Abraham asked. If I were to say, "Hey, next Tuesday you are going to get a job," and then it happens, I am a prophet. But the job came because I called those things that are not as though they were. Abraham was the first man to pray to God for someone to be healed and they were healed (see Gen. 20:17). This had never happened before. Abraham was defining what we know of God today in a way that had never been defined. He understood God without any help from a preacher and without having a Bible on his nightstand.

Abraham's approach to God was a change from the way people thought about "the gods" in his day. People in this day worshiped many gods, and presented sacrifices to them. They realized that creation was too great to be happenstance; they considered that someone (lots of someones) greater and more intelligent must be in charge. They reasoned that sacrifices would appease these gods. They hoped that the smoke of burnt sacrifices would rise into the air and reach their gods.

They had malevolent gods, too. The god Molech required them to give up their firstborn children. This ultimate sacrifice would ensure that the god Molech would bless their crops with rain.

The God of Abraham acted very differently. He gave man authority over the earth and asked him to subdue it. He was a healing God and a God who gave first. Whereas Abraham's God was concerned for man and loved him, the other gods were indifferent to man, almost annoyed by mankind. The only way to please other gods was with a sacrifice.

Abraham's God was pleased by faith. He was a God who answered prayer. Abraham began to accurately define God and name His attributes. Infinite power resides in the name of God. Out of that name Abraham pulled out descriptive "titles" such as *Jehovah Jireh* (see Gen. 22:14). Abraham called Him that because He provided. *Jehovah Ropheka* is the God who heals (see Exod. 15:26). These names are in the name of God, but they provide us with greater understanding of the promises. Abraham understood God so well that he was naming God and God was OK with it.

Remember that the Israelites were described as not entering the rest of the Lord because they *"have not known My ways"* (Heb. 3:10).

Abraham did know God's ways.

How Did Abraham Receive?

The Book of Hebrews leads us down the same journey, starting with its description of the rest and the relationship the Israelites had with the journey. The book then talks about grace, the covenant, our need to enter in to see God in our hearts, and more.

The book whose theme is entering the rest of the Lord then discusses the heroes of faith. The writer, like me, shares the secrets of entering the rest, although not all of the heroes named actually entered in. We are left to discern the differences among them. Abel, who was killed by Cain, did not receive the promises. Neither did Enoch (who was taken up by God in Genesis 5:22) or Noah. But Abraham is different. When Abraham is mentioned, the writer of Hebrews continually reminds us that he received the promises.

> *By faith Abraham, when called to go to a place he* ***would later receive as his inheritance,*** *obeyed and went, even though he did not know where he was going* (Hebrews 11:8).

Here you see that he did receive the inheritance of the Promised Land. There is mention that he was also awaiting a city with foundations whose architect and builder is God. This is only available to you and me *after* Christ's sacrifice. Abraham is mentioned more in the heroes of faith than any other person:

> *By faith Abraham, even though he was past age—and Sarah herself was barren—was enabled to become a father because he considered Him faithful who had made the promise* (Hebrews 11:11).

Abraham had faith in God, and considered Him faithful. Faith is the seed we plant and faithfulness is the fruit that grows. Abraham had a grasp of God's ways; he understood God's faithfulness.

> *By faith Abraham, when God tested him, offered Isaac as a sacrifice. He who had* ***received the promises*** *was about to sacrifice his one and only son* (Hebrews 11:17).

Again, Abraham was described as having "received the promises." It seems surprising that God would ask Abraham to sacrifice his son. In Abraham's age, however, it was not uncommon for a person to make this sort of sacrifice. Yet, God was making a statement; He differentiated Himself from the false gods. Remember that Molech asked for children to be sacrificed all the time. Now Abraham is asked by God to sacrifice his son and agrees to do so, because He trusts God.

Abraham and his son set out on a three-day journey up a mountain. Just before Abraham sacrifices Isaac, an angel of the Lord stops him. God provides the sacrifice, a ram caught in the thicket (see Gen. 22:11-13). God is different than the other gods. He shows that instead of us sacrificing our children to God, He will, in fact, be sacrificing His Son for us.

Abraham's son, Isaac, was a picture of Christ. This reveals a completely unique attribute compared to the false gods of that time. Abraham's God gives first. God sees things finished, so when Abraham decides to obey God and sacrifice his son, Isaac dies, symbolically speaking, on that first day. It was still three days until the actual sacrifice. So on the third day Isaac lives, just as Christ would.

> *Even though God had said to him, "It is through Isaac that your offspring will be reckoned." Abraham reasoned that God could raise the dead, and figuratively speaking, he did receive Isaac back from death* (Hebrews 11:18-19).

No man had been raised from the dead to this point and yet Abraham had already attributed this power to God. Abraham knew God's ways. Continuing on in Hebrews 11, is again referred Abraham to as having received what was promised as he is lumped into the group of heroes with this passage: *"who through faith conquered kingdoms, administered justice, and gained what was promised..."* (Heb. 11:33).

These heroes were destined to rule so that they could administer justice and gain what had been promised by God. Heroes! Imagine how elevated a status is when God calls someone a hero!

> *Therefore, since we are surrounded by such a great cloud of witnesses, let us throw off everything that hinders and the sin that so easily entangles, and let us run with perseverance the race marked out for us* (Hebrews 12:1).

The Book of Hebrews now adds more key elements for our understanding of how to complete the journey. We already know to address our Ites (the distractions of sin). We have covered the need to stay within our anointed purpose and run the unique race that is ours. We understand the role of perseverance as the transitional seed that leads us into experiencing God's promises.

So how did Abraham receive the promises, when so many others struggled even though they loved God?

> *We want each of you to show this same diligence to the very end, in order to make your hope sure. We do not want you to become lazy, but to imitate those who* ***though faith and patience inherit what has been promised*** (Hebrews 6:11-12).

Show diligence for how long? God says to show it until the very end. Not just the end, but the very end. There's perseverance one more time. God is saying that we are not to give up because pushing on enhances our hope. It makes our hope sure, meaning it converts our hope into faith.

Remember, hope does not disappoint because you empower the God of the supernatural to reward your diligence. You want your diligence to call in a greater-than-normal reward. But here we are confronted with Abraham's key! We are asked to imitate it. The first element is faith. We know of faith by now. We need faith in every move of our journey. We leave Egypt by faith. We have faith that the Passover Lamb, Christ, has redeemed us. This is our *salvation*. We learn to trust God in the Wilderness for our needs. And as our attempts at self-justification bring us to the realization that we cannot be justified without Christ, we receive justification by faith in Him.

Next we battle in the Promised Land. We become free of guilt. We recognize that we are due the land because of our faith in Christ's righteousness and not our own. We succeed in the Promised Land by faith in God's divine nature and eternal power. We then receive prosperity by faith so we can enter the rest of the Lord, fully armed with the resources necessary to attain to glory.

Faith is a key! But Abraham gives us another key. Faith and something else. Faith and *patience.* To inherit what is promised we must have faith *and* patience. Abraham possessed these qualities.

Perseverance and Patience Together

In Chapter 22, I described the seed we plant and the fruit we grow. We plant the seeds of faith, goodness, knowledge, self-control, perseverance, godliness, brotherly kindness, and love.

The first fruit to grow is self-control. I cannot grow any other fruits of the Spirit until I learn to control myself. I can plant all the seeds I want, but the fruit grow in God's order. Let's look at the seed and fruit chart again.

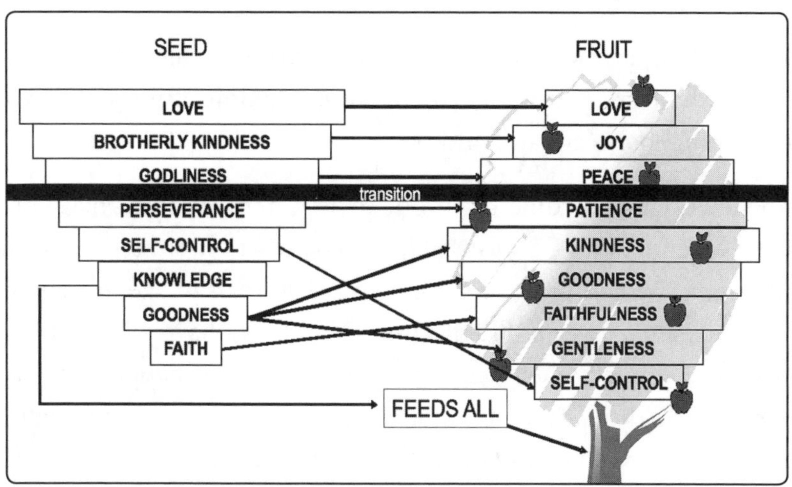

[Figure 8a]

I have drawn a black line, like a wall above patience and perseverance. The black line indicates the transition in seed and fruit that takes place here. This is the point of entering rest. I touched on this in Chapter 22. Let me now continue.

Patience is the true catalyst to experiencing the next fruit after patience, which is peace. Peace and godliness are alike. Both represent the actual experience of the promises of God. Peace is rest as I have described it throughout this book.

In the boat during the storm (see Matt. 8; Mark 4; Luke 8), Jesus did more than act in faith; He operated in complete peace. One of the Greek words used in the New Testament for "peace" is *eirēnē.* It means "security," "prosperity," and "felicity," among other things.[2] Nothing missing, and nothing broken.

The Hebrew word for peace is *shalom*. It also means "completeness," "safety," "welfare," "health," and "prosperity."[3] Again, there is nothing missing and nothing broken. This may be a redefining of what you thought peace was until now. It is so much more than not worrying. It is experiencing the Promises of God daily, free of fear or doubt, and walking in the resources you need to become a ruler.

Now looking at the chart, we see that faith working through patience takes on a whole new meaning. There are many other things it is working through as well, between faith and patience.

Patience is hard to come by in our society. Yet, Abraham had faith and patience. When he was 75 years old, Abraham was promised a son, Isaac. He did not receive this promise until he was 100 years of age. Abraham held faith patiently for 25 years. He did not give up. We have a hard time waiting more than a week when we pray for something to happen. We assume that our prayer didn't work. Right now, many single girls and guys who have been praying a whole six months for the perfect mate have cried out, "It's not working."

"Jason, I've been praying for my marriage. I'm holding on with both hands. I'm tired." Faith and patience. I didn't say it was easy. Patience starts to feel a lot like perseverance here. The two are so closely related. The perseverance grows the patience.

The seed of perseverance grows the fruit of patience. Doubt is the interrupter of that growth. That is why we must allow our perseverance to create character, hope, and diligence, which turn our hope to faith. If we allow doubt to live here, we will be inhibited. If I'm working hard toward a goal, I'm tired, I'm sweating, I'm suffering, and then doubt enters in...well, I'm at risk of quitting.

Patience is better than perseverance; it is the product of perseverance that has matured. Perseverance indicates there is still a struggle happening, a battle that is tempting me to quit (but I won't). Patience is not about struggling. When patience is present, I am OK with the circumstances and ready to overcome them.

Patience is uncommon in our society. Sit at an intersection after the light turns green and count how many seconds pass before the honking starts. (Maybe you are the honker?)

Looking to the chart, peace, joy, and love mark out the destination. Patience is the transitional fruit that will get me through the wall.

Peace, Joy, and Love

This is not just a great saying on a Christmas greeting. These three fruit are our focus now.

In Figure 8a the transition that leads us to love shows a significant change in the type of fruit and seed. Love is an infinite quality; it contains all the qualities of God named underneath it in both the seed and fruit categories. Now let's bring up a passage that I mentioned at the beginning of this book:

> *I tell you the truth, anyone who has faith in Me will do what I have been doing. He will do even greater things than these, because I am going to the Father. And I will do whatever you ask in My name, so that the Son may bring glory to the Father* (John 14:12-13).

Remember that glory is the victory that creates influence. It is the fruit of your physical and spiritual labor. When you win, God wins! The resulting influence brings God more influence through us. Glory to the Father.

According to Jesus, this starts with faith. With faith we can accomplish even greater works than Christ. Through our faith, He will do whatever we ask in His name.

What is in a name? Jesus' entire teaching here is interlaced with the promise of the Holy Spirit who would soon reside inside us and make His home with us. The life this brings will allow this fruit to grow inside. But first, let's discuss this "name" business. There is authority *in the name* of Jesus. What promises are *in His name*?

Abraham and others who went before us found that God's name had other names within it, names that defined certain attributes of God. They would pull these names out at the appropriate time: Jehovah M'Kaddesh, my sanctification (see Lev. 20:7-8). Jehovah Nissi, my banner (see Exod. 17:15). El Shaddai, the Almighty God who is sufficient to meet my needs (see Gen. 17:1). These names existed within the infinite goodness of God's name. They were in His name. Our spiritual forbears understood the principle of a name.

For us, names are random identifiers that we pick out of books before a baby is born. But God names us, too. He is very interested in our names. To God, the name is more than a random identifier. A name defines you. That is why God does not have a single, all-encompassing name. Some theologians may pin *Yahweh* on Him. But even scholars agree that the name of the Lord is unknown. He said to Moses *"I AM, WHO I AM"* (Exod. 3:14). This answer was not an answer, but an existence.

God is so many names. We can ask for anything *in the name of Jesus Christ*, the anointed one. We pull things out of this name that are in line with our anointings and individual purposes. This drives us toward the glory God has for us, if indeed we will persevere through the trouble and be diligent in enduring. Glory! *"There Abram called upon the name of the Lord"* (Gen. 13:4).

Abraham did what Christ told us to do. Abraham understood the power of pulling from the name of the Lord. Abraham did not call upon *the Lord;* he called upon *the name of the Lord*. This is something Abraham did often. Abraham would build an altar, offer a gift, and call upon the name of the Lord.

The name reminds us in our heart of God's responsibilities: Healer... Provider...Freedom...Blessing...Justification...Salvation...Prosperity... Success...Redemption...Forgiveness...Love...and more. Our faith is stirred with these reminders.

Notice also that we do not seek to receive things that are not *in* Jesus' name. There are many things Christians pray for that are not in Jesus' name. God is Jehovah Jireh. He will provide for us. The provision has a purpose—the resource to get us to the place of rulership, administering justice, and creating fruit that leads to influence. Glory.

Jesus introduces His name as the source now. *Christ* means "Anointed One." This is a reminder that the provision must be for the purpose of the Lord. As I place God's purpose first in my own heart, then all the "things" are added to me (see Matt. 6:33). God may want you to have a shiny fast car, but not first. He wants you to have the desires of your heart, but first He wants you to put the resources He provides into the Kingdom. The purpose is the expansion of God's will here on earth!

Now back to what Christ was getting at: *"Peace I leave with you; My peace I give you..."* (John 14:27).

Remember the definition of peace: nothing missing, nothing broken. He's telling the disciples, "Hey, you know how I'm never stressed and always walking in abundance? You can have that, too. Always healthy. This can be you. I'm giving it to you."

Christ is planting in us through the power of the Word of God the ability to produce the fruit of the Spirit, which is peace.

Abraham left Egypt at the age of 75 after hearing God make a promise to give him a son. He has arrived in the Promised Land, where he enters into covenant with God, and then goes into battle. God gives him victory, and just after the victory he tithes. This was his Jericho. He is now 86 years old. He has remained persevering for a son. It is perseverance because a struggle is involved. If we fast forward just a bit in his life, we see that he is struggling as he attempts to gain the promise by sleeping with Hagar, his wife's maidservant.

Ah yes, in all of this, Abraham made mistakes. (Good to know.) He is struggling to hold on to the promise. These struggles sometimes lead to mistakes. Keep in mind, this is just after his battle and his tithe to the King of Salem. The King of Salem, which is the King of Peace blesses him: *"...Blessed be Abram by God Most High, Creator of heaven and earth"* (Gen. 14:19).

Hear this again. Abraham gave of his wealth to God. He had become very wealthy. This is part of what is in godliness. Looking back to our chart, godliness is the seed that grows peace. The peace cannot grow until we get through the transitional fruit, which is patience.

Just after this, in a conversation with God, Abraham expresses his struggle. "Hey God, I am still childless over here!" (See Genesis 15.) This is a reminder. Abraham is now beginning to make a transition from perseverance to patience, as God shows him an image of how many children he will have. He shows him the stars and the sand. God is getting Abraham to "see" the unseen. He is getting Abraham to look far beyond just one kid. There will be a gajillion of them. Just as Christ plants His peace in us, He planted his peace in Abraham.

In John 14:27, Jesus talked about His peace being in us. In John 15, Jesus moves on to the next fruit. Notice he is doing this in order. Jesus says, *"I have told you this so that My joy may be in you and that your joy may be complete"* (John 15:11).

Now He is planting His most perfect joy in you. This fruit grows from the seed of brotherly kindness, as our chart demonstrates. Brotherly kindness is a giving to your brother. So closely related is the action that you plant before your harvest that Christ mentions in the same breath that we need to be willing to give our lives for others. The path we are on is the path of love.

As Abraham grows his perseverance into patience, he undergoes a name change. What's in a name? Well, in this case, a lot. He is now 99 years old and the Lord visits him:

> *No longer will you be called Abram; your name will be Abraham, for I have made you a father of many nations* (Gen. 17:5).

Right smack dab in the middle of his name he puts the letters *AH,* which I believe was taken from the name Jehov**ah**. God places His name inside of Abraham's name. This changes his name to mean "Father of many." What's in a name? God is very concerned with a name. Now every time someone calls for Abraham they are calling something that is not as though it were.

This is God's way. Upon this message from God Abraham falls to his knees and laughs. As I mentioned earlier, God placed His joy inside of Abraham—just as Jesus has asked that His joy be in us. The fruit of the Spirit, joy, is God's kind of joy. This is how God defines it:

> *Consider it pure joy, my brothers, whenever you face trials of many kinds, because you know that the testing of your faith develops perseverance. Perseverance must finish its work so that you may be mature and complete, not lacking anything* (James 1:2-4).

This would be, of course, the seed of joy. Planting and toiling to be in joy is what will grow joy. When you face a trial, joy is not a normal reaction. Doubt and fear are normal. Anyone can be happy when everything is perfect. But can we be happy in crisis? Choosing to rejoice in all things develops that perseverance to become and grow patience. Patience is not worried about the crisis. It is sleeping in the storm. You have reached beyond trying not to be afraid. Instead, you are trying to be happy.

This is like God getting Abraham to reach beyond one child to see the many. The fruit of patience springs to life in Abraham, and just one year later, he receives the promise!

The fruit of joy can begin to grow now, making it natural for you to rejoice in crisis. How can you rejoice in crisis? Well, forgive me for answering a question with a question. Who wins in the end? God does. In the game of chess, if you are going to beat a formidable opponent, you must know the ending before you move. You must lead your opponent into defeat. Often, the only way to do this is to make a sacrifice. The greatest victory will happen when your opponent is sure he is going to win, but there is something you see that he does not. You see the victory five moves away. Now, as he takes a piece from you, a spectator gasps. It appears you have lost. Are you worried? Are you in fear? No. You are excited, even at the crisis, because you know the ending. You win!

Although joy has been planted in Abraham, he is not experiencing joy. First the patience produces peace, the resources. The fruit of joy will be experienced after the patience springs to life. As the Scripture describes, *"Perseverance must finish its work so that you may be mature and complete, not lacking anything"* (James 1:4).

The finished work of perseverance is patience, which transitions you to peace, the state of "not lacking anything." Remember the seed of peace was planted when the first harvest of resource came to Abraham in the form of seed, and he sowed 10 percent of it to God, instead of spending it on himself. This moved the seed of godliness into the planting of peace, having been blessed by the King of Peace. The planting was brotherly kindness (which is giving). Brotherly kindness is the fellowship of the brethren, our partnership with the Body of Christ in the expansion of the Kingdom. It is recognition of the team effort that we must join. We are to unite our purposes to forcefully advance the Kingdom of God, the army of the Lord. We're connected to the Church, giving 10 percent of all the resources God gives us to create a combined effort, where the many can do far more than the one ever could accomplish alone.

Abraham paints this picture just before the tithe as he fights four kings to rescue his nephew, Lot. He was not fighting for himself, but for the team—for others. Because Abraham had a deep understanding of God's ways he finds himself advancing to the primary three fruits of the Spirit. Peace, joy, and love, the final destination being love. Having given birth to the fruit, peace, now the fruit of joy can grow.

Initially, though, it is a toil of joy, a forced decision. It is not coming naturally. Abraham has the name change, but it may take some time before it matures into a physical change of attitude. Toiling always indicates seed. Once that seed is bearing fruit, the fruit allows a natural and easy godly reaction, no matter what is going on.

This is not a joy for which you must toil. You are just happy. It is not a difficult choice to capture your thoughts and be happy. You just are. The battles are over now. You are truly at rest within your own heart. When you are no longer feuding inside, you are in agreement. That is wholeness. The power of agreement demands that the fruit you produce easily and effortlessly continue to manifest God's promises into the natural. Now you sit down next to Christ; He has made your enemies your footstool.

Jesus continues in his discussion of the fruit: *"My command is this: Love each other as I have loved you"* (John 15:12).

Initially it will be a toil of love, but it will grow. Love can be natural and effortless. To love someone who persecutes you can be no work at all, when it is the fruit of love. Remember, whatever is growing in your heart has the most power over your chooser, that is, your will. Love is the destination—to imitate God, who is love.

Abraham is sitting in the heat of the day. Patience has been borne as fruit. Abraham is resting. The transition has happened. The Lord appears and Abraham runs to greet Him, eager to serve the Lord a gift. Upon receiving the gift the Lord promises Abraham what he has been longing for:

Then the Lord said, "I will surely return to you about this time next year, and Sarah your wife will have a son" (Gen. 18:10).

And she did. *Abraham received what was promised.*

CHAPTER 24

JUST TOO MUCH

JUST...JUSTICE? Where did justice come from? This is not a fruit of the Spirit. However, justice is arrived at through life experience and godly knowledge.

Justice is wisdom acting through the fruit of the Spirit.

Justice is personified in the famous story of the wise King Solomon who suggested sawing a baby in half in order resolve the dispute between the baby's real mother and an imposter. The real mother was quickly identified because of her reaction of love. The baby lived.

Solomon's rest and rulership allowed him to administer justice. That justice resulted in peace, a nation without crisis, for 40 years.

*"Abraham was now old and well advanced in years, and the Lord had blessed him in **every** way"* (Gen. 24:1). Picture Abraham in this stage of life. Remember when he was resting in front of the great trees of Mamre, but still had not

received the promised Isaac? He was at peace. That fruit allowed the spiritual promise to manifest in the physical.

So, was Abraham waiting on God for the son, or was God waiting on Abraham? You know the answer. In Genesis 24:1 we see Abraham, and something is different. It is the first time a man is considered in the Word of God as being blessed in every way. It is the first time since Adam and Eve kicked themselves out of The Garden, that is.

Read Genesis 24:1 slowly: *"blessed in* every *way."* Not most ways. Abraham here has nothing missing and nothing broken. This is a rare thing. He has Isaac; he has received the promise. He is Abraham, hear him roar.

At the beginning of this book I mentioned that being in rest is having the miraculous manifested in your life daily. It is when you have no crisis (or anything that you view as a crisis). More than everything you need is there for you. You speak to the mountain and it really does move. And while you wait for it to move you are completely at rest. The Word is working on your behalf.

Abraham had nothing missing, nothing broken. This is when you bring the will of the Lord to the earth—like Jesus, who brought life to death everywhere He went. Sight to the blind and hearing for the deaf were daily experiences for Jesus.

Now, about justice. This is important, because God is asking us to administer justice after we conquer the kingdoms. To do this let's rewind in Abraham's life to the day that he meets the Lord face to face at the great trees of Mamre.

> *The Lord appeared to Abraham near the great trees of Mamre while he was sitting at the entrance to his tent in the heat of the day. Abraham looked up and saw three men standing nearby. When he saw them, he hurried from the entrance of his tent to meet them and bowed low to the ground* (Genesis 18:1-2).

The Bible tells us this is the Lord, but then refers to "three men," which would indicate that Abraham didn't realize at first that he was being visited by God.

He saw three dudes coming out of the trees. Mamre is in *Hebron*, which means "association"[1] or fellowship. Abraham has positioned himself, metaphorically speaking, among the strong oaks of Mamre as though they are a gathering of great men, a fellowship. This is a picture of the Church. This points to the seed mentioned in Second Peter 1:7 as brotherly kindness. It is the joining together of the Body of Christ, the team of the Lord.

The Lord has made His dwelling in the Body of Christ, so it is no surprise that He has emerged from this location. It is the direction that Abraham was facing. What is Abraham's reaction to seeing three men come out of the forest? Remember that he is a great man, in charge over a vast land, riches, and servants. He even has an army of 300 men at his beck and call. Would he not wave dismissively at these men, thinking to himself, "Who are these who approach me? Please, get me more grapes."

Abraham here shows the maturity of one who has been on the journey of the Lord; the maturity of a man of service. He excitedly begs them to stay so he can present them with a gift. It appears that he was suspicious that this was perhaps the Lord. Abraham runs to enlist Sarah's help in preparing the food and water. Everyone is urged to hurry: "Come on…come on…come on, let's go!"

He is literally tripping over himself to be a blessing. How excited was he to give? How excited to serve? This is maturity. We are often so quick to seek rulership so that we can have others wait on us hand and foot. Certainly Abraham had servants, but here we see that he himself is not afraid to serve. As far as we can tell, Abraham does not know this is the Lord yet. Neither does Sarah. After the gift is given, the Lord lets on that Abraham's son will be born next year. Sarah laughs to herself with sarcasm saying, "Oh now that I'm worn out and my master is old will I have this pleasure?" (see Gen. 18:12).

It doesn't appear that Sarah laughed loudly, yet the Lord tells Abraham that He heard her. At this Abraham was probably pretty sure who it was he was talking to.

Let's get back to the gift for a second.

Thinking in Abundance

Abraham has Sarah use three seahs of flour for bread (see Gen. 18:6). This is about 20 quarts of flour. Remember, she is feeding three people. This is 80 cups of flour. Three dudes. A loaf of bread requires about three cups of flour. This would be 26 loaves of bread. Three people. Then Abraham has an entire calf prepared for three people. What is going on here? Abraham thinks the way God does; he thinks in terms of abundance, overflow, more than enough. Almost nine loaves of bread per person. A smaller 600-pound calf would produce 225 pounds of meat—for three people! Maybe they were big people?

Abraham has now acclimated his godly thinking and reactions to his environment. Just as with Jesus, he did not come to be served, but to serve, not so that there might be life, but so that there would be life more abundantly. Like 26 loaves worth of life. That is some serious daily bread.

The Lord begins to reveal His intentions of the visit. For one thing, He stops off to give Abraham the good news about his son: *"Then the Lord said, "I will surely return to you about this time next year, and Sarah your wife will have a son"* (Gen. 18:10).

He was there for another reason—Sodom and Gomorrah. As they finished lunch, Abraham and the three visitors set out toward Sodom and Gomorrah. The Lord decides to clue Abraham in to what He's about to do:

> *Then the Lord said, "Shall I hide from Abraham what I am about to do? Abraham will surely become a great and powerful nation, and all nations on earth will be blessed through him. For I have chosen him, so that he will direct his children and his*

> *household after him to keep the way of the Lord by doing what is right and* ***just,*** *so that the Lord will bring about for Abraham what He has promised him"* (Genesis 18:17-19).

God here exhibits His high regard for Abraham. He confides in Abraham and listens to his concerns over Sodom. He is going to allow Abraham to counsel Him. God gives His reasons for including Abraham in the business of Sodom and Gomorrah. First, Abraham will become a powerful nation. He is becoming what God has called us all to be. His story will go on to influence all of us, even to this day. That is a great ruler, one who continues to influence the world after he dies. It's called posterity. Very few attain to this.

Another reason God includes Abraham is because God has chosen him. God has chosen all of this, before the creation of the world! Next, God mentions that Abraham will influence his children and household in the ways of the Lord. This godly influence again indicates that Abraham understood and knew God's ways. He had knowledge of the Lord. We see here God's view of the importance of instructing our children. Chew on that for a bit. Abraham will instruct them to be just.

For these reasons God not only shares His decision with Abraham and allows him to offer input, but He also gives him what was promised, the completion of the fruit of peace.

I want to expand now on this word *just.* The King James Version says it like this:

> *For I know him, that he will command his children and his household after him, and they shall keep the way of the Lord, to do justice and judgment; that the Lord may bring upon Abraham that which He hath spoken of him* (Genesis 18:17 KJV).

Here it is to "do justice." This word "just" is the Hebrew word *tsedaqah,* which can indicate meanings such as "judge," "ruler," "king," "salvation," "righteousness," "prosperity," and "justice" or "justification."[2]

To administer justice is one of the points Abraham has gotten here. Yet, he has gone beyond just doing justice, because he will also teach others to be just. In fact, he is teaching you right now. How influential is that?

We are asked to be rulers who are just; that is, administering justice. This is a foreign thought for us today. We do not think of our current rulers and influencers as just. God would like us to change this distortion back to a godly norm. Become the ruler.

This word *tsedaqah* is not used in the Word of God until it describes Abraham. Abraham is the first to be called "just." The definition states that it is in relationship to ruler, king, and judge. This is the purpose of learning to be just. We are here to subdue, but we cannot become the influence God wants us to be without gaining the wisdom first.

There are many Christians who love God but are in no position to administer justice; they do not yet know God's ways. The bridge to rulership is out. This is actually a form of protection from ourselves. If we attempt to rule without knowing God's ways, we will cause ourselves and others harm.

Again, looking at the definition of tsedaqah, we find the words *salvation, righteousness, prosperity,* and *justification*. This is the pattern of our journey. We leave Egypt with *salvation*. We pass through the Wilderness as we learn that Christ is our *justification*. We battle in the Promised Land, free from guilt as we partner with Christ in His *righteousness* and not our own (this is the revelation of grace). And, finally, we enter His rest (symbolized on our map by the *Euphrates*, which means peace and *prosperity*.

Tsedaqah is the wisdom we gain by traveling the road of life as God instructs. It is the wisdom resulting from the journey. Reading this book will not give you this wisdom. This book gives you direction, directing you back to the genius of the Word of God. Wisdom comes from God.

Justice is the wisdom that results from the sum total of life's experiences—our obedience and our mistakes alike—when we live according to God's Word.

Abraham's conversation with the Lord reaches interesting heights as they and the two other men move toward Sodom. Now the Lord and Abraham stay back to discuss the coming destruction.

> *Then the Lord said, "The outcry against Sodom and Gomorrah is so great and their sin so grievous that I will go down and see if what they have done is as bad as the outcry that has reached Me. If not, I will know"* (Genesis 18:20-21).

God reveals here that He isn't up in Heaven hitting the smite button at the first smell of sin. He shows us that the life of His creation is of utmost importance to Him and worthy of a personal visit. We understand that God is omnipotent; we know that the visit is for our benefit. God is just; we have no need to question that. Of course, Sodom and Gomorrah were destroyed by sin, which always leads to destruction.

Now there is a meeting—between the ruler of Heaven and Abraham. Abraham seems to take his position humbly here as ruler of the earth. He asks God a question.

> *Then Abraham approached Him and said: "Will You sweep away the righteous with the wicked? What if there are fifty righteous people in the city? Will you really sweep it away and not spare the place for the sake of the fifty righteous people in it? Far be it from You to do such a thing—to kill the righteous with the wicked, treating the righteous and the wicked alike. Far be it from You! Will not the Judge of all the earth do right?"* (Genesis 18:23-25)

Abraham is communicating with God in His language—the language of justice. We might wonder: "Why Abraham? Why not just let them all die? This is not directly impacting your life. These people are full of sin. Let them die."

A religious person might say, "Good. That is exactly what they deserve." In the language of legalism, one might even call it justice.

"If a good man gets too close to sin, well, it's his own fault. I mean, they are, after all, hanging out with the wrong crowd."

Abraham has become others-conscious. He is making a strong move toward love. He is risking so much by questioning the Creator of Heaven and earth. He has taken his position as ruler over earth, still submitted to God, but standing confidently in his role. As a good leader, God submits to the authority He has delegated to another. He can do this if he can trust the leader to have His heart and the right intentions.

Abraham honors the Lord in his conversation. At the same time, Abraham seemingly goes way out of bounds as he questions the source of justice, the Lord. He continues to respectfully ask the Lord about this coming wrath, apparently negotiating how many righteous people it will take to save the city.

They negotiate down to ten. Then the Lord is finished talking to Abraham. God agreed not to destroy Sodom and Gomorrah for the sake of ten righteous. There were not ten, however. We know this because Sodom and Gomorrah were destroyed. But the two men who were with the Lord went down and warned Abraham's nephew Lot, in an attempt to save his whole household. For Lot, this was like leaving Egypt.

> *So when God destroyed the cities of the plain, He remembered Abraham, and He brought Lot out of the catastrophe that overthrew the cities where Lot had lived* (Genesis 19:29).

Abraham was asking God to save Lot. From this Scripture, it appears that Lot was not saved because he was righteous but because he was Abraham's nephew. Lot would probably tell you that sometimes who you know is very important in life!

Given a face-to-face encounter with God, what would you do? I can only imagine what I would do. Actually, both you and I can more than imagine. God has asked us to draw near to Him now, not waiting until we die. Abraham was not dead, and he approached God and made his requests known. His requests, however, look different than most. He did not ask the Lord for the promised son during this encounter. The Lord brought that up. He asked for something for others. What would you ask for? To have some debt cancelled? Most of us might ask for something for ourselves.

That would be OK, but Abraham shows us maturity; he has become others-conscious.

This is the fruit of the Spirit, love. Abraham laid down his needs for the needs of others Well, this is no surprise, I guess. As you learn to be ruler, conquer kingdoms, administer justice, and receive what has been promised, then you will surely have a heart that responds like Abraham's or Christ's—a heart that has enough love to lay down one's life for another. (And somehow enjoy doing it.) Abraham was just. He was seeking God for others before himself; he was faithful and patient. And, within a year's time, he and Sarah would have their promised son!

This can be you. You can live in the lush place of God's rest. No. It's not a sprint. It's not even a marathon. It is a life of seeking God in all kinds of weather—and the result is life more abundantly.

You were born to be blessed in every way—a hero or heroine of faith.

> *And without faith it is impossible to please God, because anyone who comes to Him must believe that He exists and that He rewards those who earnestly seek Him* (Hebrews 11:6).

POSTFACE

IF WE CAN HAVE A Preface, we can have a Postface, right? (Glad you agree!)

Did you have fun? Yeah, me too. If I could take a moment to sandwich in what I mentioned in the Preface: these are my views on the Scripture today. I believe that the Spirit of the Lord has given me revelation but, as always, when handling the Word of God, you must refine all that you hear, take it to the Holy Spirit, and find the nutrition you need.

If you disagree with something I said, check it against the Scripture. If I have made any conclusion that contradicts the Bible, then I am the one who is wrong here. Lord, please wash all of this in the blood of Jesus.

I would like to close with one last thought. It is the beginning of my next teaching—most likely, the follow-up to this book. God has asked us to subdue and influence the world. It is time for us to do this. I literally mean *now.*

This is the first time in the history of the world that the time is right. The Church is ready to launch a body of people into the world who will take their rightful place in rulership and the administration of justice. The Church has broken the bondages of poverty off of her. She has cut loose misinterpretations of suffering and the Pharisaic hypocrisy of false righteousness. We are being set free!

If you have understood this book, then this next Scripture is going to blow you away. (Sorry for the bad confession there.)

> *And He made known to us the mystery of His will according to His good pleasure, which He purposed in Christ, to be put into effect when the times will have reached their fulfillment—to bring all things in heaven and on earth together under one head, even Christ* (Ephesians 1:9-10).

The mystery of His will has been revealed. He wishes us to step into rulership and bring the will of Heaven onto the earth. He purposed it in Christ. *In Christ* is the recognition of the Bride of Christ, His Body, the Church. He has purposed this through the team—all of us being together, in one place. This will all happen when the times will have reached their fulfillment—which is *now*. Finally, *now.*

When our purpose is in effect, then the anointing is released. It will flow to and through anyone who will step into the flow of divine purpose. That means accepting our assignments! Our purpose is now in effect! We are ready, Lord.

Ready for what? To bring all things in Heaven and on earth together under one head, even Christ. Christ is the head, we are the Body. Are you getting this? Are you getting it? This is ridiculously amazing! Now let's return to where we started.

> *In Him was life, and that life was the light of men. The light shines in the darkness, but the darkness has not understood it* (John 1:4-5).

Him here is Christ. In Him was life. The life was the light of men. Light influences darkness by removing it. Think of light as the tool to drive back sin. Think of influence as that light. Influence is leadership. It is the ability to change something or someone. If you have influence over an individual, you can make adjustments. This means you are leading or in authority.

Christ is ruler of all authorities. King of kings. High Priest. Lord of lords. Now then, what was it that gave Him that sort of influence? The light (the influence that drives back sin) was the result of the life that was in Him.

What is in Christ? Life. Light is part of life; the life of Christ is infinite and light can be drawn from it. In this dark, sinful world, it is up to us, the Body of Christ, to draw upon His life and shed His light throughout the world: *"You are the light of the world..."* (Matt. 5:14).

Are we in a position to influence the world? Are we driving back darkness? When we enter the Lord's rest we are!

You have received the promises of God. Your life is no longer governed by death; in you now is life. Now take that life to the high places and drive back the darkness. God has always wanted light to be seen in a high place. That is why the sun is in the sky.

"...a city on a hill cannot be hidden" (Matt. 5:14). God wants you on top of a hill! Now what are you waiting for" Put down this book and go get 'em!

Endnotes

Chapter 2: A Magical Land

1. Blue Letter Bible 1996-2010, "Dictionary and Word Search," s.v. Yepheth (Strong's3315),http://www.blueletterbible.org/lang/lexicon/lexicon.cfm?Strongs=H3315&t=KJV (accessed July 2, 2010).

Chapter 5: Turning up the Heat

1. Blue Letter Bible 1996-2010, "Dictionary and Word Search," s.v. towb (Strong's2896),http://www.blueletterbible.org/lang/lexicon/lexicon.cfm?Strongs=H2896&t=KJV (accessed June 24, 2010).

2. Blue Letter Bible 1996-2010, "Dictionary and Word Search," s.v. chalab (Strong's2461),http://www.blueletterbible.org/lang/lexicon/lexicon.cfm?Strongs=H2461&t=KJV (accessed June 24, 2010).

Chapter 6: Are Your Peeps Eagles or Beagles?

1. "Why Is the Ocean Salty?" Herbert Swenson, The U.S. Geological Survey, http://www.palomar.edu/oceanography/salty_ocean.htm (accessed June 24, 2010).

2. Smith's Bible Dictionary, PC Study Bible formatted electronic database, (Biblesoft, Inc., 2003, 2006), s.v. "Number"

3. Lyrics007, http://www.lyrics007.com/'N%20Sync%20Lyrics/Bye%20Bye%20Bye%20Lyrics.html (accessed July 14, 2010).

Chapter 8: I Like to Eat Eat Eat Apples and Ba-Mannas

1. Blue Letter Bible 1996-2010, "Dictionary and Word Search," s.v. tsela (Strong's6763),http://www.blueletterbible.org/lang/lexicon/lexicon.cfm?Strongs=H6763&t=KJV (accessed June 25, 2010).

2. Blue Letter Bible 1996-2010, "Dictionary and Word Search," s.v. Marah (Strong's4785),http://www.blueletterbible.org/lang/lexicon/lexicon.cfm?Strongs=H4785&t=KJV (accessed June 25, 2010).

3. Blue Letter Bible 1996-2010, "Dictionary and Word Search," s.v. Ciyn (Strong's5512),http://www.blueletterbible.org/lang/lexicon/lexicon.cfm?Strongs=H5512&t=KJV (accessed June 25, 2010).

4. Blue Letter Bible 1996-2010, "Dictionary and Word Search," s.v. man (Strong's4478),http://www.blueletterbible.org/lang/lexicon/lexicon.cfm?Strongs=H4478&t=KJV (accessed June 25, 2010).

5. Blue Letter Bible 1996-2010, "Dictionary and Word Search," s.v. am (Strong's5971),http://www.blueletterbible.org/lang/lexicon/lexicon.cfm?Strongs=H5971&t=KJV (accessed June 25, 2010).

6. Blue Letter Bible 1996-2010, "Dictionary and Word Search," s.v. malaq (Strong's4454),http://www.blueletterbible.org/lang/lexicon/lexicon.cfm?Strongs=H4454&t=KJV (accessed June 25, 2010).

Chapter 9: Are You Distinguished or Extinguished?

1. Arie Uittenbogaard, Abarim Publications Biblical Name Vault, (© www.abarim-publications.com 2000-2007) http://www.abarim-publications.com/Meaning/Kenite.html (accessed July 5, 2010).

Chapter 10: Earn More When Paid Less

1. Josephus, *Antiquities of the Jews,* bk. II, ch. ix, § 1.

Chapter 11: Forgiving the Unforgivable

1. Blue Letter Bible 1996-2010, "Dictionary and Word Search," s.v. Yarden (Strong's3383),http://www.blueletterbible.org/lang/lexicon/lexicon.cfm?Strongs=H3383&t=KJV (accessed June 25, 2010).

2. Blue Letter Bible 1996-2010, "Dictionary and Word Search," s.v. Tsĕredah (Strong's 6868), http://www.blueletterbible.org/lang/lexicon/Lexicon.cfm?Strongs=H6868&t=KJV, and s.v. Tsarĕthan (Strong's 6891), http://www.blueletterbible.org/lang/lexicon/lexicon. cfm?Strongs=H6891&t=KJV (accessed June 25, 2010).

Chapter 12: Doing the Undoable

1. Blue Letter Bible 1996-2010, "Dictionary and Word Search," s.v. sōzō (Strong's 4982), < http://www.blueletterbible.org/lang/lexicon/lexicon.cfm?Strongs=G4982&t=KJV > (accessed June 28, 2010).

2. Warren W. Wiersbe, The Bible Exposition Commentary: Old Testament, (Colorado Springs: Victor, 2001-2004).

Chapter 14: Half of Infinity Is Still Infinity

1. Blue Letter Bible 1996-2010, "Dictionary and Word Search," s.v. heach (Strong's 1889), http://www.blueletterbible.org/lang/lexicon/lexicon.cfm?Strongs=H1889&t=KJV (accessed July 10, 2010).

2. Blue Letter Bible 1996-2010, "Dictionary and Word Search," s.v. Abraham (Strong's 85), http://www.blueletterbible.org/lang/lexicon/lexicon.cfm?Strongs=H85&t=KJV (accessed July 10, 2010).

Chapter 15: Hear the Light, See the Night

1. Blue Letter Bible 1996-2010, "Dictionary and Word Search," s.v. Ciyn (Strong's 5512), http://www.blueletterbible.org/lang/lexicon/lexicon.cfm?Strongs=H5512&t=KJV (accessed July 10, 2010).

2. Blue Letter Bible 1996-2010, "Dictionary and Word Search," s.v. Emoriy (Strong's 567), http://www.blueletterbible.org/lang/lexicon/lexicon.cfm?Strongs=H567&t=KJV (accessed June 28, 2010).

3. Arie Uittenbogaard, Abarim Publications Biblical Name Vault, (© www.abarim-publications.com 2000-2007), http://www.abarim-publications.com/Meaning/Jebusite.html (accessed June 28, 2010).

4. "Genesis 10—The Table of Nations," s.v. Hittite, http://www.biblebelievers.org.au/bb000319.htm (accessed June 28, 2010) and Lazer Gurkow, Chabad.org Parshah, "Abraham and the Hittites," http://www.chabad.org/parshah/article_cdo/aid/328234/jewish/Abraham-and-the-Hittites.htm (accessed June 28, 2010).

Chapter 16: Sow, Grow, It's How I Roll

1. Biblesoft's New Exhaustive Strong's Numbers and Concordance with Expanded Greek-Hebrew Dictionary. CD-ROM. Biblesoft, Inc. and International Bible Translators, Inc., 1994, 2003, 2006, s.v. "Yerechow," (OT 3405) and s.v. "yareach" (OT 3394).

Chapter 17: Don't Throw Me in the Briar Patch

1. Nelson's Illustrated Bible Dictionary, Herbert Lockyer, Sr., ed. (Nashville: Thomas Nelson Publishers, 1986), s.v. Weights and Measures.

Chapter 19: Holding on to Win With Both Hands

1. Blue Letter Bible 1996-2010, "Dictionary and Word Search," s.v. pimplēmi (Strong's 4130), http://www.blueletterbible.org/lang/lexicon/lexicon.cfm?Strongs=G4130&t=KJV (accessed June 29, 2010).

2. Ibid.

Chapter 20: How to Take a Load Off

1. Blue Letter Bible 1996-2010, "Dictionary and Word Search," s.v. sympaschō (Strong's 4841), http://www.blueletterbible.org/lang/lexicon/lexicon.cfm?Strongs=G4841&t=KJV (accessed July 13, 2010).

Chapter 23: How to Wait at a Green Light

1. Blue Letter Bible 1996-2010, "Dictionary and Word Search," s.v. Shalem (Strong's 8004), http://www.blueletterbible.org/lang/lexicon/lexicon.cfm?Strongs=H8004&t=KJV (accessed July 14, 2010).

2. Blue Letter Bible 1996-2010, "Dictionary and Word Search," s.v. eirēnē (Strong's 1515), http://www.blueletterbible.org/lang/lexicon/lexicon.cfm?Strongs=G1515&t=KJV (accessed July 14, 2010).

3. Blue Letter Bible 1996-2010, "Dictionary and Word Search," s.v. shalowm (Strong's 7965), http://www.blueletterbible.org/lang/lexicon/lexicon.cfm?Strongs=H7965&t=KJV (accessed June 29, 2010).

Chapter 24: Just Too Much

1. Blue Letter Bible 1996-2010, "Dictionary and Word Search," s.v. Chebrown (Strong's 2275), http://www.blueletterbible.org/lang/lexicon/lexicon.cfm?Strongs=H2275&t=KJV (accessed July 14, 2010).

2. Blue Letter Bible 1996-2010, "Dictionary and Word Search," s.v. tsadaq (Strong's 6663), < http://www.blueletterbible.org/lang/lexicon/lexicon.cfm?Strongs=H6663&t=KJV (accessed June 29, 2010).

About Jason Anderson

Published in association with the literary agency of
Credo Communications, LLC, Grand Rapids, Michigan,

www.credocommunications.net
www.livingwordonline.org
www.thewordforwinners.com
www.takingaminute.com

In the right hands, This Book will Change Lives!

Most of the people who need this message will not be looking for this book. To change their lives, you need to put a copy of this book in their hands.

> *But others (seeds) fell into good ground, and brought forth fruit, some a hundred-fold, some sixty-fold, some thirty-fold* (Matthew 13:8).

Our ministry is constantly seeking methods to find the good ground, the people who need this anointed message to change their lives. Will you help us reach these people?

> *Remember this—a farmer who plants only a few seeds will get a small crop. But the one who plants generously will get a generous crop* (2 Corinthians 9:6).

EXTEND THIS MINISTRY BY SOWING
3 BOOKS, 5 BOOKS, 10 BOOKS, **OR MORE TODAY,**
AND BECOME A LIFE CHANGER!

Thank you,

Don Nori Sr., Publisher
Destiny Image
Since 1982